FOLLOW YOUR STARS FOR A WONDERFUL YEAR IN 1996!

Whatever it is you seek—love, adventure, good health, or good fortune—Sydney Omarr has an astonishingly accurate forecast for every aspect of your life. Packed with 18 months of on-target predictions from July 1995 to December 1996, this remarkable guide shows you:

- how to make your love connections strong and sexy
- how to fine-tune your life by coordinating your activities with the rhythms of the universe
- how your rising sign affects the outer "you"
- how to use the moon and planets for prosperity
- how to relieve your stress and live a healthier life

So chart your very own star-studded course now—and make 1996 your most extraordinary year ever!

SYDNEY OMARR'S DAY-BY-DAY ASTROLOGICAL GUIDE FOR GEMINI IN 1996

SYDNEY OMARR'S

DAY-BY-DAY ASTROLOGICAL GUIDE FOR

GEMINI

May 21–June 20

1996

A SIGNET BOOK

SIGNET
Published by the Penguin Group
Penguin Books USA Inc., 375 Hudson Street,
New York, New York 10014, U.S.A.
Penguin Books Ltd, 27 Wrights Lane,
London W8 5TZ, England
Penguin Books Australia Ltd, Ringwood,
Victoria, Australia
Penguin Books Canada Ltd, 10 Alcorn Avenue,
Toronto, Ontario, Canada M4V 3B2
Penguin Books (N.Z.) Ltd, 182–190 Wairau Road,
Auckland 10, New Zealand

Penguin Books Ltd, Registered Offices:
Harmondsworth, Middlesex, England

First published by Signet, an imprint of Dutton Signet,
a division of Penguin Books USA Inc.

First Printing, July, 1995
10 9 8 7 6 5 4 3 2 1

Sydney Omarr is syndicated worldwide by
Los Angeles Times Syndicate.

Cover art by Faranak

REGISTERED TRADEMARK—MARCA REGISTRADA

Printed in the United States of America

Contents

CHAPTER 1

Introduction

> God helps those who help themselves.
> Lost time is never found again.
> A penny saved is a penny earned.
> Early to bed, early to rise, makes a man healthy,
>   wealthy, and wise.
> Never put off till tomorrow, what you can do
>   today.

These sayings are so familiar to us that they're a part of American folklore. Yet how many readers know that they came from an ancestor of today's popular astrology books? The venerable sage who wrote those words was the author of *Poor Richard's Almanac*, named for an actual eighteenth-century English astrologer, Richard Saunders. The name, if not the astrological knowledge, was adopted by Benjamin Franklin, an ambitious young printer who later became one of the founding fathers of this country. Astrology was popular in the early eighteenth century and an almanac was an indispensable book for Colonial settlers, standing side by side with the Bible in Colonial homes, so why not combine the two and add some practical, pithy advice of my own? Franklin thought. For spiritual guidance, the early colonists relied on the Bible. But for daily affairs, an almanac was a "must," consulted to forecast the weather, give the best times for planting, and also for advice on how to live one's life.

To kick off the first edition in 1732, Franklin, posing as astrologer Saunders, predicted the demise of his competition—a highly successful publicity stunt (which no astrologer would do today, even in jest). "Poor Richard" certainly made Ben wealthy and wise, since he is probably the most quoted American philosopher in our history.

Franklin, who was also one of America's first scientists,

7

took his astrology with a light, jocular touch. Like many of our forefathers, however, he had more than a smattering of knowledge about such things—and the concept of planetary happenings affecting our daily lives was a familiar one. Though sun sign forecasts were not uncommon, more extensive astrological knowledge was the privilege of an elite few until this century.

In this year blessed by Jupiter, the planet of good fortune, traveling through the sign of Capricorn (and Ben Franklin, of course, was a Capricorn), it seems especially fitting to relate the aims of this book to the almanacs of old. It's your personal astrological weather forecast, to help you move your life in harmony with the rhythms of nature, as determined by the position of the moon and planets.

So let this guide be your "almanac" for the exciting year 1996, which starts off with a "special event"—the entry of the planet Uranus into Aquarius, the sign it rules, where it will send its most powerful rays. One of the nicknames for Uranus is "The Awakener"—and in Aquarius, it should wake us up to possibilities we'd never realized before.

Uranus is also the ruler of high technology, which is transforming astrology as it is other areas of our lives. Telecommunications have put astrology fans in touch with each other over online computer bulletin boards, where you can ask questions, get information, and connect with kindred souls. Computer innovations are racing so far ahead, that by the time this book is published, there are sure to be many more exciting products that make astrology easier to learn and use than ever! Already CD-ROMS, Windows programs, and many levels of chart interpretation are available. We'll tell you where to look for the hottest new products for your commuter system.

If you're new to astrology, you may feel just as bewildered as you did when you got a new PC. You have a marvelous tool available, but it takes some learning to operate in your life. Fortunately a little knowledge can get you up and running quickly. We'll give you basic information, so you'll know what astrology is all about. We'll tell you everything you need to know about your sun sign. And you can look up other planets in your horoscope and find out how each contributes to your total personality. Many readers are fascinated by astrology's insights into relationships. This year, we give you all the possible sun sign relationships, the pros and cons of each, as well as ways to use

8

astrology to take charge of your life, by creating better health, by timing the events in your life according to key planetary happenings.

As "Poor Richard" said: "Let all things have their places; let each part of your business have its time." Let this guide be your companion, like the almanacs of old, to help you make this year, on the cusp of the millennium, one of the happiest, most prosperous ever!

CHAPTER 2

The Top Trends in 1996: Uranus Enters Aquarius

Moving Toward the Millennium

The end of this century is in sight and the planetary forces now gathering indicate that this will be a time of great breakthroughs, not only in technology, but in our vision of how to use it. And the signals now are that we're using this technology to reach out and touch one another. More people will be talking to each other than ever before—exchanging ideas over long distances. You can now chat with a group of people from all over the world for the price of a phone call thanks to computer bulletin boards. We'll be exchanging ideas, philosophies, customs, making friends and meeting lovers electronically, experiencing the freedom of roaming wherever we want without leaving our home. It has been estimated that half of all American homes will have interactive devices such as high-end PCs, interactive TV systems, or video games. The challenge is to create a universal operating system which will enable everyone to speak the same technological language.

Uranus, the planet of high technology, is now solidly moving forward in the sign of its greatest strength, Aquarius, which represents humanitarianism, universality, and hope. This planet can cause sudden changes and shakeups, overturns of the status quo. In its "home" sign, it's sure to revolutionize the way we use technology to reach out to others. Already, we see forces leading to the convergence of computers, information sources, telecommunications, and entertainment, leading to powerful commercial alliances which will control the content of the media.

Science and technology will make our lives easier and enable us to contact each other easily, but they will not tell us how to express ourselves or how to live life to the fullest, as we adapt to sweeping changes. That is the territory of Pluto, another planet that effects long-term changes in our collective con-

10

sciousness. This planet of transformation and regeneration is now beginning a long journey through the spiritual sign of Sagittarius, which is designed to eliminate outworn beliefs and prepare us philosophically for the future. That means, after the boom and bust of the 1980s, we are now asking what it all means and will be going on a collective spiritual quest, taking religion into new areas and creating new blends of Eastern and Western religions.

Since Sagittarius rules advertising and publishing, we are now seeing a great transformation in these areas. The old, intrusive advertising commercials and print ads will be replaced by far more subtle and well-disguised sales messages. Books and magazines are now available on computer which makes them instantly accessible. And desktop publishing is making it possible for many authors to publish their own manuscripts.

Along with a new emphasis on spirituality, look for reinterpretations of ancient manuscripts. We astrologers are reclaiming our roots, after centuries of misinterpretations, by digging into the past for new light on ancient techniques, translating early writings in a scholarly but more astrology-friendly way. These writings are being published and circulated in professional circles, and they're eye-openers!

The Sagittarian symbol of a hunter with bow and arrow now greets visitors to one of the gambling casinos on a Native American reservation. Because Sagittarius rules gambling and sporting events, expect these to translate into the electronic Aquarian world. By the time this is published, gambling via your PC may be in the works.

Capricorn Is Lucky

As we know, the most rapidly growing segment of the population is that of the elderly. We're living longer and healthier lives, but Jupiter in Capricorn this year should bring age-related and elder market issues much more to the forefront of our attention. Look for such developments as "universal" housing designs—housing and furniture that is created to accommodate the physical needs of the elderly in a much more attractive, style-conscious way. Rather than being isolated in adult communities, the over-70 generation will have a much more active role in society. The entertainment world will have more programs catering to this market. Romance and sexual activity in the older generation also becomes a new theme.

CHAPTER 3

How to Do Your Own Predictions

You can look into the future using one of the same techniques that astrologers use. Each planet represents a kind of energy and the sign it is passing through shows how that energy will be expressed. Therefore, by pairing up the key words that describe the planet's energy and what it rules with the key words for what each sign rules, you can make a prediction. For example, Jupiter represents the principles of abundance and expansion; it rules writers and writing. This year it is passing through the sign of Capricorn. Therefore there should be expansion in Capricorn areas such as real estate, issues of old age, and such, and much writing will be done about these subjects. Since the five outer, or most distant, planets (Jupiter, Saturn, Uranus, Neptune, and Pluto) are those that most affect our collective conscious, they are the ones most used to make predictions. Try the "one from column A, one from column B method" to make your own predictions for 1996, using the following lists.

In 1996, Jupiter is in Capricorn.

JUPITER	CAPRICORN
abundance	builders, building
expansion	business, corporations
cheerfulness	chiropractors
commerce	minerals, mountains
foreign travel	aging, old-age issues
accumlation of wealth	politicians
welfare	real estate, property
writers and writing	organization, order
religion and spirituality	tradition

12

philosophy
gambling, risk taking
advertising

the joints and bones
farms, farming
antiques

In 1996, Saturn is in Aries.

SATURN	**ARIES**
contraction	the head, baldness, hats, the brain,
testing	headaches
aging, maturity	diamonds
structures	operations, operating rooms
limitation	sheep, lambs
rules	sharp-edged tools
obedience	courage, pioneering exploration
obstructions	partisan guerillas
discipline	Palestine and Israel
thrift	England
hard work	fire, things connected with fire

In 1996, Uranus is in Aquarius.

URANUS	**AQUARIUS**
surprise	modern architecture
sudden, unexpected happenings	blood circulation
high tech, electricity	broadcasting
the bizarre	telephones
shock	computers
disruptions	television
faith healers	research
feminism	humanitarianism
rebellions	friends
freedom, freelancing	moderization
metaphysics, magic	social affairs, society in general
paradoxes	airplanes
overthrowing, overhauling	Congress

In 1996, Neptune is in Capricorn.

NEPTUNE	**CAPRICORN**
artists of all kinds	builders, building

drugs, intoxicating
substances
inspiration, imagination

crime, criminals
deception
glamour
the homeless, destitute
hospitals
hidden forces
secrets
oceans, petroleum
psychic experiences

business, corporations

joints, bones, bone
diseases
chiropractors
politicians
old age, age-related issues
tradition
real estate, property
organization, order
antiques
minerals, crystals
mountains

In 1996, Pluto is in Sagittarius.

PLUTO
transformation,
transmutation
nuclear power
violence

sexuality, passion, sexual
issues
toxins, waster matter
recycling, waste disposal
elimination
viruses
purification
monsters

SAGITTARIUS
horses, horse-related
things
gambling
religion, the religious
world
literature of higher
wisdom
hunting, hunters
higher education
teachers
space exploration
distant or foreign travel
the legal profession

CHAPTER 4

How's Your Sign Language?

The Magical Symbols of Astrology ... and Why You Should Learn Them!

If you've never seen an astrological chart before, your first reaction might be: What is this—Russian, Sanskrit, Japanese? How am I supposed to make sense of these weird-looking things? In fact, that is exactly why the symbols were adopted—to help you make sense of the chart, whether you're from Japan, Russia, India, or Kansas City. The astrological symbols, or glyphs, belong to a universal language written by astrologers throughout the world, meaning that a chart set up in Moscow can be interpreted by an astrologer in New York. And, because there are only 12 signs and 10 planets (not counting a few asteroids and other space creatures some astrologers use), it's a lot easier than learning to read Chinese!

You may well ask why you should bother to make the effort at all! There are several good reasons. First, it's interesting. The glyphs are much more than little drawings. They are magical codes that contain within them keys to the meanings of the planets. Cracking the code can teach you immediately, in a visual way, much about the deeper meaning of a planet or sign.

If you ever get your chart done by computer, the printout will be covered with glyphs! Though many charts have a list of the planets in plain English, many do not, leaving you mystified if you don't know the glyphs. Some glyphs are instantly identifiable, like the crescent for the moon. And perhaps you recognize the Mars and Venus glyphs as popular male and female gender symbols, often used in jewelry or decoration.

You might pick out the symbol for the sun and the tri-

15

dent of Neptune, but then there's Jupiter (is that a number 4?) and Mercury, who looks like Venus wearing a hat.

Here's a code-cracker for the glyphs, beginning with the glyphs for the planets. To those who already know their glyphs, don't just skim over the chapter! There are hidden meanings to discover, so test your glyph-ese.

The Glyphs for the Planets

Almost all the glyphs of the planets are combinations of the most basic forms—the circle, the half-circle or arc, and the cross. Artists and glyph designers have stylized these forms over the years, but the basic concept is always visible. Each component of the glyph has a special meaning in relation to the others, which combines to create the meaning of the completed symbol.

The circle, which has no beinning or end, is one of the oldest symbols of spirit or spiritual forces. All of the early diagrams of the heavens—spiritual territory—are shown in circular form. The semicircle or arc symbolizes the receptive, finite soul, which contains spiritual potential in the curving line. The vertical line of the cross symbolizes movement from heaven to earth. The horizontal line describes temporal movement, here and now, in time and space. Superimposed together the vertical and horizontal planes symbolize manifestation in the material world.

The Sun Glyph ☉

The sun is always shown by this powerful solar symbol, a circle with a point in the center. It is you, your spiritual center, your infinite personality incarnating (the point) into the finite cycles of birth and death.

This symbol was brought into common use in the sixteenth century, after a German occultist and scholar, Cornelius Agrippa (1486–1535), wrote a book entitled *Die Occulta Philosophia*, which became accepted as the standard work in its field. Agrippa collected many medieval astrological and magical symbols in this book, which were used by astrologers thereafter, copied from those found in Agrippa's book.

The Moon Glyph ☽

This is surely easiest symbol to spot on a chart. The moon glyph is a left-facing arc stylized into the crescent moon, which perfectly captures the reactive, receptive, emotional nature of the moon.

As part of a circle, the arc symbolizes the potential fulfillment of the entire circle. It is the life force that is still incomplete.

The Mercury Glyph ☿

This is the "Venus with a hat" glyph. With another stretch of the imagination, can't you see the winged cap of Mercury the messenger? The upturned crescent could be antennae that tune in and transmit messages from the sun, signifying that Mercury is the way you communicate, the way your mind works. The upturned arc is receiving energy into the spirit or solar circle, which will later be translated into action on the material plane, symbolized by the cross. All the elements are equally sized because Mercury is neutral—it doesn't play favorites! This planet symbolizes objective, detached, unemotional thinking.

The Venus Glyph ♀

Here the relationship is between two elements, the circle or spirit above the cross of matter. Spirit is elevated over matter, pulling it upward. Venus asks, "What is beautiful? What do you like best, what do you love to have done to you?" Venus determines both your ideal of beauty and what feels good sensually. It governs your own allure and power to attract, as well as what attracts and pleases you.

The Mars Glyph ♂

In this glyph, the cross of matter is stylized into an arrowhead pointed up and outward, propelled by the circle of spirit. You can deduce that Mars embodies your spiritual energy projected into the outer world. It's your assertiveness, your initiative, your aggressive drive, what you like to do to others, your temper. If you know someone's Mars, you know whether they'll blow up when angry or do a slow

17

burn. Your task is to use your outgoing Mars energy wisely and well.

The Jupiter Glyph ♃

Jupiter is the basic cross of matter, with a large stylized crescent perched on the left side of the horizontal, temporal plane. You might think of the crescent as an open hand—one meaning of Jupiter is "luck," what's handed to you. You don't work for what you get from Jupiter—it comes to you, if you're open to it.

The Jupiter glyph might also remind you of a jumbo jet plane with a huge tail fin, about to take off. This is the planet of travel, mental and spiritual, of expanding your horizons via new ideas, new spiritual dimensions, and new places. Jupiter embodies the optimism and enthusiasm of the traveler about to embark on an exciting adventure.

The Saturn Glyph ♄

Flip Jupiter over and you've got Saturn. (This might not be immediately apparent, because Saturn is usually stylized into an "h" form like the one shown here.) But the principle it expresses is the opposite of Jupiter's expansive tendencies. Saturn pulls you back to earth—the receptive arc is pushed down underneath the cross of matter. Before there are any rewards or expansion, the duties and obligations of the material world must be considered. Saturn says, "Stop, wait, finish your chores before you take off!"

Saturn's glyph also resembles the sickle of old "Father Time." Saturn was first known as Chronos, the Greek god of time, for time brings all matter to an end. When it was thought to be the most distant planet (before the discovery of Uranus), Saturn was belived to be the place where time stopped. After the soul, having departed from earth, journeyed back to the outer reaches of the universe, it finally stopped at Saturn, or at "the end of time."

The Uranus Glyph ♅

The glyph for Uranus is often stylized to form a capital H after Sir William Herschel, the name of the planet's discoverer. But the more esoteric version curves the two pillars of the H into crescent antennae, or "ears" or like satellite disks receiving signals from space. These are perched on the horizontal material line of the cross (matter) and pushed from below by the circle of the spirit. To many sci-fi fans, Uranus looks like an orbiting satellite.

Uranus channels the highest energy of all, the white electrical light of the universal spiritual sun, the force that holds the cosmos together. This pure electrical energy is gathered from all over the universe. Because it doesn't follow an ordinary celestial drumbeat, it can't be controlled or predicted (which is also true of those who are strongly influenced by this eccentric planet). In the symbol, this energy is manifested through the balance of polarities (the two opposite arms of the glyph) like the two polarized wires of a light bulb.

The Neptune Glyph Ψ

Neptune's glyph is usually stylized to look like a trident, the weapon of the Roman god Neptune. On a more esoteric level, however, it shows the large upturned crescent of the soul pierced through by the cross of matter. Neptune nails down, or materializes, soul energy, bringing impulses from the soul level into manifestation. That is why Neptune is associated with imagination or "imagining in," making an image of the soul. Neptune works through feeling, sensitivity, and mystical capacity to bring the divine into the earthly realm.

The Pluto Glyph ♇

Pluto is written two ways. One is a composite of the letters PL, the first two letters of the word *Pluto* and coincidentally in the initial Percival Lowell, one of the planet's discoverers. The other, more esoteric symbol is a small circle, above a large open crescent which surmounts the cross of matter. This depicts Pluto's power to regenerate—you might imagine from this glyph a new spirit emerging from the sheltering cup of the soul. Pluto rules the forces of life and death—after a Pluto experience, you are transformed, reborn in some way.

Sci-fi fans might visualize this glyph as a small satellite (the circle) being launched. It was shortly after Pluto's discovery that we learned how to harness the nuclear forces that made space exploration possible. Pluto rules the transformative power of atomic energy, which totally changed our lives and from which there was no turning back.

The Glyphs for the Signs

On an astrological chart, the glyph for the sign will appear after that of the planet. When you see the moon glyph followed by a number and the glyph for the sign, this means that the moon was passing over a certain degree of an astrological sign at the time of the chart. On the dividing points between the segments or "houses" on your chart, you'll find the symbol for the sign that rules the house.

Because sun-sign symbols do not always bring together the same basic components of the planetary glyphs, where do their meanings come from? Many have been passed down from ancient Egyptian and Chaldean civilizations with few modifications. Others have been adapted over the centuries. In deciphering many of the glyphs, you'll often find that the symbols reveal a dual nature of the sign, which is not always apparent in sun-sign descriptions. For instance, the Gemini glyph is similar to the Roman numeral for two, and reveals this sign's longing to discover a twin soul. The Cancer glyph may be interpreted as either resembling the nurturing breasts, or the self-protective claws of the crab. Libra's glyph embodies the duality of the spirit balanced with material reality. The Sagittarius glyph shows that the aspirant must also carry along the earthly animal nature in his quest. The Capricorn sea goat is another symbol with dual emphasis. The goat climbs high, yet is always pulled back by the deep waters of the unconscious. Aquarius embodies the double waves of mental detachment, balanced by the desire for connection with others in a friendly way. And finally, the two fishes of Pisces, which are forever tied together, show the duality of the soul and the spirit that must be reconciled.

The Aries Glyph ♈

Since the symbol for Aries is the ram, this glyph's most obvious association is with a ram's horns, which characterizes one aspect of the Aries personality—an aggressive, me-first, leaping-headfirst attitude. But the symbol may have other meanings for you, too. Some astrologers liken it to a fountain of energy, which Aries people also embody. The first sign of the zodiac bursts on the scene eagerly, ready to go. Another analogy is to the eyebrows and nose of the human head, which Aries rules, and the thinking power that is initiated in the brain.

One theory of the origin of this symbol links it to the Egyptian god Amun, represented by a ram. As Amon-Ra, this god was believed to embody the creator of the universe, the leader of all the other gods. This relates easily to the position of Aries as the leader (or first sign) of the zodiac, which begins at the spring equinox, a time of the year when nature is renewed.

The Taurus Glyph ♉

This is another easy glyph to draw and identify. It takes little imagination to decipher the bull's head with long curving horns. Like the bull, the archetypal Taurus is slow to anger, but ferocious when provoked, as well as stubborn, steady, and sensual. Another association is the larynx (and thyroid) of the throat area (ruled by Taurus) and the eustachian tubes running up to the ears, which coincides with the relationship of Taurus to the voice, song, and music. Many famous singers, musicians, and composers have prominent Taurus influences.

Many ancient religions involved a bull as the central figure in fertility rites or initiations, usually symbolizing the victory of man over his animal nature. Another possible origin is the sacred bull of Egypt, which embodied the incarnate form of Osiris, god of death and resurrection. In early Christian imagery, the Taurean bull represented St. Luke.

The Gemini Glyph ♊

The standard glyph immediately calls to mind the Roman numeral for two and the symbol for Gemini, the "twins." In almost all images for this sign, the relationship between two persons is emphasized. This is the sign of communication, human contact, and manifests the desire to share.

Many of the figurative images for Gemini show twins with their arms around each other, emphasizing that they are sharing the same ideas and the same ground. In the

21

glyph, the top line indicates mental communication, whereas the bottom line indicates shared physical space.

The most famous Gemini legend is that of the twin sons, Castor and Pollux, one of whom had a mortal father, while the other was the son of Zeus, king of the gods. When it came time for the mortal twin to die, his grief-stricken brother pleaded with Zeus, who agreed to let them spend half the year on earth, in mortal form, and half in immortal life, with the gods on Mt. Olympus. This reflects the basic nature of humankind, which possesses an immortal soul, yet is also subject to the limits of mortality.

The Cancer Glyph ♋

Two convenient images relate to the Cancer glyph. The easiest to picture is the curving claws of the Cancer symbol, the crab. Like the crab, Cancer's element is water. This sensitive sign also has a hard protective shell to protect its tender interior. It must be wily, to escape predators, scampering sideways and hiding shyly under rocks. The crab also responds to the cycles of the moon, as do all shellfish. The other image is that of two female breasts, which Cancer rules, showing that this is a sign which nurtures and protects others as well as itself.

In ancient Egypt, Cancer was also represented by the scarab beetle, a symbol of regeneration and eternal life.

The Leo Glyph ♌

Lions have belonged to the sign of Leo since earliest times, and it is not difficult to imagine the king of beasts with his sweeping mane and curling tail from this glyph. The upward sweep of the glyph easily describes the positive energy of Leos, the flourishing tail, their flamboyant qualities. Another analogy, which is a stretch, is that of a heart leaping up with joy and enthusiasm, also very typical of Leo. Notice that the Leo glyph seems to be an extension of Cancer's glyph, with a significant difference. In the Cancer glyph, the figures are folding inward, protectively, while the Leo glyph expresses energy outwardly and there is no duality in the symbol (or in Leo). In early Christian imagery, the Leo lion represented St. Mark.

The Virgo Glyph ♍

You can read much into this mysterious glyph. For instance, it could represent the initials of "Mary Virgin," or a young woman holding a staff of wheat, or stylized female genitalia, all common interpretations. The M shape might also remind you that Virgo is ruled by Mercury. The cross beneath the symbol could indicate the grounded, practical nature of this earth sign.

The earliest zodiacs link Virgo with the Egyptian goddess Isis, who gave birth to the god Horus after her husband Osiris had been killed, in the archetype of a miraculous conception. There are many statues of Isis nursing her baby son, which are reminiscent of medieval Virgin and Child motifs. This sign has also been associated with the image of the Holy Grail, when the Virgo symbol was substituted with a chalice.

The Libra Glyph ♎

It is not difficult to read the standard image for Libra, the scales, into this glyph. There is another meaning, however, that is equally relevant: the setting sun as it descends over the horizon. Libra's natural position on the zodiac wheel is the descendant or sunset position (as Aries' natural position is the ascendant, or rising sign). Both images relate to Libra's personality. Libra is always weighing pros and cons for a balanced decision. In the sunset image, the sun (male) hovers over the horizontal Earth (female) before setting. Libra is the space between these lines, harmonizing yin and yang, spiritual and material, ideal and real worlds. The glyph has also been linked to the kidneys, which are ruled by Libra.

The Scorpio Glyph ♏

With its barbed tail, this glyph is easy to identify with the sign of the Scorpion. It also represents the male sexual parts, over which the sign rules. However, some earlier symbols for Scorpio, such as the Egyptian, represent it as an erect serpent. You can also draw the conclusion that Mars is its ruler by the arrowhead.

Another image for Scorpio, which is not identifiable in this glyph, is the eagle. Scorpios can go to extremes, soaring like the eagle or self-destructing like the scorpion. In early Christian imagery, which often used zodiacal symbols, the Scorpio eagle was chosen to symbolize the intense apostle St. John the Evangelist.

The Sagittarius Glyph ♐

This glyph is one of the easiest to spot and draw—an upward-pointing arrow lifting up a cross. The arrow is pointing skyward, while the cross represents the four elements of the material world, which the arrow must convey. Elevating materiality into spirituality is an important Sagittarius quality, which explains why this sign is associated with higher learning, religion, philosophy, travel—the aspiring professions. Sagittarius can also send barbed arrows of frankness in their pursuit of truth. (This is also the sign of the super-salesman.)

Sagittarius is symbolically represented by the centaur, a mythological creature who is half-man, half-horse, aiming his arrow toward the skies. Though Sagittarius is motivated by spiritual aspiration, it also must balance the powerful appetites of the animal nature. The centaur Chiron, a figure in Greek mythology, became a wise teacher, after many adventures and world travels.

The Capricorn Glyph ♑

One of the most difficult symbols to draw, this glyph may take some practice. It is a representation of the seagoat—a mythical animal that is a goat with a curving fish's tail. The goat part of Capricorn wants to leave the waters of the emotions and climb to the elevated areas of life. But the fish part is the unconscious, the deep chaotic psychic level that draws the goat back. Capricorn is often trying to escape the deep, feeling part of life by submerging himself in work, steadily climbing to the top. To some people, the glyph represents a seated figure with a bent knee, a reminder that Capricorn governs the knee area of the body.

An interesting aspect of this figure is how the sharp pointed horns of the symbol, which represent the penetrating, shrewd, conscious side of Capricorn, contrast with the swishing tail, which represents its serpentine, unconscious, emotional force. One Capricorn legend, which dates from Roman times, tells of the earthy fertility god, Pan, who

24

tried to save himself from uncontrollable sexual desires by jumping into the Nile. His upper body then turned into a goat, while the lower part became a fish. Later, Jupiter gave him a safe haven in the skies, as a constellation.

The Aquarius Glyph ≈≈

This ancient water symbol can be traced back to an Egyptian hieroglyph representing streams of life force. Symbolized by the water bearer, Aquarius is distributor of the waters of life—the magic liquid of regeneration. The two waves can also be linked to the positive and negative charges of the electrical energy that Aquarius rules, a sort of universal wavelength. Aquarius is tuned in intuitively to higher forces via this electrical force. The duality of the glyph could also refer to the dual nature of Aquarius, a sign that runs hot and cold, is friendly but also detached in the mental world of air signs.

In Greek legends, Aquarius is represented by Ganymede, who was carried to heaven by an eagle in order to become the cup bearer of Zeus, and to supervise the annual flooding of the Nile. The sign became associated with aviation and notions of flight.

The Pisces Glyph)(

Here is an abstraction of the familiar image of Pisces, two fish swimming in opposite directions, bound together by a cord. The fish represent spirit, which yearns for the freedom of heaven, while the soul remains attached to the desires of the temporal world. During life on earth, the spirit and the soul are bound together and when they complement each other, instead of pulling in opposite directions, this facilitates the creative expression for which Pisceans are known. The ancient version of this glyph, taken from the Egyptians, had no connecting line, which was added in the fourteenth century.

Another interpretation is that the left fish indicates the direction of involution or the beginning of the cycle, the right-hand fish, the direction of evolution, the way to completion of a cycle. It's an appropriate meaning for Pisces, the last sign of the zodiac.

Test Your Knowledge of the Glyphs

1. Draw two glyphs that represent dual principles.
2. Draw a planetary glyph that contains the circle, cross, and semicircle.
3. Draw the glyphs for two signs that are not represented by an animal or fish.
4. Draw the glyphs that are reversed to represent two planets with opposite meanings.
5. Draw the easiest glyph to recognize.
6. What two planetary glyphs are often used to represent male and female?
7. Draw the ancient water symbol that represents an air sign.
8. Which planetary glyph looks like a weapon?
9. Which sun sign glyph looks like a weapon?
10. Which sun sign glyph is most difficult to draw? Can you draw it?

Answers

1. The glyphs for Gemini, Cancer, Libra, Sagittarius, Capricorn, Aquarius, or Pisces all embody dual principles.
2. The glyphs for Mercury, Pluto, and Uranus all contain combinations of the three basic forms.
3. Virgo, Gemini, Aquarius, Libra
4. Jupiter and Saturn
5. The moon
6. Venus and Mars
7. Aquarius
8. Neptune
9. Sagittarius' arrow
10. Capricorn

CHAPTER 5

Get Connected!

A Guide to Getting Involved with the Astrology Community by Computer, Clubs, Conferences, Tapes, and More

Astrology is zooming ahead with all kinds of electronic ways to get connected. Perhaps it's to be expected, now that Uranus, the planet that rules computers and high tech, has entered Aquarius, the sign it rules, which is its strongest position. There are now astrology CDs, programs for Windows and MACs, online bulletin boards for you to explore. In this chapter, we have only space to briefly cover some of the ways you can link up with other astrology fans, take part in the exciting events, or get more involved yourself at home. So get connected with your fellow astrologers and try out some of the exciting new products and services available.

There are conferences all over the country and very well-organized groups of astrologers dedicated to promoting the image of astrology in the most positive way. The National Council for Geocosmic Research (NCGR) is one nation-wide group that is dedicated to bringing astrologers together, promoting fellowship and high-quality education. They have an accredited course system, with a systematized study of all the different specialties within astrology. Whether you'd like to know more about such specialties as financial astrology or techniques for timing by the stars, or if you'd prefer a psychological or mythological approach, you'll find the experts at NCGR conferences.

Those of you with computers have a terrific tool for connecting with other astrology buffs of all levels of expertise. If you have a modem, you can sign on to the GEnie bulletin board, which, at this writing, has the most active and lively astrology area. Online at GEnie, you can attend workshops or seminars, find the answers to whatever is puzzling you. There is a section called "Frequently Asked Questions" which covers just about every question you can think of, as well as a beginner's section. You can often get charts of famous people in the news—at this writing: O. J. Simpson, Michael Jackson, and Lisa Marie Presley were there for downloading. If you are thinking about buying an astrology program for your computer, there are many demo versions here that you can preview. So, computer buffs, check it out! Though astrologers do not advertise their services on the bulletin board, you can find out about happenings in your local area. Nationwide astrology conferences are also covered (you may want to combine a vacation with an astrology conference). The key word is ASTROLOGY to access the astrologer's area. If you are a serious modem fan, you can link up with other astrologers around the world via this service's access to INTERNET.

You'll also find astrologers on Prodigy (check under HOBBIES), CompuServe and American Online, though the offerings are not as extensive at this writing as those on GEnie.

If you do not yet own a computer and are thinking about buying a new or used one, have no fear. In spite of the breakneck pace of technology, there will still be plenty of software available for your computer. Even if you are using a "dinosaur" from the early 1980s, there are still excellent calculation and interpretation programs available.

If you are a newcomer to astrology, it is a good idea to learn the glyphs (astrology's special shorthand language) before you purchase a program. That way, you'll be able to read the charts without consulting a book. One program, however, Astrolabe's Solar Fire for Windows, has pop-up definitions. Just click your mouse on the glyph and a definition appears.

The more sophisticated astrology programs are fairly expensive (approximately $200 to $250) at this writing, but you may not want all the features they provide. In that case, investigate some of the lower-priced programs—there are many available for under $100. Call some of the companies on our list, state your needs and the type of computer you have, to find the right program for you.

If you cannot go to conferences, you can still listen to many of the lectures and workshops on tape in your home or car. See the resource list to order catalogs of local or nationwide conferences. Taped instruction is also advertised in the more specialized astrology magazines such as *Planet Earth* or *Mountain Astrologer*.

Another option, which might interest those who live in out-of-the-way places or who are unable to fit classes into their schedule, are study-by-mail courses offered by several astrological computing services. Some courses will send you a series of tapes; others use workbooks or computer printouts.

Your Astrology Resource List

Nationwide Astrology Organizations

(Contact these organizations for information on conferences, workshops, local meetings, conference tapes, referrals)

National Council for Geocosmic Research
(Educational workshops, tapes, conferences, directory of professional astrologers available.)
Contact by mail, phone, or FAX
NCGR Membership Secretary
P.O. Box 501078
Malabar, FL 32950-1078
407-722-9500
FAX: 407-728-2244

American Federation of Astrologers (A.F.A.)
P.O. Box 22040
Tempe, AZ 85382

A.F.A.N.
(Networking, Legal Issues)
8306 Wilshire Blvd
Berkeley Hills, CA 90211

ARC Directory
(Listing of astrologers worldwide)
2920 E. Monte Vista
Tucson, AZ 85716
602-321-1114

Conference and Lecture Tapes

National Council for Geocosmic Research
(Class, lecture, conference tapes)
P.O. Box 501078
Malabar, FL 32950-1078
407-722-9500
FAX 407-728-2244

Pegasus Tapes
(Lectures, conference tapes)
P.O. Box 419
Santa Ysabel, CA 92070

International Society of Astrological Research
(Lectures, workshops, seminars)
P.O. Box 38613
Los Angeles, CA 90038

ISIS Institute
P.O. Box 21222
El Sobrante, CA 94820-1222

Astro Analytics Productions
P.O. Box 16927
Encino, CA 91416-6927

For Computer Programs

Astrolabe
(Check out their Solar Fire Windows software, variety of
programs for all levels of expertise, wide selection of readings, MAC program. A good resource for innovative software as well as programs for older computers.)
Box 1750–R
Brewster, MA 02631
1-800-843-6682

Matrix Software
(Wide variety of software in all price ranges, demo disks,
student and advanced level; lots of interesting readings)
315 Marion Avenue
Big Rapids, MI 49307
1-800-PLANETS

Astro Communications Services
(Books, software for MAC and IBM compatibles, individual charts, telephone readings. Extensive free catalog and online store on GEnie BBS.)
Dept. AF693, P.O. Box 34487
San Diego, CA 92163-4487
1-800-888-9983

Air Software
115 Caya Avenue
West Hartford, CT 06110
1-800-659-1AIR

Time Cycles Research
(Programs for the MAC)
27 Dimmock Road
Waterford, CT 06385

Astro-Cartography
(Charts for location changes)
Astro-Numeric Service Box 336–B
Ashland, OR 97520
1-800-MAPPING

Microcycles
P.O. Box 3175
Culver City, CA 90231
1-800-829-2537

Astrology Online Computer Bulletin Boards

If you have a computer with a modem, then the world of online astrology is just a phone call away. By the time this book is in print, there may be many other active astrology bulletin boards, so check your favorite online service. If there is no Astrology section, you may find astrologers hanging out under the New Age, Metaphysical, or Hobbies categories.

GEnie

You can meet and chat with professional astrologers as well as beginning astrology buffs on The Astrology Roundtable, which at this writing is the only area on a major online level devoted exclusively to astrology. It will give you access to hundreds of astrology-related files of all interest levels, from beginners to professional. There is also access to the information superhighway Internet files, plus live online classes, conferences, chats, and its own astrology magazine. It's managed by professional astrologers, who are available to answer your questions. In the extensive library, there are free calculation programs, as well as demo programs for both PC and Macintosh formats. It's a great place to ask questions, find out the latest conference news, and meet other astrology buffs.

To join GEnie or get more information, call 1-800-638-9636 (GEnie client services), noon to midnight (Eastern Time).

Compuserve

(Check the New Age category)

Prodigy

(Check out Astrology under "Hobbies")

Astronet—United Kingdom

(Interesting downloads, dial up bulletin board) #011-44-458-833-000

Astrology Schools

New York School of Astrology
(Intensive curriculum, seminars, bookstore, conferences, public events. Meet other astrologers when you visit New York City.)
545 Eighth Avenue—10th floor
New York, NY 10018-4307
212-947-3609

National Council for Geocosmic Research
(Many local chapters nationwide that hold educational workshops, conferences, and special events.)
For information on a chapter near you, contact by mail, phone, or FAX:
NCGR Membership Secretary
P.O. Box 501078

Malabar, FL 32950-1078
407-722-9500
FAX: 407-728-2244

Astrology Magazines

(Most have listings of conferences, events, local happenings.)

American Astrology
475 Park Avenue South
New York, NY 10016

Dell Horoscope
P.O. Box 53352
Boulder, CO 89321-3342

Planet Earth
The Great Bear
P.O. Box 5164
Eugene, OR 97405

Mountain Astrologer
P.O. Box 970
Cedar Ridge, CA 95924-0970

Aspects
Aquarius Workshops
P.O. Box 260556
Encino, CA 91426

CHAPTER 6

How to Find an Astrologer and What to Expect from a Reading

Whether you're new to astrology or already hooked, you'll find the more you get involved, the more you'll be fascinated by its accuracy and relevance to your life. And the more there is to challenge you!

If you've caught the "astrology bug" you'll want to go even further than the scope of this book. Perhaps you'll begin by having your chart done, then deepen your knowledge by taking courses or attending conferences, subscribing to astrology-oriented magazines, or trying your hand at doing charts yourself on your personal computer. (There's a resource list in Chapter 5.)

When to Have a Reading

Though you can learn much about astrology from books such as this one, nothing compares to a personal consultation with a professional astrologer who has analyzed thousands of charts and can pinpoint the winning potential in yours. There's no question that a good astrologer can help you create a more fulfilling future by understanding your own tendencies as well as your place in the cosmic scheme. With your astrologer, you can address specific problems in your life that may be holding you back. For instance, if you are not getting along with your mate or coworker, you could leave the reading with some new insights and some constructive ways to handle the situation.

If you've been wondering about whether an astrological reading could give you the competitive edge in business, help you break through a personal dilemma, decide on the best day for a key event in your life, or help you make a career change, this may be the time to have a personal consultation. An astrologer might give you reassurance and validation at a turning point or crisis time in your life, or simply help you get where you want to go. Before your reading, a reputable astrologer will ask for the date time (as accurately as possible) and place of birth of the subject of the reading. A horoscope can be cast about anything that has a specific time and place. Most astrologers will then enter this information into a computer, which will calculate your chart in seconds. From the resulting chart, the astrologer will do an interpretation.

If you don't know your exact birth time, you can usually find it filed at the Bureau of Vital Statistics at the city hall or county seat of the state where you were born. If you have no success in getting your time of birth, some astrologers specialize in rectification, using past events of your life to estimate an approximate birth time.

How to Find a Good Astrologer

Your first priority should be to choose a qualified astrologer. Rather than relying on word of mouth or grandiose advertising claims, do this with the same care you would choose any trusted adviser such as a doctor, lawyer, or financial adviser. Unfortunately, anyone can claim to be an astrologer—to date, there is no licensing of astrologers or established professional criteria. However, there are nationwide organizations of serious, committed astrologers that can help you in your search.

Good places to start your investigation are organizations such as the American Federation of Astrologers or the National Council for Geocosmic Research (NCGR), which offers a program of study and certification. If you live near a major city, there is sure to be an active NCGR chapter or astrology club in your area; many are listed in astrology magazines available at your local newsstand. In response to many requests for referrals, the NCGR has compiled a directory of professional astrologers, which includes a glossary of terms and an explanation of specialties within the astrological field. Contact the NCGR headquarters (see the resource list at the end of Chapter 5) to order a copy.

As a potentially lucrative freelance business, astrology has always attracted self-styled experts who may not have the technique or the counseling experience to give a helpful reading. These astrologers can range from the well-meaning amateur to the charlatan or street-corner gypsy who has for many years given astrology a bad name. Be wary of astrologers who claim to have occult powers or who make pretentious claims of celebrated clients or miraculous achievements. You can often tell from the initial phone conversation if the astrologer is legitimate. He or she should ask for your time and place of birth, and conduct the conversation in a professional way. Any astrologer who gives a reading based only on your sun sign is highly suspect.

When you arrive for the reading, the astrologer should be prepared. The consultation should be conducted in a private, quiet place. The astrologer should be interested in your problems of the moment. A good reading involves feedback on your part, so if the reading is not relating to your concerns, be sure to let the astrologer know. You should feel free to ask questions and get clarifications of technical terms. The reading should be an interaction between two people, rather than a solo performance. The more you actively participate, rather than expecting the astrologer to carry the reading or come forth with oracular predictions, the more meaningful your experience will be. An astrologer should help you validate your current experience, and be frank about possible negative happenings. But he or she should be helpful about pointing you life in the most positive direction.

In their approach to a reading, some astrologers may be more literal, others more intuitive. Those who have had counseling training may take a more psychological approach. Some astrologers may seem to have an almost psychic ability, extrasensory perception, or another parapsychological talent, but these skills do not necessarily make this person a good astrologer. A very accurate picture can be drawn from factual data.

An astrologer may do several charts for each client—one for the time of birth, one for the current date, and a "progressed chart" showing the evolution from birth to the present time. According to your individual needs, there are many other possibilities, such as a chart for a different location, if you are contemplating a change of place. Relationships between any two people, things, or events can be interpreted with a synastry chart, which compares the chart of one birth date with the chart of another date. Another type of relationship chart is the composite chart, which uses the midpoint between planets in two individual charts to describe the relationship.

An astrologer will be particularly interested in transits—times when planets pass over the planets or sensitive points in your chart, which signal important times for you.

Another option is a taped reading; the astrologer will mail you a previously taped reading based on your birth chart. Although this type of reading is more personal than a computer printout and can give you valuable insights, it is not equivalent to a live reading when you can have a dialogue with the astrologer and can address your specific interests and issues of the moment.

About Telephone Readings

Telephone readings are available in two varieties—one is a dial-in taped reading, usually by a well-known astrologer. The other is a live consultation with an "astrologer." The taped readings are general daily or weekly forecasts, applied to all members of your sign and charged by the minute. The quality depends on the astrologer. One caution: be aware that these readings can run up a high telephone bill, especially if you get into the habit of calling every day. Be sure that you are aware of the per-minute cost of each call. Live telephone readings also vary with the expertise of the astrologer. Ideally the astrologer enters your birth data into a computer and refers to that chart during the consultation. The advantage of a live telephone reading is that your individual chart is used and you can ask about a specific problem. Before you invest in any reading, however, be sure that your astrologer is qualified and that you fully understand how much you will be charged.

About Computer Readings

Most of the companies that offer computer programs (such as ACS, Matrix, Astrolabe) also offer a wide variety of computer-generated horoscope interpretations. These can be quite comprehensive, offering a beautiful printout of the chart plus many pages of information. A big plus is that a basic natal chart interpretation can be an ideal way to learn about your own chart, since most readings interpret all the details of the chart in a very understandable way. However, the interpretations will be general, since there is no input from you, and thus the reading may not cover your immediate concerns. This is still a good option for a first reading, especially since these printouts cost much less than live consultations. You might consider them as either a supplement or preparation for a live reading (study one before you have a live reading to get familiar with your chart and plan specific questions), and they make a terrific gift for anyone interested in astrology.

CHAPTER 7

Mark These Days on Your 1996 Calendar

It's no secret that some of the most powerful and famous people, from Julius Caesar to financier J. P. Morgan, from Ronald Reagan to Cher, have consulted astrologers before they made their moves. If it works for the rich and famous, why not learn how to put astrology to work for you?

You can get control of your life and set it on its most successful course by letting astrology help you coordinate your activities. For instance, if you know the dates that the tricky planet Mercury will be creating havoc with communications, you'll back up that vital fax with a duplicate by Express Mail, you'll read between the lines of contracts and put off closing that deal until you have double-checked all the information. When Venus is in your sign, you'll revamp your image or invite someone special to dinner.

To find out for yourself if there's truth to the saying "timing is everything," mark your own calendar for love, career moves, vacations, and important events, using the following information and the tables in this chapter and the one titled "How to Use All Ten Planets," as well as the moon sign listings under your daily forecast. Here are the happenings to note on your agenda:

- Dates of your sun sign (high energy period)
- The month previous to your sun sign (love energy period)
- Dates of planets in your sign this year
- Full and new moons (Pay special attention when these fall in your sun sign)
- Eclipses
- Moon in your sun sign every month, as well as moon in the opposite sign (listed in daily forecast)

- Mercury retrogrades
- Other retrograde periods

Your Personal Power Time

Every birthday starts a cycle of solar energy for you. You should feel a new surge of vitality as the powerful sun enters your sign. This is the time when predominant energies are most favorable to you, so go for it! Start new projects, make your big moves. You'll get the recognition you deserve now, when everyone is attuned to your sun sign. Look in the tables in this book to see if other planets will also be passing through your sun sign at this time. Venus (love beauty), Mars (energy, drive), or Mercury (communication, mental acuity) reinforce the sun and give an extra boost to your life in the areas they affect. Venus will rev up your social and love life, making you seem especially attractive. Mars gives you extra energy and drive. Mercury fuels your brain power and helps you communicate. Jupiter signals an especially lucky period of expansion.

There are two "down" times related to the sun. During the month before your birthday period, when you are winding up your annual cycle, you could be feeling especially vulnerable and depleted, so get extra rest, watch your diet, and don't overstress yourself. Use this time to gear up for a big "push" when the sun enters your sign.

Another "down" time is when the sun is in the opposite sign (six months from your birthday) and the prevailing energies are very different from yours. You may feel at odds with the world, and things might not come easily. You'll have to work harder for recognition, because people are not on your wavelength. However, this could be a good time to work on a team, in cooperation with others or behind the scenes.

How to Use the Moon's Phase and Sign

Working with the *Phases* of the moon is as easy as looking up at the night sky. At the new moon, when both sun and moon are in the same sign, is the best time to begin new ventures, especially the activities that are favored by that sign.

You'll have powerful energies pulling you in the same direction. You'll be focused outward, toward action, doing. Postpone breaking off, terminating, deliberating, or reflecting—activities that require introspection and passive work.

Get your project underway during the first quarter, then go public at the full moon, a time of high intensity, when feelings come out into the open. This is your time to shine—to express yourself. Be aware, however, that because pressures are being released, other people are also letting off steam and confrontations are possible. So try to avoid arguments. Traditionally, astrologers often advise against surgery at this time, which could produce heavier bleeding.

During the last quarter of the new moon, you'll be most controlled. This is a winding-down phase, a time to terminate unproductive relationships, do serious thinking and inward-directed activities.

You'll feel some new and full moons more strongly than others, especially those new moons that fall in your sun sign and full moons in your opposite sign. Because that full moon occurs at your low-energy time of year, it is likely to be an especially stressful time in a relationship, when any hidden problems or unexpressed emotions could surface.

1996 Full and New Moons

Full moon in Cancer—January 5
New moon in Capricorn—January 20
Full moon in Leo—February 4
New moon in Aquarius—February 18
Full moon in Virgo—March 5
New moon in Pisces—March 19
April 4—lunar eclipse in Libra
April 17—solar eclipse in Aries
Full moon in Scorpio—May 3
New moon in Taurus—May 17
Full moon in Sagittarius—June 1
New moon in Gemini—June 16
Full moon in Capricorn—July 1
New moon in Cancer—July 15
New moon in Leo—August 14
Full moon in Pisces—August 28
New moon in Virgo—September 12

September 27—lunar eclipse in Aries
October 12—solar eclipse in Libra
Full moon in Taurus—October 26
New moon in Scorpio—November 11
Full moon in Gemini—November 25
New moon in Sagittarius—December 10
Full moon in Cancer—December 24

How to Handle Eclipses

One of the most amazing phenomena in the cosmos, which many of us take for granted, is the spatial relationship between the sun and moon. How many of us have ever noticed or marveled that, relative to our viewpoint here on earth, both the largest source of energy (the sun) and the smallest (the moon) appear to be almost exactly the same size? This is most evident to us at the time of the solar eclipse, when the moon is directly aligned with the sun and so nearly covers it that scientists use the moment of eclipse to study solar flares.

When the two most powerful forces in astrology—the sun and moon—are lined up, we're sure to feel the effects, both in world events and our personal lives. It might help us to learn how best to cope with the periods around eclipses. Both solar and lunar eclipses are times when our natural rhythms are changed, depending on where the eclipse falls in your horoscope. If it falls on or close to your birthday, you're going to have important changes in your life, perhaps a turning point.

Lunar eclipses occur when the earth is on a level plane with the sun and moon and moves exactly between them during the time of the full moon, breaking the powerful monthly cycle of opposition of these two forces. We might say the earth "short-circuits" the connection between them. The effect can be either confusion or clarity, as our subconscious energies, which normally react to the pull of opposing sun and moon, are turned off. Because we are temporarily freed from the subconscious attachments, we might have objective insights that could help us change any destructive emotional patterns, such as addictions, which normally occur at this time. This momentary "turnoff" could help us turn our lives around. On the other hand, this break in the normal cycle could cause a bewildering disorientation that intensifies our insecurities.

The solar eclipse occurs at the new moon and this time the moon blocks the sun's energies as it passes exactly between the sun and the earth. This means the objective, conscious force, represented by the sun, will be temporarily darkened. Subconscious lunar forces, activating our deepest emotions, will now dominate, putting us in a highly subjective state. Emotional truths can be revealed or emotions can run wild, as our objectivity is cut off and hidden patterns surface. If your sign is affected, you may find yourself beginning a period of work on a deep inner level, you may have psychic experiences or a surfacing of deep feelings.

You'll start feeling the energies of an upcoming eclipse a few days after the previous new or full moon. The energy continues to intensify until the actual eclipse, then disperses for three or four days. So plan ahead at least a week or more before an eclipse and allow several days afterward, for the natural rhythms to return. Try not to make major moves during this period (it's not a good time to get married, change jobs, or buy a home).

Eclipses in 1996

April 4—lunar eclipse in Libra
April 17—solar eclipse in Aries
September 27—lunar eclipse in Aries
October 12—solar eclipse in Libra

Moon Sign Timing

To forecast the daily emotional "weather," to determine your monthly high and low days, or to synchronize your activities with the cycles and the sign of the moon, take note of the moon's daily sign under your daily forecast at the end of the book. Here are some of the activities favored and moods you are likely to encounter under each sign.

MOON IN ARIES. Get moving! The new moon in Aries is an ideal time to start new projects. Everyone is pushy, raring to go, rather impatient, and short-tempered. Leave details and follow-up for later. Competitive sports or martial arts are good ways to let off steam. Quiet types could use some assertiveness, but it's a great day for dynamos. Be careful not to step on too many toes.

MOON IN TAURUS. It's time to do solid, methodical tasks. This is the time to tackle follow-through or backup work. Lay the foundations for success. Make investments, buy real estate, do appraisals, do some hard bargaining. Attend to your property—get out in the country. Spend some time in your garden. Enjoy creature comforts, music, a good dinner, sensual lovemaking. Forget starting a diet.

MOON IN GEMINI. Talk means action today. Telephone, write letters, fax! Make new contacts and stay in touch with steady customers. You can handle lots of tasks at once. It's a great day for mental activity of any kind. Don't try to pin others down—they too are feeling restless. Keep it light. Flirtations and socializing are favored. Watch gossip, and don't give away secrets.

MOON IN CANCER. This is a moody, sensitive, emotional time. People respond to personal attention, mothering. Stay at home, have a family dinner, call your mother. Nostalgia, memories, psychic powers are heightened. You'll want to hang on to people and things (don't clean out your closets now). You could have some shrewd insights into what others really need and want now. Pay attention to dreams, intuition, gut reactions.

MOON IN LEO. Everyone is in a much more confident, warm, and generous mood. It's a good day to ask for a raise, show what you can do, dress like a star. People will respond to flattery, enjoy a bit of drama and theater. You may be extravagant, treat yourself royally, and show off a bit (but don't break the bank!). Take care not to promise more than you can deliver!

MOON IN VIRGO. Do practical down-to-earth chores such as reviewing your budget, making repairs, being an efficiency expert. This is not a day to ask for a raise. Have a health checkup, revamp your diet, and buy vitamins or health food. Make your home spotless by taking care of details and piled-up chores. Reorganize your work and life so they run more smoothly and efficiently. Save money. Be prepared for others to be in a critical, fault-finding mood.

MOON IN LIBRA. Attend to legal matters—negotiate contracts, arbitrate. Do things with your favorite partner. This is a day to socialize and be romantic. Buy a special gift, a beautiful object. Decorate yourself or your surroundings. Buy some new clothes and throw a party. Have an elegant, romantic evening. Smooth over any ruffled feathers, and avoid confrontations by sticking to unemotional discussions.

MOON IN SCORPIO. This is a day to do things with passion. You'll have excellent concentration and focus. Try not to get too intense emotionally, however, and avoid sharp exchanges with loved ones. Others may tend to go to extremes, get jealous and overreact. This is a great day for troubleshooting, problem solving, research, scientific work—and for making love. Pay attention to psychic vibes.

MOON IN SAGITTARIUS. It's a good time for travel, to have philosophical discussions, and set long-range career goals. Work out, do sports, or buy athletic equipment. Others will be feeling upbeat, exuberant, and adventurous. Risk taking is favored—you may feel like taking a gamble, betting on the horses, visiting a local casino, buying a lottery ticket. Teaching, writing, and spiritual activities also get the green light. Relax outdoors. Take care of animals.

MOON IN CAPRICORN. You can accomplish a lot today, so get on the ball! Issues concerning your basic responsibilities, duties, family, and parents could crop up. You'll be expected to deliver on promises now. Weed out the dead wood from your life. Get a dental checkup.

MOON IN AQUARIUS. This is a great day for doing things with groups—clubs, meetings, outings, political parties, campaigning for your candidate. Work for a worthy cause; focus on larger issues that affect humanity: the environment, metaphysical questions. It's a good day to buy a computer or an electronic gadget. Wear something outrageous, and try something you've never done before. Present an original idea; don't stick to a rigid schedule—go with the flow. Take a class in meditation, mind control, or yoga. Watching television is favored.

MOON IN PISCES. This can be a very creative day, so let your imagination work overtime. Film, theater, music, ballet could inspire you. Spend some time alone, resting and reflecting, reading or writing poetry. Daydreams can also be profitable. Help those less fortunate or lend a sympathetic ear to someone who may be feeling blue. Don't overindulge in self-pity or escapism, however. People are especially vulnerable to substance abuse now. Turn your thoughts to romance and someone special.

When the Planets Go Backward

All the planets, except for the sun and moon, at times appear to move backward—or retrograde—in the sky, or so it seems from our point of view on earth. At these times, planets do not work as they usually do, so it's best to "take a break" from that planet's energies in our life and do some work on an inner level.

Mercury Retrograde

Mercury goes retrograde most often, and its effects can be especially irritating. When it reaches a short distance ahead of the sun three times a year, it seems to move backward from our point of view. Astrologers often compare retrograde motion to the optical illusion that occurs when we ride on a train that passes another train traveling at a different speed—the second train appears to be moving in reverse.

What this means to you is that the Mercury-ruled areas of your life—analytical thought processes, communications, scheduling, and such—are subject to all kinds of confusion. Be prepared: People will change their minds, renege on commitments. Communications equipment can break down, and schedules must be changed on short notice. People are late for appointments or don't show up at all. Traffic is horrendous. Major purchases malfunction, or are delivered in the wrong color. Letters don't arrive or are delivered to the wrong address. Employees will make errors that have to be corrected later. Contracts don't work out or must be renegotiated.

Since most of us can't put our lives on "hold" for nine weeks every year (three Mercury retrograde periods), we should learn to tame the trickster and make it work for us. The key is in the prefix "re." This is the time to go back over things in your life. Reflect on what you've done during the previous months. Look for deeper insights, spot errors you've missed, take time to review and reevaluate what has happened. This time is very good for inner spiritual work and meditations. REst and REward yourself—it's a good time to take a vacation, especially if you revisit a favorite place. REorganize your work and finish projects that are backed up. Clean out your desk and closets. Throw away what you can't REcycle.

If you must sign contracts or agreements, do so with a contingency clause that lets you reevaluate the terms later.

Postpone major purchases or commitments. Don't get married (unless you're remarrying the same person). Try not to rely on other people keeping appointments, contracts, or agreements to the letter—have several alternatives. Double-check and read between the lines. Don't buy anything connected with communications or transportation (if you must, be sure to cover yourself). Mercury retrograding through your sun sign will intensify its effect on your life.

If Mercury was retrograde when you were born, you may be one of the lucky people who don't suffer the frustrations of this period. If so, your mind probably works in a very intuitive, insightful way.

The sign Mercury is retrograding through can give you an idea of what's in store—as well as the sun signs that will be especially challenged.

Mercury Retrograde Periods in 1996

Mercury retrograde in Aquarius—January 9
Mercury direct in Capricorn—January 30
Mercury turns retrograde in Taurus—May 3
Mercury direct in Taurus—May 27
Mercury turns retrograde in Libra—September 4
Mercury direct in Virgo—September 26
Mercury turns retrograde in Capricorn—December 23

Venus Retrograde

Retrograding Venus can cause your relationships to take a backward step or it can make you extravagant and impractical. It's *not* a good time to redecorate—you'll hate the color of the walls later on. Postpone getting a new hairstyle and try not to fall in love either. But, if you wish to make amends in an already troubled relationship, make peaceful overtures.

Venus Retrograde Period in 1996

Venus turns retrograde in Gemini—May 20
Venus direct in Gemini—July 2

When Other Planets Retrograde

The slower-moving planets stay retrograde for months at a time (Saturn, Jupiter, Neptune, Uranus, and Pluto). When Saturn is retrograde, you may feel more like hanging out at the beach than getting things done. It's an uphill battle with self-discipline at this time. Neptune retrograde promotoes a dreamy escapism from reality, whereas Uranus retrograde may mean setbacks in areas where there have been sudden changes. Think of this as an adjustment period, a time to think things over and allow new ideas to develop. Pluto retrograde is a time to work on establishing proportion and balance in areas where there have been recent dramatic transformations.

When the planets start moving forward again, there's a shift in the atmosphere. Activities connected with each planet start moving ahead, plans that were stalled get rolling. Make a special note of those days on your calendar and proceed accordingly.

Other Retrogrades in 1996

Pluto turns retrograde in Sagittarius—March 5
Neptune turns retrograde in Capricorn—April 29
Jupiter turns retrograde in Capricorn—May 4
Uranus turns retrograde in Aquarius—May 8
Saturn turns retrograde in Aries—July 18
Pluto direct in Sagittarius—August 10
Jupiter direct in Capricorn—September 3
Neptune direct in Capricorn—October 6
Uranus direct in Aquarius—October 9
Saturan direct in Aries—December 3

CHAPTER 8

The First Easy Steps to Learning Astrology

This chapter should come in handy for those who want to know more about astrology—maybe you've just been bitten by the "astrology bug"—in a no-pain, no-strain way. You'll pick up some useful information so you can move on to the more enjoyable things, such as analyzing the latest love of your life, or figuring out when to make that big career move. Here you'll learn the difference between a sign and a constellation. What a "house" is and who lives there, and lots more basic information that will help you understand the sometimes complex terminology of astrology. So come along with us, as we take a fast trip through the world of astrology.

The Horoscope Chart: A Frozen Moment in Time

When you first see your chart you'll probably find the page filled with mysterious symbols placed on a circle divided into 12 sectors, somewhat bewildering. It looks like another language—and not an easy one to read, at first. But as you get acquainted with your chart, you'll see how it makes common, cosmic sense.

What you are looking at is a picture of a moment in time as seen from a particular place on Earth. The earth is the center of the chart, surrounded by the zodiac portion of the sky, divided into wedge-shaped segments. This is simply a graphic depiction of the energies occurring at a given moment at a certain place. On a deeper, more esoteric level, the horoscope actually materializes the qualities present in a moment in time. It shows how the energies will be used in real life and establishes a continuing link between the attributes of certain signs and specific kinds of experience.

Anything that happens can have a horoscope—a meeting, a person, a marriage—anything that can be pinned down to a time and a place. There are horoscopes for countries, cities, businesses, events as well as people.

Each wedge-shaped segment of the chart is called a "house" and deals with a specific area of life. The house reflects the character of *two* signs. First, the sign that rules the house, which has a natural affinity for it. You might think of this as the house's owner. The planet that rules this sign is also naturally at home in this house. The other important sign is the one that is passing over the house at the moment the chart is cast, which colors the house individually—this sign is what makes the house uniquely "yours," because it is passing over at "your" moment in time at your place of birth. If there were no house system, the horoscope would apply to anyone born at that time anyplace on earth.

The houses rotate counterclockwise from the left center horizontal spoke (that would be the number 9 on a clock), which is the 1st House or ascendant. The signs were moving clockwise around the chart at the time they were "frozen" in place on the chart.

The sequence of the houses is an integrated cycle, somewhat like a "hero's journey," an evolution toward growth and maturity. As houses progress around the chart, starting with the birth of the self in the first chart and evolving through the different areas of life, the "hero" becomes mature and finally "dissolves" in the 12th House, which prepares for the next cycle. Follow along as each house tells you about a stage in your development.

The 1st House: Natural place of Aries and Mars

How you assert yourself—what others see first.

This is the house of "firsts"—the first gasp of independence, the first impression you make, how you initiate matters, the image you choose to project, the seeds that are planted. This is where you advertise yourself. Planets that fall here will intensify how you come across to others. Often the 1st House will project an entirely different type

51

of personality than the sun sign. For example, a Capricorn with Leo in the 1st House will come across as much more flamboyant than the average Capricorn. The sign passing over this house is known as your ascendant or rising sign.

The 2nd House: Home of Taurus and Venus

How you experience the material world—what you value.

Here is your contact with the material world—your attitudes about money, possessions, finances, whatever belongs to you—what you own, your earning and spending capacity. On a deeper level, this house reveals your sense of self-worth, the inner values that draw wealth in various forms.

The 3rd House: Home of Gemini and Mercury

How well you communicate with others—are you understood?

This house shows how you reach out to others nearby and interact with the immediate environment. Here is how your thinking process works, how you communicate, if you are misunderstood. It shows your first relationships, experiences with brothers and sisters. How you deal with people close to you, such as your neighbors or pals. It's where you take short trips, write letters, or use the telephone. It shows how your mind works in terms of left-brain logical and analytical functions.

The 4th House: Natural place of Cancer and the moon

How you are nurtured and made to feel secure.

At the bottom of the chart, the 4th House, like the home, shows the foundation of life, the psychological underpinnings. Here is where you have the deepest confrontations with who you are, how you make yourself feel secure. It shows your early home environment and the circumstances of the end of your life—your final "home"—as well as the place you call home now. Astrologers look here for information about the parental nurturers in your life.

The 5th House: Home of Leo and the sun

How you express yourself creatively—your idea of play.

The Leo house is where creative potential develops. Here you express yourself and procreate (children), in the sense that children are outgrowths of your creative ability. But this house most represents your inner childlike self who delights in play. Assuming inner security has been established by the time you reach this house, you are now free to have fun, romance, love affairs, and to *give* of yourself. This is also the place astrologers look for carefree love affairs, brief romantic encounters (rather than long-term commitments).

The 6th House: Home of Virgo and Mercury

How you function in daily life.

The 6th House has been called the "repair and maintenance" department. Here is the shop where you get things done, how you look after others and fulfill responsibilities such as taking care of pets. Here is your daily survival, your "job" (as opposed to your career, which is the domain of the 10th House), your diet, health, and fitness regimens. This house shows how you take care of your body and maintenance systems so you can perform efficiently in the world.

The 7th House: Natural place of Libra and Venus

How you form a partnership.

Here is how you relate to others; your close, intimate one-on-one relationships. Your attitudes toward partners and those with whom you enter into commitments, contracts, or agreements develop in this house. Open hostilities, lawsuits, divorces as well as marriages happen here. If the 1st House is the "I"—the 7th or opposite house is the "Not-I"—the complementary partner you attract by the way you come across. If you are having trouble with partnerships, consider what you are attracting by the energies of your 1st and 7th houses.

53

The 8th House: Home of Scorpio and Pluto (also Mars)

How you merge with something greater than yourself.

This is one of the most mysterious and powerful houses, where your energy transforms itself from "I" to "we." As you give up power and control, you unite with what is larger than yourself—two kinds of energies merge and become something greater—and lead to a regeneration of the self. Here are your attitudes toward sex, shared resources, debt, taxes. Because this house involves what belongs to others, you face issues of control and power struggles, or undergo a deep psychological transformation as you bond with another. Here you transcend yourself with the occult, dreams, drugs, or psychic experiences which reflect the collective unconscious.

The 9th House: Home of Sagittarius and Jupiter

How you search for wisdom and higher knowledge, your belief system.

As the 3rd House represents the "lower mind," its opposite on the wheel, the 9th House, is the "higher mind," the abstract, intuitive, spiritual mind which asks "big" questions such as why are we here? The 9th House shows what you believe in. After the 3rd House explored what was close at hand, the 9th stretches out to explore more exotic territory, either by traveling, broadening mentally with higher education, or stretching spiritually with religious interest. Here is where you write a book or extensive thesis, where you pontificate, philosophize, or preach.

The 10th House: Natural place of Capricorn and Saturn

Your public image and how you handle authority.

This house is located directly overhead at the "high noon" position. This is the most "visible" house in the chart, the one where the world sees you. It deals with your public image, your career (but not your routine "job"), your reputation. Here is where you go public, take on responsibilities (as opposed to the 4th House, where you stay home). This will affect the career you choose and your "public relations." This house is also associated with the father figure or the person who was the authority figure in your life.

The 11th House: Home of Aquarius and Uranus

Your support system, how you relate to society, your goals.

Here you extend yourself to a group, a goal, a belief system. This house is where you define what you really want, what kinds of friends you have, your political affiliations, the kind of groups you identify with as an equal. Here is where you could become a socially-conscious humanitarian—or a party-going social butterfly, where you look to others to stimulate you, where you discover your kinship to the rest of humanity. The sign on this house can help you understand what you gain and lose from friendships.

The 12th House: Home of Pisces and Neptune

How you become self-less.

Here is where the boundaries between yourself and others are blurred. In your trip around the zodiac, you've gone from the "I" of self-assertion in the 1st House to the final house symbolizing the dissolution that happens before a rebirth, a place where the accumulated experiences are processed in the unconscious. Spiritually oriented astrologers look to this house for your past lives and karma. Places where we go to be alone and do spiritual or reparatory work belong here, such as retreats, religious institutions, hospitals. Here is also where we withdraw from society— or are forced to withdraw because of antisocial activity. Self-less giving through charitable acts is part of this house. In your daily life, the 12th House reveals your deepest intimacies, your best-kept secrets—especially those you hide from yourself, repressed deep in the unconscious. It is where we surrender a sense of a separate self to the deep feeling of wholeness that comes from selfless service in religion or any activity that involves merging with the greater whole. Many outstanding athletes have important planets in the 12th House which enable them to "go with the flow" of the game, to rise above competition and find an inner, almost mystical, strength that transcends their limits. Madonna, the rock star, has a strong 12th-House emphasis in her horoscope, and reflects the religious, psychological, and sexual concerns of this house.

Who's Home in Your Houses?

Houses are stronger or weaker depending on how many planets are inhabiting them. If there are many planets in a given house, it follows that the activities of that house will be especially important in your life. If the planet that rules the house is also located there, this too adds power to the house.

The Anatomy of a Sign

What is the difference between a sign and a constellation? This is one of the most frequently asked questions. Everyone knows that the constellations of the zodiac are specific configurations of stars. But not everyone knows that the sign which the constellation represents may be in a different place!

A sign is actually a 30-degree division of a circular belt of sky called the zodiac, which means "circle of animals" in Greek. Originally, each division was marked by a constellation (some of which were named after animals—a lion, a bull, a goat, a ram—or sea creatures—fish, a crab). But as the earth's axis changed over thousands of years, so did the signposts. Even though the "animals" have moved, however, the division of the circle—which is what astrologers call a "sign"—remains the same.

A *sun sign* is the sign (or division of the zodiac) the sun was passing through at the time of your birth. This is really the foundation of your horoscope, the base of your astrological character. It takes on color and nuances with nine other planets (the moon is most often referred to as a planet) and the signs in which they fall.

You may have heard that each sign is associated with an element. Pisces is a water sign, Aquarius is an air sign, for instance. How did this happen?

The definitions of the signs evolved systematically from four interrelated components: a sign's *element*, its *quality* (or mode), its *polarity* or sex, and its *order* in the circle of the zodiac. These components work together to tell us what the sign is like and how it behaves.

The system is mathematical, in a magical way: The number 12—as in the 12 signs of the zodiac—is divisible by 4, by 3, and by 2. Perhaps it is no coincidence that there are four elements, three qualities, and two polarities. These follow each other in sequence around the zodiac, starting with Aries. And it happens that no two signs have the same combination of element, quality, or polarity.

The four elements (earth, air, fire, and water) are the "building blocks" of astrology. The use of an element to describe a sign probably dates from man's first attempts to categorize what and who he saw in the world. Sages of old believed that all things were composed of combinations of earth, air, fire, and water. This included the human character, which was fiery/choleric, earthy/melancholy, airy/sanguine, or watery/phlegmatic. The elements also correspond to our emotional (water), physical (earth), mental (air), and spiritual (fire) natures. The energies of each of the elements were then observed to relate to the time of year when the sun was passing through a certain segment of the zodiac.

The fire signs—Aries, Leo, and Sagittarius—embody the characteristics of that element. Optimism, warmth, hot tempers, enthusiasm, and "spirit" are typical of these signs. Taurus, Virgo, and Capricorn are "earthy"—more grounded, physical, materialistic, organized, and deliberate than fire people. Air signs—Gemini, Libra, and Aquarius—are mentally oriented communicators. Water signs—Cancer, Scorpio, and Pisces—are emotional and creative.

Think of what each element does to the others: water puts out fire or evaporates with heat. Air fans the flames or blows them out. Earth smothers fire, drifts and erodes with too much wind, becomes mud or fertile soil with water. Those are often perfect analogies for the relationships between signs of these elements! This astro-chemistry was one of the first ways man described his relationships. Fortunately, no one is entirely "air" or "fire." We all have some, or a lot, of each element in our horoscopes, this unique mix that defines each astrological personality.

Within each element, there are three qualities, that describe how the sign behaves, how it works. (The qualities are sometimes referred to as "modes.") Cardinal signs are the activists, the go-getters. These signs—Aries, Cancer, Libra, and Capricorn—begin each season. Fixed signs are the builders that occur in the middle of the season. You'll find that Taurus, Leo, Scorpio, and Aquarius are gifted with concentration, stubbornness, and stamina. Mutable signs—Gemini, Virgo, Sagitarrius, and Pisces—are catalysts for change at the end of each season, these are flexible, adaptable, mobile signs.

The polarity of a sign is its positive or negative "charge." It can be masculine, active, positive, or yang like the air and fire signs. Or it can be feminine, reactive, negative, or yin like the water and earth signs. These polarities alternate like the poles of a battery, sending energy around the chart.

Finally, we consider the sign's place in the order of the zodiac. This is vital to the balance of all the forces and the transmission of energy moving through the signs. You may have noticed that your sign is quite different from your neighboring sign on either side. Yet each seems to grow out of its predecessor like links in a chain, and transmits a synthesis of energy gathered along the "chain" to the following sign, beginning with the fire-powered active positive charge of Aries.

What if a person has no planets in an element? Usually that person will be especially challenged in the areas of that low-function element. For instance, someone who has no planets in earth signs may have to work very hard to manifest the material side of life. Or the person may overcompensate in that area, want to be around earthy things—have a beautiful garden, for instance.

It's appropriate here to remember that, in astrology, there are no pat answers. How a chart works out depends on the individual: a missing element could be an area of great self-expression and self-development, as well as a difficult area. One example is a famous TV commentator, renowned for his intellectual approach, who has no planets in air signs. The missing element could also be emphasized in the placement of the houses. Someone with no water might have a water sign in a powerful angular position.

Each sign has a "ruling Planet" that is most compatible with its energies. Mars rules the fiery, assertive Aries. The sensual beauty- and comfort-loving side of Venus rules Taurus, while the more idealistic side rules Libra. The quick-moving Mercury rules both Gemini and Virgo, showing its mental agility in Gemini, its critical analytical side in Virgo. Emotional Cancer is ruled by the moon, while outgoing Leo is ruled by the sun. Scorpio was originally given Mars, but when Pluto was discovered in this century, its powerful magnetic energies were deemed more suitable to Scorpio (though many astrologers still consider Mars the coruler of Scorpio). Disciplined Capricorn is ruled by Saturn; expansive Sagittarius, by Jupiter. Unpredictable Aquarius is ruled by Uranus and creative, impressionable Pisces by Neptune.

Quick Reference Chart

Sign	Element	Quality	Polarity	Ruling Planet
Aries	Fire	Cardinal	Positive	Mars
Taurus	Earth	Fixed	Negative	Venus
Gemini	Air	Mutable	Positive	Mercury
Cancer	Water	Cardinal	Negative	Moon
Leo	Fire	Fixed	Positive	Sun
Virgo	Earth	Mutable	Negative	Mercury
Libra	Air	Cardinal	Positive	Venus
Scorpio	Water	Fixed	Negative	Pluto
Sagittarius	Fire	Mutable	Positive	Jupiter
Capricorn	Earth	Cardinal	Negative	Saturn
Aquarius	Air	Fixed	Negative	Uranus
Pisces	Water	Mutable	Negative	Neptune

CHAPTER 9

How to Use All Ten Planets

Astrology gives you not one, but *ten* ways to get to know yourself and others. If you only know your sun sign, you've been missing out on the nine other planetary forces that are great sources of information. Think of the other planets as your own special task force, which can be put to work for you, supplying you with tips you can use in every area of your life, to help you focus your goals, define your objectives, deal with other people, and get what you want.

The planets can be your key allies in personal relationships. Want to know what turns someone on? Consult their Venus. How about mastering a fear, phobia, or anxiety? Look up Saturn. Having a power struggle? Pluto might shed some light. Knowing a person's planets will reveal what that person needs for fulfillment in the area each planet represents. The *sign* a planet is in will show how the planet is used. For instance, the moon (emotional needs) in Cancer (maternal, nurturing) indicates that a person might be emotionally fulfilled through nurturing others, have a close relationship with Mother, and a very caring, sensitive nature. If that moon is located in the 10th house (career, public life, status in the world), the person would live out the moon's need for nurturing in some public way, perhaps through a career in a nurturing or feeding profession, such as the hotel, child care, or restaurant business.

The planets in a horoscope will play starring or supporting roles, depending on their position in the chart. For instance, a planet in the 1st house, particularly near your rising sign, is sure to be especially influential. Planets that are grouped together usually operate together, like a team, playing off each other, rather than expressing their energy singularly. A planet that stands alone, away from the others, is usually outstanding and sometimes steals the show.

Each planet has two signs where it is especially at home.

The most favorable place for a planet is in the sign or signs it rules, or in a sign where it is "exalted," that is, especially harmonious. Conversely, there are places in the horoscope where a planet works harder to play its role. These places are called the planet's "detriment" and "fall." The sign opposite a planet's rulership (which embodies the opposite area of life), is its detriment. The sign opposite its exaltation is its fall. Though the terms may suggest unfortunate circumstances for the planet, that is not necessarily the case. In fact, a planet that is under stress can actually be more powerful, because it must struggle to meet the challenges of living in a more difficult sign. Like world leaders who have had to struggle for greatness, this planet may actually develop strength and character.

Use the charts following this chapter to look up most of the following planets. Then apply them to your coworkers, family, lovers, friends. Check out the potential of those around you—or tap some of your own hidden powers!

What a Person's Sun Sign Reveals

Want to know about someone's basic ego, their central focus, what they want to accomplish? Look to the sun. It is always center stage in the horoscope, the star of the show, even when surrounded by other strong planetary players. Astrologers focus on the sun sign in general books such as these, because the qualities of the sun are the most typical of people who were born when the sun was passing through a given sign. This is the common denominator. Though you might share other planets with someone, it's your sun sign that will color your outward personality most strongly. It rules the sign of Leo, gaining strength through the pride, dignity, and confidence of Leo's fixed fire personality. It is exalted in "me-first" Aries. In its detriment, Aquarius, the sun ego is strengthened through group participation and social consciousness (think of the Aquarius celebrities like Paul Newman who amplify their fame by identifying themselves with charitable and political causes). In its fall, in Libra, the sun needs the strength of a partner, an "other," for balance and self-expression. You can read all about your sun sign from the individual chapters at the end of this book.

Uncover Someone's Emotional Needs with the Moon

The moon's role is to dig beneath the surface, to reflect your subconscious needs and longings, and the kind of mothering and childhood conditioning you had. The moon rules maternal Cancer and is exalted in Taurus, both comforting home-loving signs where the natural emotional energies of the moon are easily and productively expressed. But, when the moon is in the opposite signs, in its Capricorn detriment and Scorpio fall, the moon leaves the comfortable nest and deals with emotional issues of power and achievement in the outside world. Those of you with the moon in these signs will find your emotional role more challenging in life.

(Since accurate moon tables are too extensive to include in this book, we suggest you consult an astrologer or have a computer chart made to determine your correct moon position.)

MOON IN ARIES. Emotionally, you are independent and ardent. You are fulfilled by meeting challenges, overcoming obstacles, by being "first." You have exceptional courage. You love the challenge of an emotional pursuit, and difficult situations in love only intensify your excitement. But the catch-22 is that, once you attain your goal or conquer your pursuit, your ardor cools. To avoid continuous "treat 'em rough" situations, work on developing patience and tolerance.

MOON IN TAURUS. Solid, secure, comfortable situations and relationships are fulfilling to you. You need plenty of open displays of affection and gravitate to those who provide you with material comforts and sensual pleasures. Your emotions are steady and nurturing in this strong moon sign, but could lean toward stubbornness when pushed. You could miss out on some of life's excitement by sticking to the safe straight and narrow road.

MOON IN GEMINI: You need constant emotional stimulation and enjoy an outgoing, diversified lifestyle. You could have difficulty with commitment, and therefore marry more than once or have a love life of changing partners.

An outgoing, interesting, talented partner could merit your devotion, however. Be careful not to spread yourself too thin to accomplish major goals—and beware a tendency to be emotionally fragmented. Find a creative way to express the range of your feelings, possibly through developing writing, speaking, or other communicative talents.

MOON IN CANCER: The moon is strongest here, making you the zodiac nurturer—one who needs to be needed. You have an excellent memory and an intuitive understanding of the needs of others. You are happiest at home and may work in a home office or turn your corner of the company into a home away from home. Work that supplies food and shelter, nurtures children, involves occult studies and psychology could take advantage of this lunar position.

MOON IN LEO: You need to be treated like royalty! Strong support, loyalty, and loud applause win your heart. You rule over your territory and resent anyone who intrudes on your turf. Your attraction to the finer things in people and in your lifestyle could give you a snobbish outlook. But basically you have a warm, passionate, loyal, emotional nature that gives generously to those you deem worthy. Children and leadership roles which express your creativity can bring you great satisfaction.

MOON IN VIRGO: This moon often draws you to situations where you play the role of healer, teacher, or critic. You may find it difficult to accept others as they are or enjoy what you have. Because you must analyze before you can give emotionally, the Virgo moon can be hard on others and equally tough on yourself. Be aware that you may have impossible standards, and be more flexible with others. A little tolerance goes a long way and so does a sense of humor to see if they measure up. Take it easy!

MOON IN LIBRA: Your emotional role is partnership oriented—you won't live or work alone for long! You may find it difficult to do things alone. You need the emotional balance of a strong "other." You thrive in an elegant, harmonious atmosphere, where you get attention and flattery. This moon needs to keep it light. Heavy emotions cause your Libran moon's scales to swing precariously. So does an overly possessive or demanding partner.

MOON IN SCORPIO: The moon is not really comfortable in intense Scorpio, which is emotionally drawn to extremes and can be obsessive, suspicious, and jealous. You take disappointments very hard and are often drawn to extreme situations, dealing with issues of power and control. It's important to learn when to tone down those all-or-nothing feelings. Finding a healthy outlet in meaningful work could diffuse your intense needs. Medicine, occult work, law-enforcement, or psychology are good possibilities.

MOON IN SAGITTARIUS: This moon needs freedom—you can't stand to be possessed by anyone. You have emotional wanderlust and may need a constant dose of mental and spiritual stimulation. But you cope with the fluctuations of life with good humor and a spirit of adventure. You may find great satisfaction in exotic situations, foreign travels, and spiritual studies, rather than in intense one-on-one relationships.

MOON IN CAPRICORN: Here the moon is cool and calculating—and very ambitious. You get a sense of security from achieving prestige and position in the outside world, rather than creating a cozy nest at home. Though you are dutiful toward those you love, your heart is in your climb to the top of the business or social ladder. Concrete achievement and improving your position in life bring you great satisfaction.

MOON IN AQUARIUS: This is a gregarious moon, happiest when surrounded by people. You're everyone's buddy—as long as no one gets too close. You'd rather stay pals. You make your own rules in emotional situations and may have a radically different life- or love-style. Intimate relationships may feel too confining, for you need plenty of space.

MOON IN PISCES: This watery moon needs an emotional anchor to help you keep grounded in reality. Otherwise, you tend to look for means of escape from the harshness of life, either by creating a fantasy world (many actors have this placement) or through intoxicating substances. Creative work could give you a far more productive way to express yourself and get away from it all. Working in a healing or helping profession is also good for you because you get satisfaction from helping the underdog. But, though you naturally attract people with sob stories, try to cultivate friends with a positive upbeat point of view.

Mercury Helps You Discover How the Mind Works

Mercury shows how a person thinks and speaks, how logically someone's mind works. Since it stays close to the sun, never more than a sign away, and often shares the same sign as the sun, it often reinforces the sun's communicative talents. Mercury functions easily in the signs it rules—Gemini and Virgo—which are naturally analytical signs. A person with sun in Gemini (Mercury ruled), and Mercury placed in Taurus, will have a more disciplined mind, capable of great concentration (like President John F. Kennedy). Mercury in Sagittarius and Pisces, signs where logic often takes second place to visionary ideas, and where Mercury is "debilitated," can still provide visionary thinking and poetic expression when this planet is properly used.

Since Mercury never moves more than a sign away from the sun, check your sun sign and the signs preceding and following it, to see which Mercury position most applies to you.

MERCURY IN ARIES never shies away from a confrontation. You say what you think; you are active and assertive. Your mind is sharp, alert, impatient, but you may not be thorough.

MERCURY IN TAURUS is deliberate, thorough, has good concentration. You'll take the slow, methodical approach, and leave no stone unturned. You'll see a problem through to the end, stick with a subject until you become an expert. You may talk very slowly, but in a melodious voice.

MERCURY IN GEMINI is a quick study. You can handle many subjects at once, jumping from one to the other easily. You may, however, spread yourself too thin. You express yourself easily both verbally and in writing. You are a "people person" who enjoys having others buzzing around and communicating with a large audience.

MERCURY IN CANCER has great empathy for others—you can read their feelings. You are intuitive, rather than logical. And your thoughts are always colored by your emotions. You have an excellent memory and imagination.

MERCURY IN LEO has a flair for dramatic expression which can hold the attention of others (and sometimes hog the limelight). This is also a placement of mental overconfidence. You think big and prefer to skip the details. However, you might be an excellent salesperson or public speaker.

MERCURY IN VIRGO is a strong position. You're a natural critic, with an analytic, orderly mind. You pay attention to details and have a talent for thorough analysis, good organization, though you tend to focus on the practical side of things. Teaching and editing come naturally to you.

MERCURY IN LIBRA. You are a smooth talker, with a graceful gift of gab. Though gifted in diplomacy and debate, you may vacillate in making decisions, forever juggling the pros and cons. You speak in elegant, well-modulated tones.

MERCURY IN SCORPIO has a sharp mind, which can be sarcastic and given to making cutting remarks. You have a penetrating insight and will stop at nothing to get to the heart of matters. You are an excellent and thorough investigator, researcher, or detective. You enjoy problems that challenge your skills in digging and probing.

MERCURY IN SAGITTARIUS has a great sense of humor, but a tendency toward tactlessness. You enjoy telling others what you see as the truth "for their own good." This can either make you a great teacher or visionary, like poet Robert Bly, or it can make you dogmatic. When you feel you're in the right, you may expound endlessly on your own ideas. Watch a tendency to puff up ideas unrealistically (however, this talent could make you a super salesman).

MERCURY IN CAPRICORN has excellent mental discipline. You take a serious, orderly approach and play by the rules. You have a super-organized mind that grasps structures easily, though you may lack originality. You have a dry sense of humor.

MERCURY IN AQUARIUS is "exalted" and quite at home in this analytical sign. You have a highly original point of view, combined with good mental focus. An independent thinker, you'll break the rules, if this will help make your point. You are, however, fixed mentally, and reluctant to change your mind once it is made up. Therefore, you could come across as a "know-it-all."

MERCURY IN PISCES has a poetic mind that is receptive to psychic, intuitive influences. You may be vague, unclear in your expression and forgetful of details, and find it difficult to work within a structure, but you are strong on creative communication and thinking. You'll express yourself in a very sympathetic, caring way. You should find work that uses your imaginative talents.

For Attractions and Reactions, Look at Venus

Venus is the planet of romantic love, of pleasure and artistry. It shows what you react to, your tastes, what (or who) turns you on. It shows what you'll attract without trying— and that includes income. Your Venus will show you how to charm others in a way that is suited to you.

Venus is naturally at home in Libra, the sign of relating, or Taurus, the sign of physical pleasures, both of which it rules. Yet in Aries, its detriment, Venus is daring and full of energy (though self-serving). In Pisces, where Venus is exalted, this planet can go overboard, loving to the point of self-sacrifice. While Venus in Virgo, its fall, can be a perfectionist in love, it can also offer affectionate service and true support.

You can find your Venus placement on the chart in this book. Look for the year of your birth in the left-hand column, then follow the line across the page until you read the time of your birthday. The sign heading that column will be your Venus. If you were born on a day when Venus was changing signs, check the signs preceding or following that day. Here are the roles your Venus plays—and sings.

VENUS IN ARIES: Scarlett O'Hara probably had Venus here! You love a challenge that adds spice to life, and might even pick a fight now and then to shake 'em up. Since a good chase revs up your romantic motor, you could abandon a romance if the going becomes too smooth. You're first on the block with the newest styles. And first out the door if you're bored or ordered around.

VENUS IN TAURUS: Venus is literally "at home" in Taurus. Here is a "material girl" or boy who loves to surround yourself with the very finest smells, tastes, sounds, visuals, textures. You'd run from an austere lifestyle or uncomfortable surroundings. Creature comforts turn you on. And so does a beautiful, secure nest—and nest egg. Not one to rush about, you take time to enjoy your pleasures and treasures.

VENUS IN GEMINI: You're a sparkler, like singer Cher, who loves the nightlife, with constant variety, a frequent change of scenes—and loves. You like lots of stimulation, a varied social life, and are better at light flirtations than serious romances. You may be attracted to younger playful lovers who have the energy to keep up with you.

VENUS IN CANCER: You can be daddy's girl or mama's boy. You love to be babied, coddled, and protected in a cozy, secure home. You are attracted to those who make you feel secure, well provided for. You could also have a secret love life or clandestine arrangement with a "sugar daddy." You love to "mother" others as well.

VENUS IN LEO: You're an "uptown" girl or boy who loves "Putting on the Ritz," where you can consort with elegant people, dress extravagantly, and be the center of attention. Think of Coco Chanel, who piled on the jewelry and decorated tweed suits with gold braid. You dress and act like a star, but you may be attracted to hangers-on and flatterers, rather than cultivating relationships with solid value.

VENUS IN VIRGO: You are attracted to perfect order, but underneath your pristine white dress is some naughty black lace! You fall for those who you can make over or improve in some way. You may also fancy those in the medical profession. Here Venus may express itself best through some kind of service—giving loving support. You may find it difficult to show your true feelings, to really let go in intimate moments. "I Can't Get No Satisfaction" could sometimes be your theme song.

VENUS IN LIBRA: "I Feel Pretty" sings this Venus. You love a beautiful, harmonious, luxurious atmosphere. Many artists and musicians thrive with this Venus, with its natural feeling for the balance of colors and sounds. In love, you make a very compatible partner in a supportive relationship where there are few confrontations. You can't stand arguments or argumentative people. The good looks of your partner may also be a deciding factor.

VENUS IN SCORPIO: "All or Nothing at All" could be your theme song. This Venus wants "Body and Soul." You're a natural detective who's attracted to a mystery. You know how to keep a secret, and have quite a few of your own. This is a very intense placement, where you can be preoccupied with sex and power. Living dangerously adds spice to your life, but don't get burned. All that's intense appeals to you: heady perfume, deep rich colors, dark woods, spicy foods.

VENUS IN SAGITTARIUS: "On the Road Again" sums up your Venus personality. Travel, athletics, religious or philosophical studies, and a casual, carefree lifestyle appeal to you. You are attracted to exciting, idealistic types who give you plenty of space. Large animals, especially horses, are part of your life. You probably have a four-wheel drive vehicle—or a motorized skateboard—anything to keep moving.

VENUS IN CAPRICORN: "Diamonds Are a Girl's Best Friend" could characterize this ambitious Venus. You may seem cool and calculating, but underneath you're insecure and want a substantial relationship you can count on. It wouldn't hurt if your beloved could help you up the ladder professionally, either. This Venus is often attracted to objects and people of a different generation (like Clark Gable, you could marry someone much older—or younger)—antiques, traditional clothing (sometimes worn in a very "today" way, like Diane Keaton) and dignified, conservative behavior are trademarks.

VENUS IN AQUARIUS: "Just Friends, Lovers No More" is often what happens with Venus in Aquarius. You love to be surrounded by people, but are uncomfortable with intense emotions (steer clear of Venus in Scorpio!). You like a spontaneous lifestyle, full of surprises. You make your own rules in everything you do, including love. The avant-garde, high technology, and possibly unusual sexual experiences attract you.

VENUS IN PISCES: "Why Not Take All of Me?" sings this exalted Venus, who loves to give. You may have a collection of stray animals, lost souls, the underprivileged, the lonely. (Try to assess their motives in a clear light.) You're a natural for theater, film, anything involving fantasy. Psychic or spiritual life also draws you, as does selfless service for a needy cause.

Want to Know What Drives Someone? How Energetic and Aggressive a Person Can Be? Look to Mars

This planet is your driving force, your active sexuality. Mars is what makes you run. In Aries, which it rules, and Scorpio, which it corules, Mars is at his most powerful. Yet this drive can be self-serving and impetuous. In Libra, the sign of its detriment, Mars demands cooperation in a relationship. In Capricorn, where it is exalted, Mars becomes an ambitious achiever, headed for the top. On the other hand, Mars in Cancer, the sign of its "fall," expresses itself through the emotions. The end can never justify the means for a sensitive Mars in Cancer. To find your Mars, refer to the Mars chart in this book. If the following description of your Mars sign doesn't ring true, you may have been born on a day when Mars was changing signs, so check the adjacent sign descriptions.

MARS IN ARIES runs in high gear, showing the full force of its energy. You have a fiery explosive disposition, but are also very courageous, with enormous drive. You'll tackle problems head on and mow down anything that stands in your way. Though you're supercharged and can jump-start others, you are short on perseverance, especially when a situation requires diplomacy, patience, and tolerance.

MARS IN TAURUS could claim the motto: "Persistance alone is omnipotent." You're in it for the long haul—and win the race with a slow, steady steamrolling pace. Gifted with stamina and focus, this Mars may not be first out of the gate, but you're sure to finish. You tend to wear away or outlast your foes rather than bowl them over. Like Bruce Willis, this Mars is super-sensual sexually—you take your time and enjoy yourself all the way. You'll probably accumulate many collections and material possessions.

MARS IN GEMINI holds the philosophy: "two is better than one," which could create havoc with your love life. Your restless nature searches out stimulation and will switch rather than fight. Your life gets complicated, but that only makes it more interesting for you. You have a way with words and can "talk" with your hands. Since you tend to go all over the lot in your interests, you may have to work to develop focus and concentration.

MARS IN CANCER is given to moods and can be quite crabby. This may be due to a fragile sense of security. You are quite self-protective and secretive about your life, which might make you appear untrustworthy or manipulative to others. Try not to take things so much to heart—cultivate a sense of impersonality or detachment. Sexually, you are tender and sensitive, a very protective lover.

MARS IN LEO fills you with self-confidence and charisma. You'll use your considerable drive to get attention, coming on strong, with show-biz flair, like Cher, who has this placement. In fact you'll head right for the spotlight. Sexually, you're a giver—but you do demand the royal treatment in return. You enjoy giving orders and can create quite a scene if you're disobeyed. At some point, you may have to learn some lessons in humility.

MARS IN VIRGO is a worker bee, a "Felix Unger" character who notices every detail. This is a thorough, painstaking Mars that worries a great deal about making mistakes. This "worrier" tendency may create tightly strung nerves under your controlled facade. Your energy can be expressed positively in a field such as teaching or editing, but your tendency to find fault could make you a hard-to-please lover. Learning to delegate and praise, rather than do everything perfectly yourself, could make you easier to live with. You enjoy good mental companionship, with less emphasis on sex and no emotional turmoil. If you do find the perfect lover, you'll tend to take care of that person.

MARS IN LIBRA is a passive-aggressor who avoids confrontations and charms people into doing what you want. You'll do best in a position where you can exercise your great diplomatic skills. Mars is in its detriment in Libra, and expends much energy deciding which course of action to take. However, setting a solid goal in life—perhaps one that expresses your passion for beauty, justice, or art—could give you the vantage point you need to achieve success. In love, like Michael Douglas, you'll go for beauty in your partner and surroundings.

MARS IN SCORPIO has a powerful drive (relax, sometimes!) that could become an obsession. Learn to use this energy wisely and well, for Mars in Scorpio hates to compromise, loves with all-or-nothing fervor (while it lasts), and can get jealous or manipulative if you don't get your way! But your powerful concentration and nonstop stamina is an asset in challenging fields like medicine or scientific research. You're the master planner, a super-strategist who, when well-directed, can achieve important goals, like actors Larry Hagman and Bill Cosby, and scientist Jonas Salk.

MARS IN SAGITTARIUS is the conquering hero off on a crusade. You're great at getting things off the ground; however, your challenge is to consider the consequences of your actions. In love with freedom, you don't always make the best marriage partner. "Love 'em and leave 'em" could be your motto. You may also gravitate toward risk and adventure, and may have great athletic skill. You're best off in a situation where you can express your love of adventure, philosophy, and travel, or where you can use artistic talents to elevate the lives of others, like Johann Sebastian Bach.

MARS IN CAPRICORN is exalted. This "chief executive" placement gives you both a drive for success and the discipline to achieve it. You deliberately aim for status and a high position in life, and you'll keep climbing, despite the odds. This Mars will work for what you get. You are well organized and persistent—a winning combination. Sexually, you have a strong, earthy drive, but may go for someone who can be useful to you, rather than someone flashy or fascinating.

MARS IN AQUARIUS is a visionary and often a revolutionary who stands out from the crowd. You are innovative and highly original in your methods. Sexually, you could go for unusual relationships, like Hugh Hefner or Howard Hughes. You have a rebellious streak and like to shake people up a bit. Intimacy can be a problem—you may keep lots of people around you or isolate yourself to keep anyone from getting too close.

MARS IN PISCES likes to play different roles. Your ability to tune in and project others' emotions makes you a natural actor. There are many film and TV personalities with this placement, including Mary Tyler Moore, Jane Seymour, Cybill Shepherd, Burt Reynolds, and Jane Fonda. You understand how to use glamour and illusion for your own benefit. You can switch emotions on and off quickly, and you're especially good at getting sympathy. You'll enjoy romance, though real life relationships never quite live up to your fantasies.

Luck, Risks, Enthusiasm, and Salesmanship are Jupiter's Territory

Jupiter is often viewed as the "Santa Claus" of the horoscope, a jolly, happy planet that brings good luck, gifts, success, and opportunities. Jupiter also embodies the functions of the higher mind, where you do complex, expansive thinking, and deal with the big overall picture rather than the specifics (the province of Mercury). Jupiter functions naturally in Sagittarius, the sign of the philosopher, or Pisces, which it corules with Neptune. In Gemini, its detriment, Jupiter can be scattered, a jack-of-all-trades. On the other hand, it can also be a lighthearted, effective communicator. In Cancer, where it is exalted, Jupiter becomes the protective "big brother." In Capricorn, its fall, Jupiter is brought down to earth, its vision harnessed to practical goals.

Be sure to look up your Jupiter "lucky spot" in the tables in this book. But bear in mind that Jupiter gives growth without discrimination or discipline. A person with a strong Jupiter may be weak in common sense. This is also the place where you could have too much of a good thing, resulting in extravagance, excess pounds, laziness, or carelessness.

JUPITER IN ARIES. You have big ambitions and won't settle for second place. You are luckiest when you are pioneering an innovative project, pushing to be "first." You can break new ground with this placement, but watch a tendency to be pushy and arrogant. You'll also need to learn patience and perseverance in the house where Jupiter falls in your horoscope.

JUPITER IN TAURUS. You have expensive tastes and like to surround yourself with the luxuries money can buy. You acquire beauty and comfort in all its forms. You could tend to expand physically—from overindulgence to good tastes! Dieting could be a major challenge. Land and real estate are especially lucky for you.

JUPITER IN GEMINI. You love to be in the center of a whirlwind of activity, talking a blue streak, with all phone lines busy. You have great facility in expressing yourself verbally or in writing. Work that involves communicating or manual dexterity is especially lucky for you. Watch a tendency to be too restless—slow down from time to time. Try not to spread yourself too thin!

JUPITER IN CANCER. This Jupiter has a big safe-deposit box, an attic piled to overflowing with boxes of treasures. You may still have your christening dress or your beloved high school sweater. This Jupiter loves to accumulate things, to save for a rainy day, or gather collections. Negatively, you could be a hoarder with closets full of things you'll never use. Protective, nurturing Jupiter in Cancer often has many mouths to feed—human or animal. Naturally, this placement produces great restaurateurs and hotel keepers. The shipping business is also a good bet.

74

JUPITER IN LEO. Naturally warm, romantic, and playful, you can't have too much attention or applause. You bask in the limelight while others are still trying to find the stage! Politics or show business—anywhere you can perform for an audience—are lucky for you. You love the good life and are happy to share your wealth with others. Negatively, you could be extravagent and tend to hog center stage. Let others take a bow from time to time. Also, be careful not to overdo or overspend.

JUPITER IN VIRGO. You like to work! In fact, work can be more interesting than play for you. You have a sharp eye for details and pick out every flaw! Be careful not to get caught up in nitpicking. You expect nothing short of perfection from others. Finding practical solutions to problems and helping others make the most of themselves are better uses for this Jupiter. Consider a health field such as nutrition, medicine, or health education. Coaching and teaching are other good outlets for this energy.

JUPITER IN LIBRA. You function best when you have a stimulating partner. You also need harmonious, beautiful surroundings. Chances are, you have closets full of fashionable clothes. The serious side of this Jupiter has an excellent sense of fair play, and can be a good diplomat or judge. Careers in law, the arts, or fashion are favored.

JUPITER IN SCORPIO. You love the power of handling other people's money—or lives! Others see you as having nerves of steel. You have luck in detective work, sex-related ventures, psychotherapy, research, the occult, or tax work—anything that involves a mystery. You're always going to extremes; testing the limits gives you a thrill. Your timing is excellent—you'll wait for the perfect moment to make your moves. Negatively this Jupiter could use power to achieve selfish ends.

JUPITER IN SAGITTARIUS. In its strongest place, Jupiter compels you to expand your mind, travel far from home, collect college degrees. This is the placement of the philosopher, the gambler, the animal trainer, the publisher. You have an excellent sense of humor and a cheerful disposition. This placement often works with animals, especially horses.

JUPITER IN CAPRICORN. You are lucky working in an established situation, within a traditional structure. In the sign of caution and restraint, Jupiter is frugal, definitely not a big spender. You accumulate duties and responsibilities, which is fine for business leadership. You'll expand in any area where you can achieve respect, prestige, or social position. People with this position are especially concerned that nothing be wasted. You might have great luck in a recycling or renovation business.

JUPITER IN AQUARIUS. You are lucky when doing good in the world. You are extremely idealistic and think in the most expansive terms about improving society at large. This is an excellent position for a politician or labor leader. You're everybody's friend, who can relate to people of diverse backgrounds. You are luckiest when you can operate away from rigid rules and conservative organizations.

JUPITER IN PISCES. You work best in a creative field or in one where you are helping the downtrodden. You exude sympathy and gravitate toward the underdog. Watch a tendency to be too self-sacrificing, overly emotional. You should also be careful not to overindulge in alcohol or drugs. Some lucky work areas: oil, perfume, dance, footwear, alcohol, pharmaceuticals, the arts—especially film.

How Disciplined Is this Person? How Does Someone Get the Job Done? What Are You Afraid Of? Saturn Will Tell

Saturn has suffered from a bad reputation, always cast as the "heavy" in the horoscope. However, the flip side of Saturn is the teacher, the one whose class is the toughest in school, but, when you graduate, you never forget the lessons well learned. (They are the ones you came here on this planet to learn.) And the tests of Saturn, which come at regular seven-year "exam periods," are the ones you need to pass to survive as a conscious, independent adult. Saturn gives us the grade we've earned—so, if we have studied and prepared for our tests, we needn't be afraid of the big bad wolf. Saturn in Capricorn, its ruler, is comfortable with this sign's emphasis on structure and respect for authority. In Cancer, Saturn's detriment, it suggests both that feeling must become responsible and that authority cannot operate effectively without concern for nurturing the individual.

Your Saturn position can illuminate your fears, your hang-ups, your important lessons in life. Remember that Saturn is concerned with your maturity, what you need to know to survive in the world. Be sure to look it up in the Saturn chart in this book.

SATURN IN ARIES. "Don't push me around!" says this Saturn, which puts the brakes on Aries' natural drive and enthusiasm. You'll have to learn to cooperate, tone down self-centeredness, and respect authorities. Bill Cosby, who has this placement, may have had the same lessons to learn.

SATURN IN TAURUS. "How am I going to pay the rent?" You'll have to stick out some lean periods and get control of your material life. Learn to use your talents to their fullest potential. In the same boat, Ben Franklin had the right idea: "A penny saved is a penny earned."

SATURN IN GEMINI. You're a deep thinker, with lofty ideals—a good position for scientific studies. You may be quite shy, speak slowly, or have fears about communicating, like Eleanor Roosevelt. Yet when you master those fears, you'll be able to sway the masses, just as she did. You'll take shelter in abstract ideas, like Sigmund Freud, when dealing with emotional issues.

SATURN IN CANCER. This placement is in its detriment. Some very basic fears could center on your early home environment, overcoming a negative childhood influence to establish a sense of security. You may fear being mothered or smothered and be tested in your female relationships. You may have to learn to be objective and distance yourself emotionally when threatened or when dealing with negative feelings such as jealousy or guilt. Bette Midler and Diane Keaton have this placement.

SATURN IN LEO. This placement can create ego problems. If you have not received the love you crave, you could be an overly strict, dictatorial parent. You may demand respect and a position of leadership at any cost. You may have to watch a tendency toward rigidity and withholding affection. You may have to learn to relax, have fun, lighten up!

SATURN IN VIRGO. You can be very hard on yourself, making yourself nauseated by worrying about every little detail. You must learn to set priorities, discriminate, and laugh!

SATURN IN LIBRA. This placement is exalted. You may have your most successful marriage (or your first) later in life, because you must learn to stand on your own first. How to relate to others is one of your major lessons. Your great sense of fairness makes you a good judge or lawyer, or a prominent diplomat like former Secretary of State Henry Kissenger.

SATURN IN SCORPIO. Your tests come when you handle situations involving the control of others. You could fear depending on others financially or sexually, or there could be a blurring of the lines between sex and money. Sexual tests, periods of celibacy (resulting from fear of "merging" with another), sex for money, are some ways this placement could manifest.

SATURN IN SAGITARIUS. You accept nothing at face value. You are the opposite of the "happy-go-lucky" Sagittarius. With Saturn here, your beliefs must be fully examined and tested. Firsthand experience, without the guidance of dogma, gurus, or teachers is your best education. This Saturn has little tolerance for another authority. You won't follow a "dream" unless you understand the idea behind it.

SATURN IN CAPRICORN. Those with this placement tend to be sensitive to public opinion and achieving a high-status image. You are not a big risk taker here, because you do not want to compromise your position. In its most powerful place, Saturn is the teacher par excellence, giving structure, form, and discipline to your life. Your persistence will assure you a continual climb to the top.

SATURN IN AQUARIUS. This is a Greta Garbo position where you feel like an outsider, one who doesn't fit into the group. There may be a lack of trust in others, a kind of defensiveness that could engender defensiveness in return. Not a superficial social butterfly, your commitment to groups must have depth and humanitarian meaning.

SATURN IN PISCES. This position generates a feeling of helplessness, of being a victim of circumstances. You could underestimate yourself, lack a sense of self-power. However, this can give great wisdom if you can manage, like Edgar Cayce, to look inward to contemplation and meditation, rather than outward, for solutions.

The Outer Planets—Uranus, Neptune, and Pluto

The three outer planets, Uranus, Neptune, and Pluto are slow moving but powerful forces in our lives. Because they stay in a sign at least seven years, you'll share the sign placement with everyone you went to school with and probably your brothers and sisters. The specific place (house) in the horoscope where each one operates is yours alone, and depends on your "moment in time"—the exact time you were born. That's why it is important to have an exact birth chart. Look at the charts on pages 108–111 to find the location of your outer planets.

How Does a Person Handle Freedom? How Independent Are You? Look at Uranus

Uranus is the brilliant, highly original, unpredictable planet that shakes us out of a rut and propels us forward. When Uranus hits a critical area of your life, such as a planet, or moves into a new area of your chart, nothing is ever the same again. Uranus strikes hardest at the fixed signs, where a shakeup is sometimes desperately needed. Uranus is right at home in the fixed air sign of Aquarius, where its brilliant ideas have universal applications, but in the fixed fire sign of Leo, its detriment, Uranus breaks up rigid patterns, seems to thumb its nose at proud, sometimes pompous Leo. Exalted in Scorpio, its insights lead to transformation, but in Taurus, Uranus becomes focused on revolutioniaizng earthly affairs, turning daily life topsy-turvy.

URANUS IN ARIES. Yours was the generation that pioneered in electronics, developing the first computers and high-tech gadgets. Your powerful mixture of fire (Aries) and electricity (Uranus) propels you into exploring the unknown. Those of you born here, like Jacqueline Onassis, Grace Kelly, Andy Warhol, and Yoko Ono probably have had sudden, violent changes in your lives and have a very strong individualistic streak.

URANUS IN TAURUS. This generation became the "hippies" who rejected the establishment (Taurus) and shook us out of deep-rooted ideas. The rise of communism and socialism occurred during this period. You have bright ideas about making money and are natural entrepreneurs, but can have sudden financial shakeups.

URANUS IN GEMINI. The age of information begins. This generation was the first to be brought up on television. You stock up on cordless telephones, answering machines, faxes, modems, and car phones—any new way to communicate. You have an inquiring, curious, highly original mind. You're the talk-show fan.

URANUS IN CANCER. You have unorthodox ideas about parenting, shelter, food, and child rearing. You are the New Age people, fascinated with understanding subconscious motivation, memories, dreams, and psychic research. During this time period, the home was transformed with electronic gadgets. Many of you are sure to have home computers.

URANUS IN LEO. This period coincided with the rise of rock 'n' roll and the heyday of Hollywood. Self-expression led to the exhibitionism of the sixties. Electronic media was used skillfully for self-promotion and self-expression. This generation will probably have an unusual approach to romance (perhaps creatively using electronic media) and extraordinary children. You'll show the full force of your personalty in a unique way.

URANUS IN VIRGO. This generation arrived at a time of student rebellions, the civil rights movement, and general acceptance of health foods. You'll be concerned with pollution and cleaning up the environment. You may revolutionize the healing arts, making nontraditional methods acceptable. This generation also has compaigned against the use of dangerous pesticides and smoking in public places.

URANUS IN LIBRA. Born at a time when the divorce rate soared and the women's liberation movement gained ground, this generation will have some revolutionary ideas about marriage and partnerships. You may have an on-again, off-again relationship, prefer unusual partners, or prefer to stay uncommited. This generation will pioneer concepts in justice and revolutionize the arts.

URANUS IN SCORPIO. Uranus here shook up our sexual ideas. And this generation, just beginning to enter adulthood, will have unorthodox sex lives. You'll delve beneath the surface of life to explore life after death, past lives, and mediumship. This time period signaled the public awareness of the New Age. Body and mind control will be an issue with this generation. You may make great breakthroughs in scientific research and the medical field, especially in surgery.

URANUS IN SAGITTARIUS. This generation rebels against orthodoxy and may invest some unusual modes of religion, education, or philosophy. In Sagittarius, Uranus will make great advances in long-distance travel—these children may be the first to travel in outer space. When this placement happened earlier, the Wright Brothers began to fly and the aviator Charles Lindbergh was born.

URANUS IN CAPRICORN. For the past few years, Uranus shook up the established structures of society in Capricorn. Stock market ups and downs, the crumbling of the Berlin Wall, and practical high-tech gadgets changed our lives. Long-established financial and technological structures suddenly crashed. Those born with this placement will take an innovative approach to their careers. Capricorn likes tradition, whereas Uranus likes change. Therefore, this generation's task is to reconcile the two forces.

URANUS IN AQUARIUS. Uranus shines brightest in Aquarius, the sign it rules. During its previous transit, innovators such as Orson Welles and Leonard Bernstein were born, and breakthroughs in science and technology changed the way we view the world. Uranus entered Aquarius in 1995, where it will remain until 2002, when we can look forward to this planet performing at its most revolutionary, eccentric, and brilliant peak. Though this planet promises many surprises, we can be sure that the generation born during this time will be very concerned with global issues that are shared by all humanity, and with experimentation and innovation on every level.

URANUS IN PISCES. Many of the first TV personalities were born with this placement, because this was the first generation to exploit the electronic media. This was the time of Prohibition (Pisces rules alcohol) and the development of the film industry (also Pisces ruled). The next go-round in the early 2000s, could bring on the Hollywood of the twenty-first century!

What Are Your Favorite Fantasies? Neptune Will Tell

Neptune shows how well you and those of your generation create a world of illusion (very useful in creative work). Do you have an innate glamour you can tap? With Neptune, what you see is not what you get. Neptune is the planet of dissolution (it dissolves hard reality). It is not interested in the world at face value: it dons tinted glasses or blurs the facts with the haze of an intoxicating substance. Where Neptune is, you don't see things quite clearly. This planet's function is to express our visions, and it is most at home in Pisces, which it rules.

Neptune was in the following signs in this century:

NEPTUNE IN CANCER. Family ties were glamorized and extended to the nation. Motherhood and home cooking were cast in a rosy glow. (Julia Child was born with this placement.) People born then read Dr. Spock and watched Walt Disney. Many gave their lives for their homeland.

NEPTUNE IN LEO. Neptune in Leo brought the lavish spending and glamour of the 1920s, which blurred the harsh realities of the age. When Neptune left Leo and moved into Virgo in 1929, the stock market fell. This Neptune, which favored the entertainment industry, brought the golden age of Broadway and the rise of the "star system." Those born with this placement have a flair for drama, may idealize fame without realizing there is a price to pay.

NEPTUNE IN VIRGO. Neptune in Virgo glamorizes health and fitness (Jane Fonda). This generation invented fitness videos, marathon running, TV sports. You may include psychotherapy as part of your mental health regime. You glamorized the workplace and many became workaholics.

NEPTUNE IN LIBRA. Born at a time when "Ozzie and Harriet" was the marital ideal, this generation went on to glamorize "relating" in ways that idealized sexual equality, and is still trying to find its balance in marriage. There have been many divorces as this generation tries to adapt traditional marriage to modern times and allow both sexes free expression.

NEPTUNE IN SCORPIO. This generation was born at a time that glamorized sex and drugs, and matured at a time when the price was paid in AIDS and drug wars. The Berlin Wall was erected when they were born, torn down when they matured. Because of your intense powers of regeneration, part of your mission will be healing and transforming the earth after damage resulting from the delusions of the past is revealed.

NEPTUNE IN SAGITTARIUS. Spiritual and philosophical values were glamorized in the New Age period. Neptune brought out the truth-teller who revealed Watergate and unethical conduct in business. Space travel became a reality, and children born with the placement could travel mentally or physically to other worlds.

NEPTUNE IN CAPRICORN. Now in Capricorn, Neptune brings illusions of material power, which have been tested as Saturn passed by and are now being shaken up by Uranus. It is a time when spiritual interests are commercialized and gain respectability. The business world, however, has been rocked with scandals and broken illusions as management distances itself from the "product" and becomes engrossed in power plays. Those born during this period will embody these Neptune energies in some way and express them at maturity.

How Does Someone Feel about Power and Control? Look at Pluto

Pluto is slow-moving, covering only seven signs in the last century. It reveals how your generation handles power, what makes it seem "cool" to others. This planet brings our deep subconscious feelings to light, digging out our secrets through painful probing. Nothing escapes—or is sacred—with Pluto. Because Pluto was only discovered recently, the signs of its exaltation and fall are still debated. But in Scorpio, which Pluto rules, we have been able to witness its fullest effect as it traveled through this sign in the past several years. Pluto symbolizes death and rebirth, violence, elimination, and renewal.

PLUTO IN GEMINI. Some of our most transformative writers were born with Pluto in Gemini, including Hemingway and F. Scott Fitzgerald. Sex taboos were broken by other writers such as Henry Miller, D. H. Lawrence, and James Joyce. Muckraking journalism became an agent for transformation. Psychoanalysis (talk therapy) was developed.

PLUTO IN CANCER. Motherhood, security, and the breast became fetishes for this generation, as well as the rise of women's rights, dictators who swayed the masses with emotional appeals, and the rise of nationalism. This generation is deeply sentimental, places great value on emotional security. This was also the time of the depression, deprivation of food and security. This is the sign of mother power: intense, emotional sympathies and an understanding of where others are emotionally dependent. Power issues center around using the understanding of where others need mothering to either "feed" them psychologically or to manipulate them.

PLUTO IN LEO. Self-expression becomes a power play for this generation, which invented rock 'n' roll. The rise of television and development of the entertainment business emphasize Leo's transformative power. This was the generation that "did its own thing" and demanded sexual freedom. This generation will go to great lengths to get attention and recognition. This desire for personal recognition can lead to self-aggrandizement and extremes of self-promotion, such as baring innermost secrets on a talk show or to a tabloid. This generation also produced some of the most flamboyant entrepreneurs of the 1980s—the big-spending billionaries who lived in the grand style. Pluto in Leo loves to see itself in everything. As this generation ages, it will remain extremely visible and demanding of attention.

PLUTO IN VIRGO. This generation returned to traditional values and became workaholics. Fitness, health, and career interests took over mass consciousness. To increase efficiency, this generation stocked up on high-tech gadgets such as faxes, computer dictionaries, time planners, and portable telephones. This generation used power by discrimination. They became the "yuppies," who want the best of everything. A keen, judgmental mind, good organizational skills, and an extremely dutiful attitude characterize their exercise of power.

PLUTO IN LIBRA. This generation is now coming into its own. At their birthtime, there was landmark legislation on life-or-death issues such as abortion and euthanasia. The ERA and gay rights movements were receiving mass attention. Marriage is now being redefined by this generation as an equal partnership, and parental roles are being shared. Those of this generation may feel compelled to be in a relationship and to link with others, working better in partnerships than independently. They will exercise power in a diplomatic way. This is more of a "we" person than an independent operator.

PLUTO IN SCORPIO. During the time Pluto came the closest to earth that its irregular orbit will allow. So it is no wonder that we experienced the full force of this tiny planet. Somewhere in each of our lives, we felt Pluto's transforming power, especially in 1989, when Pluto was at its perhelion (most powerful). Sexually transmitted diseases such as AIDs, nucleur power controversies, extreme turnabouts in international politics are all signs of Pluto power. We've also seen the rise of Pluto-ruled stars in mass culture: Julia Roberts, Goldie Hawn, and Jodie Foster to name a few. Madonna and Michael Jackson also have powerful Pluto placements. Sex in the mass media became pervasive and more graphic than ever. For those of you who have felt "nuked" by Pluto (Scorpios and those with Scorpio rising, especially), however, it may be helpful to remember one of the key symbols for Scorpio: the phoenix rising from the ashes. Pluto "clears the decks" in order to create anew. In the Scorpio area of your life, you will go through changes in order to be "born again" and to make way for a period of optimism and expansion. Scorpion themes such as sexuality, birth, and death—and the transcendence of death—will be reflected in the concerns of the generation born now.

PLUTO IN SAGITTARIUS (JANUARY 17, 1995–2008). This should signal a time of great optimism and spiritual development, bringing the century to an exciting close. The generation born now will be expansive on a mass level. In Sagittarius, the traveler, there's a good possibility that Pluto, the planet of extremes, will make space travel a reality for many of us. Look for new dimensions in publishing, emphasis on higher education, and a concern with animal rights issues. Religion will have a new emphasis in our lives and we'll certainly be developing far-reaching philosophies designed to elevate our lives with a new sense of purpose. The following tables are provided so that you can look up the signs of seven major planets—Venus, Mars, Saturn, Jupiter, Uranus, Neptune, and Pluto. We do not have room for tables for the moon and Mercury, which change signs often.

How to Use the Venus Table

Find the year of your birth in the vertical column on the left, then follow across the page until you find the correct date. The Venus sign is at the top of that column.

How To Use the Mars, Saturn, and Jupiter Tables

Find the year of your birth date on the left side of each column. The dates the planet entered each sign are listed on the right side of each column. (Signs are abbreviated to the first three letters.) Your birthday should fall on or between each date listed, and your planetary placement should correspond to the earlier sign of that period.

VENUS SIGNS 1901–2000

	Aries	Taurus	Gemini	Cancer	Leo	Virgo
1901	3/29-4/22	4/22-5/17	5/17-6/10	6/10-7/5	7/5-7/29	7/29-8/23
1902	5/7-6/3	6/3-6/30	6/30-7/25	7/25-8/19	8/19-9/13	9/13-10/7
1903	2/28-3/24	3/24-4/18	4/18-5/13	5/13-6/9	6/9-7/7	7/7-8/17 9/6-11/8
1904	3/13-5/7	5/7-6/1	6/1-6/25	6/25-7/19	7/19-8/13	8/13-9/6
1905	2/3-3/6 4/9-5/28	3/6-4/9 5/28-7/8	7/8-8/6	8/6-9/1	9/1-9/27	9/27-10/21
1906	3/1-4/7	4/7-5/2	5/2-5/26	5/26-6/20	6/20-7/16	7/16-8/11
1907	4/27-5/22	5/22-6/16	6/16-7/11	7/11-8/4	8/4-8/29	8/29-9/22
1908	2/14-3/10	3/10-4/5	4/5-5/5	5/5-9/8	9/8-10/8	10/8-11/3
1909	3/29-4/22	4/22-5/16	5/16-6/10	6/10-7/4	7/4-7/29	7/29-8/23
1910	5/7-6/3	6/4-6/29	6/30-7/24	7/25-8/18	8/19-9/12	9/13-10/6
1911	2/28-3/23	3/24-4/17	4/18-5/12	5/13-6/8	6/9-7/7	7/8-11/8
1912	4/13-5/6	5/7-5/31	6/1-6/24	6/24-7/18	7/19-8/12	8/13-9/5
1913	2/3-3/6 5/2-5/30	3/7-5/1 5/31-7/7	7/8-8/5	8/6-8/31	9/1-9/26	9/27-10/20
1914	3/14-4/6	4/7-5/1	5/2-5/25	5/26-6/19	6/20-7/15	7/16-8/10
1915	4/27-5/21	5/22-6/15	6/16-7/10	7/11-8/3	8/4-8/28	8/29-9/21
1916	2/14-3/9	3/10-4/5	4/6-5/5	5/6-9/8	9/9-10/7	10/8-11/2
1917	3/29-4/21	4/22-5/15	5/16-6/9	6/10-7/3	7/4-7/28	7/29-8/21
1918	5/7-6/2	6/3-6/28	6/29-7/24	7/25-8/18	8/19-9/11	9/12-10/5
1919	2/27-3/22	3/23-4/16	4/17-5/12	5/13-6/7	6/8-7/7	7/8-11/8
1920	4/12-5/6	5/7-5/30	5/31-6/23	6/24-7/18	7/19-8/11	8/12-9/4
1921	2/3-3/6 4/26-6/1	3/7-4/25 6/2-7/7	7/8-8/5	8/6-8/31	9/1-9/25	9/26-10/20
1922	3/13-4/6	4/7-4/30	5/1-5/25	5/26-6/19	6/20-7/14	7/15-8/9
1923	4/27-5/21	5/22-6/14	6/15-7/9	7/10-8/3	8/4-8/27	8/28-9/20
1924	2/13-3/8	3/9-4/4	4/5-5/5	5/6-9/8	9/9-10/7	10/8-11/12
1925	3/28-4/20	4/21-5/15	5/16-6/8	6/9-7/3	7/4-7/27	7/28-8/21

Libra	Scorpio	Sagittarius	Capricorn	Aquarius	Pisces
8/23-9/17	9/17-10/12	10/12-1/16	1/16-2/9	2/9	3/5-3/29
			11/7-12/5	12/5-1/11	
10/7-10/31	10/31-11/24	11/24-12/18	12/18-1/11	2/6-4/4	1/11-2/6
					4/4-5/7
8/17-9/6	12/9-1/5			1/11-2/4	2/4-2/28
11/8-12/9					
9/6-9/30	9/30-10/25	1/5-1/30	1/30-2/24	2/24-3/19	3/19-4/13
		10/25-11/18	11/18-12/13	12/13-1/7	
10/21-11/14	11/14-12/8	12/8-1/1/06			1/7-2/3
8/11-9/7	9/7-10/9	10/9-12/15	1/1-1/25	1/25-2/18	2/18-3/14
	12/15-12/25	12/25-2/6			
9/22-10/16	10/16-11/9	11/9-12/3	2/6-3/6	3/6-4/2	4/2-4/27
			12/3-12/27	12/27-1/20	
11/3-11/28	11/28-12/22	12/22-1/15			1/20-2/4
8/23-9/17	9/17-10/12	10/12-11/17	1/15-2/9	2/9-3/5	3/5-3/29
			11/17-12/5	12/5-1/15	
10/7-10/30	10/31-11/23	11/24-12/17	12/18-12/31	1/1-1/15	1/16-1/28
				1/29-4/4	4/5-5/6
11/19-12/8	12/9-12/31		1/1-1/10	1/11-2/2	2/3-2/27
9/6-9/30	1/1-1/4	1/5-1/29	1/30-2/23	2/24-3/18	3/19-4/12
	10/1-10/24	10/25-11/17	11/18-12/12	12/13-12/31	
10/21-11/13	11/14-12/7	12/8-12/31		1/1-1/6	1/7-2/2
8/11-9/6	9/7-10/9	10/10-12/5	1/1-1/24	1/25-2/17	2/18-3/13
	12/6-12/30	12/31			
9/22-10/15	10/16-11/8	1/1-2/6	2/7-3/6	3/7-4/1	4/2-4/26
		11/9-12/2	12/3-12/26	12/27-12/31	
11/3-11/27	11/28-12/21	12/22-12/31		1/1-1/19	1/20-2/13
8/22-9/16	9/17-10/11	1/1-1/14	1/15-2/7	2/8-3/4	3/5-3/28
		10/12-11/6	11/7-12/5	12/6-12/31	
10/6-10/29	10/30-11/22	11/23-12/16	12/17-12/31	1/1-4/5	4/6-5/6
11/9-12/8	12/9-12/31		1/1-1/9	1/10-2/2	2/3-2/26
9/5-9/30	1/1-1/3	1/4-1/28	1/29-2/22	2/23-3/18	3/19-4/11
	9/31-10/23	10/24-11/17	11/18-12/11	12/12-12/31	
10/21-11/13	11/14-12/7	12/8-12/31		1/1-1/6	1/7-2/2
8/10-9/6	9/7-10/10	10/11-11/28	1/1-1/24	1/25-2/16	2/17-3/12
	11/29-12/31				
9/21-10/14	1/1	1/2-2/6	2/7-3/5	3/6-3/31	4/1-4/26
	10/15-11/7	11/8-12/1	12/2-12/25	12/26-12/31	
11/13-11/26	11/27-12/21	12/22-12/31		1/1-1/19	1/20-2/12
8/22-9/15	9/16-10/11	1/1-1/14	1/15-2/7	2/8-3/3	3/4-3/27
		10/12-11/6	11/7-12/5	12/6-12/31	

VENUS SIGNS 1901-2000

	Aries	Taurus	Gemini	Cancer	Leo	Virgo
1926	5/7-6/2	6/3-6/28	6/29-7/23	7/24-8/17	8/18-9/11	9/12-10/5
1927	2/27-3/22	3/23-4/16	4/17-5/11	5/12-6/7	6/8-7/7	7/8-11/9
1928	4/12-5/5	5/6-5/29	5/30-6/23	6/24-7/17	7/18-8/11	8/12-9/4
1929	2/3-3/7	3/8-4/19	7/8-8/4	8/5-8/30	8/31-9/25	9/26-10/19
	4/20-6/2	6/3-7/7				
1930	3/13-4/5	4/6-4/30	5/1-5/24	5/25-6/18	6/19-7/14	7/15-8/9
1931	4/26-5/20	5/21-6/13	6/14-7/8	7/9-8/2	8/3-8/26	8/27-9/19
1932	2/12-3/8	3/9-4/3	4/4-5/5	5/6-7/12	9/9-10/6	10/7-11/1
			7/13-7/27	7/28-9/8		
1933	3/27-4/19	4/20-5/28	5/29-6/8	6/9-7/2	7/3-7/26	7/27-8/20
1934	5/6-6/1	6/2-6/27	6/28-7/22	7/23-8/16	8/17-9/10	9/11-10/4
1935	2/26-3/21	3/22-4/15	4/16-5/10	5/11-6/6	6/7-7/6	7/7-11/8
1936	4/11-5/4	5/5-5/28	5/29-6/22	6/23-7/16	7/17-8/10	8/11-9/4
1937	2/2-3/8	3/9-4/17	7/7-8/3	8/4-8/29	8/30-9/24	9/25-10/18
	4/14-6/3	6/4-7/6				
1938	3/12-4/4	4/5-4/28	4/29-5/23	5/24-6/18	6/19-7/13	7/14-8/8
1939	4/25-5/19	5/20-6/13	6/14-7/8	7/9-8/1	8/2-8/25	8/26-9/19
1940	2/12-3/7	3/8-4/3	4/4-5/5	5/6-7/4	9/9-10/5	10/6-10/31
			7/5-7/31	8/1-9/8		
1941	3/27-4/19	4/20-5/13	5/14-6/6	6/7-7/1	7/2-7/26	7/27-8/20
1942	5/6-6/1	6/2-6/26	6/27-7/22	7/23-8/16	8/17-9/9	9/10-10/3
1943	2/25-3/20	3/21-4/14	4/15-5/10	5/11-6/6	6/7-7/6	7/7-11/8
1944	4/10-5/3	5/4-5/28	5/29-6/21	6/22-7/16	7/17-8/9	8/10-9/2
1945	2/2-3/10	3/11-4/6	7/7-8/3	8/4-8/29	8/30-9/23	9/24-10/18
	4/7-6/3	6/4-7/6				
1946	3/11-4/4	4/5-4/28	4/29-5/23	5/24-6/17	6/18-7/12	7/13-8/8
1947	4/25-5/19	5/20-6/12	6/13-7/7	7/8-8/1	8/2-8/25	8/26-9/18
1948	2/11-3/7	3/8-4/3	4/4-5/6	5/7-6/28	9/8-10/5	10/6-10/31
			6/29-8/2	8/3-9/7		
1949	3/26-4/19	4/20-5/13	5/14-6/6	6/7-6/30	7/1-7/25	7/26-8/19
1950	5/5-5/31	6/1-6/26	6/27-7/21	7/22-8/15	8/16-9/9	9/10-10/3
1951	2/25-3/21	3/22-4/15	4/16-5/10	5/11-6/6	6/7-7/7	7/8-11/9

Libra	Scorpio	Sagittarius	Capricorn	Aquarius	Pisces
10/6-10/29	10/30-11/22	11/23-12/16	12/17-12/31	1/1-4/5	4/6-5/6
11/10-12/8	12/9-12/31	1/1-1/7	1/8	1/9-2/1	2/2-2/26
9/5-9/28	1/1-1/3	1/4-1/28	1/29-2/22	2/23-3/17	3/18-4/11
	9/29-10/23	10/24-11/16	11/17-12/11	12/12-12/31	
10/20-11/12	11/13-12/6	12/7-12/30	12/31	1/1-1/5	1/6-2/2
8/10-9/6	9/7-10/11	10/12-11/21	1/1-1/23	1/24-2/16	2/17-3/12
	11/22-12/31				
9/20-10/13	1/1-1/3	1/4-2/6	2/7-3/4	3/5-3/31	4/1-4/25
	10/14-11/6	11/7-11/30	12/1-12/24	12/25-12/31	
11/2-11/25	11/26-12/20	12/21-12/31		1/1-1/18	1/19-2/11
8/21-9/14	9/15-10/10	1/1-1/13	1/14-2/6	2/7-3/2	3/3-3/26
		10/11-11/5	11/6-12/4	12/5-12/31	
10/5-10/28	10/29-11/21	11/22-12/15	12/16-12/31	1/1-4/5	4/6-5/5
11/9-12/7	12/8-12/31		1/1-1/7	1/8-1/31	2/1-2/25
9/5-9/27	1/1-1/2	1/3-1/27	1/28-2/21	2/22-3/16	3/17-4/10
	9/28-10/22	10/23-11/15	11/16-12/10	12/11-12/31	
10/19-11/11	11/12-12/5	12/6-12/29	12/30-12/31	1/1-1/5	1/6-2/1
8/9-9/6	9/7-10/13	10/14-11/14	1/1-1/22	1/23-2/15	2/16-3/11
	11/15-12/31				
9/20-10/13	1/1-1/3	1/4-2/5	2/6-3/4	3/5-3/30	3/31-4/24
	10/14-11/6	11/7-11/30	12/1-12/24	12/25-12/31	
11/1-11/25	11/26-12/19	12/20-12/31		1/1-1/18	1/19-2/11
8/21-9/14	9/15-10/9	1/1-1/12	1/13-2/5	2/6-3/1	3/2-3/26
		10/10-11/5	11/6-12/4	12/5-12/31	
10/4-10/27	10/28-11/20	11/21-12/14	12/15-12/31	1/1-4/4	4/6-5/5
11/9-12/7	12/8-12/31		1/1-1/7	1/8-1/31	2/1-2/24
9/3-9/27	1/1-1/2	1/3-1/27	1/28-2/20	2/21-3/16	3/17-4/9
	9/28-10/21	10/22-11/15	11/16-12/10	12/11-12/31	
10/19-11/11	11/12-12/5	12/6-12/29	12/30-12/31	1/1-1/4	1/5-2/1
8/9-9/6	9/7-10/15	10/16-11/7	1/1-1/21	1/22-2/14	2/15-3/10
	11/8-12/31				
9/19-10/12	1/1-1/4	1/5-2/5	2/6-3/4	3/5-3/29	3/30-4/24
	10/13-11/5	11/6-11/29	11/30-12/23	12/24-12/31	
11/1-1/25	11/26-12/19	12/20-12/31		1/1-1/17	1/18-2/10
8/20-9/14	9/15-10/9	1/1-1/12	1/13-2/5	2/6-3/1	3/2-3/25
		10/10-11/5	11/6-12/5	12/6-12/31	
10/4-10/27	10/28-11/20	11/21-12/13	12/14-12/31	1/1-4/5	4/6-5/4
11/10-12/7	12/8-12/31		1/1-1/7	1/8-1/31	2/1-2/24

VENUS SIGNS 1901-2000

	Aries	Taurus	Gemini	Cancer	Leo	Virgo
1952	4/10-5/4	5/5-5/28	5/29-6/21	6/22-7/16	7/17-8/9	8/10-9/3
1953	2/2-3/13	3/4-3/31	7/8-8/3	8/4-8/29	8/30-9/24	9/25-10/18
	4/1-6/5	6/6-7/7				
1954	3/12-4/4	4/5-4/28	4/29-5/23	5/24-6/17	6/18-7/13	7/14-8/8
1955	4/25-5/19	5/20-6/13	6/14-7/7	7/8-8/1	8/2-8/25	8/26-9/18
1956	2/12-3/7	3/8-4/4	4/5-5/7	5/8-6/23	9/9-10/5	10/6-10/31
			6/24-8/4	8/5-9/8		
1957	3/26-4/19	4/20-5/13	5/14-6/6	6/7-7/1	7/2-7/26	7/7-8/19
1958	5/6-5/31	6/1-6/26	6/27-7/22	7/23-8/15	8/16-9/9	9/10-10/3
1959	2/25-3/20	3/21-4/14	4/15-5/10	5/11-6/6	6/7-7/8	7/9-9/20
					9/21-9/24	9/25-11/9
1960	4/10-5/3	5/4-5/28	5/29-6/21	6/22-7/15	7/16-8/9	8/10-9/2
1961	2/3-6/5	6/6-7/7	7/8-8/3	8/4-8/29	8/30-9/23	9/24-10/17
1962	3/11-4/3	4/4-4/28	4/29-5/22	5/23-6/17	6/18-7/12	7/13-8/8
1963	4/24-5/18	5/19-6/12	6/13-7/7	7/8-7/31	8/1-8/25	8/26-9/18
1964	2/11-3/7	3/8-4/4	4/5-5/9	5/10-6/17	9/9-10/5	10/6-10/31
			6/18-8/5	8/6-9/8		
1965	3/26-4/18	4/19-5/12	5/13-6/6	6/7-6/30	7/1-7/25	7/26-8/19
1966	5/6-6/31	6/1-6/26	6/27-7/21	7/22-8/15	8/16-9/8	9/9-10/2
1967	2/24-3/20	3/21-4/14	4/15-5/10	5/11-6/6	6/7-7/8	7/9-9/9
					9/10-10/1	10/2-11/9
1968	4/9-5/3	5/4-5/27	5/28-6/20	6/21-7/15	7/16-8/8	8/9-9/2
1969	2/3-6/6	6/7-7/6	7/7-8/3	8/4-8/28	8/29-9/22	9/23-10/17
1970	3/11-4/3	4/4-4/27	4/28-5/22	5/23-6/16	6/17-7/12	7/13-8/8
1971	4/24-5/18	5/19-6/12	6/13-7/6	7/7-7/31	8/1-8/24	8/25-9/17
1972	2/11-3/7	3/8-4/3	4/4-5/10	5/11-6/11		
			6/12-8/6	8/7-9/8	9/9-10/5	10/6-10/30
1973	3/25-4/18	4/18-5/12	5/13-6/5	6/6-6/29	7/1-7/25	7/26-8/19
1974						
	5/5-5/31	6/1-6/25	6/26-7/21	7/22-8/14	8/15-9/8	9/9-10/2
1975	2/24-3/20	3/21-4/13	4/14-5/9	5/10-6/6	6/7-7/9	7/10-9/2
					9/3-10/4	10/5-11/9

Libra	Scorpio	Sagittarius	Capricorn	Aquarius	Pisces
9/4-9/27	1/1-1/2	1/3-1/27	1/28-2/20	2/21-3/16	3/17-4/9
	9/28-10/21	10/22-11/15	11/16-12/10	12/11-12/31	
10/19-11/11	11/12-12/5	12/6-12/29	12/30-12/31	1/1-1/5	1/6-2/1
8/9-9/6	9/7-10/22	10/23-10/27	1/1-1/22	1/23-2/15	2/16-3/11
	10/28-12/31				
9/19-10/13	1/1-1/6	1/7-2/5	2/6-3/4	3/5-3/30	3/31-4/24
	10/14-11/5	11/6-11/30	12/1-12/24	12/25-12/31	
11/1-11/25	11/26-12/19	12/20-12/31		1/1-1/17	1/18-2/11
8/20-9/14	9/15-10/9	1/1-1/12	1/13-2/5	2/6-3/1	3/2-3/25
		10/10-11/5	11/6-12/16	12/7-12/31	
10/4-10/27	10/28-11/20	11/21-12/14	12/15-12/31	1/1-4/6	4/7-5/5
11/10-12/7	12/8-12/31		1/1-1/7	1/8-1/31	2/1-2/24
9/3-9/26	1/1-1/2	1/3-1/27	1/28-2/20	2/21-3/15	3/16-4/9
	9/27-10/21	10/22-11/15	11/16-12/10	12/11-12/31	
10/18-11/11	11/12-12/4	12/5-12/28	12/29-12/31	1/1-1/5	1/6-2/2
8/9-9/6	9/7-12/31		1/1-1/21	1/22-2/14	2/15-3/10
9/19-10/12	1/1-1/6	1/7-2/5	2/6-3/4	3/5-3/29	3/30-4/24
	10/13-11/5	11/6-11/29	11/30-12/23	12/24-12/31	
11/1-11/24	11/25-12/19	12/20-12/31		1/1-1/16	1/17-2/10
8/20-9/13	9/14-10/9	1/1-1/12	1/13-2/5	2/6-3/1	3/2-3/25
		10/10-11/5	11/6-12/7	12/8-12/31	
10/3-10/26	10/27-11/19	11/20-12/13	2/7-2/25	1/1-2/6	4/7-5/5
			12/14-12/31	2/26-4/6	
11/10-12/7	12/8-12/23		1/1-1/6	1/7-1/30	1/31-2/23
9/3-9/26	1/1	1/2-1/26	1/27-2/20	2/21-3/15	3/16-4/8
	9/27-10/21	10/22-11/14	11/15-12/9	12/10-12/31	
10/18-11/10	11/11-12/4	12/5-12/28	12/29-12/31	1/1-1/4	1/5-2/2
8/9-9/7	9/8-12/31		1/1-1/21	1/22-2/14	2/15-3/10
9/18-10/11	1/1-1/7	1/8-2/5	2/6-3/4	3/5-3/29	3/30-4/23
	10/12-11/5	11/6-11/29	11/30-12/23	12/24-12/31	
	11/25-12/18	12/19-12/31		1/1-1/16	1/17-2/10
10/31-11/24					
8/20-9/13		1/1-1/12	1/13-2/4	2/5-2/28	3/1-3/24
		10/9-11/5	11/6-12/7	12/8-12/31	
			1/30-2/28	1/1-1/29	
10/3-10/26	10/27-11/19	11/20-12/13	12/14-12/31	3/1-4/6	4/7-5/4
			1/1-1/6	1/7-1/30	1/31-2/23
11/10-12/7	12/8-12/31				

93

VENUS SIGNS 1901-2000

	Aries	Taurus	Gemini	Cancer	Leo	Virgo
1976	4/8-5/2	5/2-5/27	5/27–6/20	6/20-7/14	7/14-8/8	8/8-9/1
1977	2/2-6/6	6/6-7/6	7/6-8/2	8/2-8/28	8/28-9/22	9/22-10/17
1978	3/9-4/2	4/2-4/27	4/27-5/22	5/22-6/16	6/16-7/12	7/12-8/6
1979	4/23-5/18	5/18-6/11	6/11-7/6	7/6-7/30	7/30-8/24	8/24-9/17
1980	2/9-3/6	3/6-4/3	4/3-5/12	5/12-6/5	9/7-10/4	10/4-10/30
			6/5-8/6	8/6-9/7		
1981	3/24-4/17	4/17-5/11	5/11-6/5	6/5-6/29	6/29-7/24	7/24-8/18
1982	5/4-5/30	5/30-6/25	6/25-7/20	7/20-8/14	8/14-9/7	9/7-10/2
1983	2/22-3/19	3/19-4/13	4/13-5/9	5/9-6/6	6/6-7/10	7/10-8/27
					8/27-10/5	10/5-11/9
1984	4/7-5/2	5/2-5/26	5/26-6/20	6/20-7/14	7/14-8/7	8/7-9/1
1985	2/2-6/6	6/8-7/6	7/6-8/2	8/2-8/28	8/28-9/22	9/22-10/16
1986	3/9-4/2	4/2-4/26	4/26-5/21	5/21-6/15.	6/15-7/11	7/11-8/7
1987	4/22-5/17	5/17-6/11	6/11-7/5	7/5-7/30	7/30-8/23	8/23-9/16
1988	2/9-3/6	3/6-4/3	4/3-5/17	5/17-5/27	9/7-10/4	10/4-10/29
			5/27-8/6	8/6-9/7		
1989	3/23-4/16	4/16-5/11	5/11-6/4	6/4-6/29	6/29-7/24	7/24-8/18
1990	5/4-5/30	5/30-6/25	6/25-7/20	7/20-8/13	8/13-9/7	9/7-10/1
1991	2/22-3/18	3/18-4/13	4/13-5/9	5/9-6/6	6/6-7/11	7/11-8/21
					8/21-10/6	10/6-11/9
1992	4/7-5/1	5/1-5/26	5/26-6/19	6/19-7/13	7/13-8/7	8/7-8/31
1993	2/2-6/6	6/6-7/6	7/6-8/1	8/1-8/27	8/27-9/21	9/21-10/16
1994	3/8-4/1	4/1-4/26	4/26-5/21	5/21-6/15	6/15-7/11	7/11-8/7
1995	4/22-5/16	5/16-6/10	6/10-7/5	7/5-7/29	7/29-8/23	8/23-9/16
1996	2/9-3/6	3/6-4/3	4/3-8/7	8/7-9/7	9/7-10/4	10/4-10/29
1997	3/23-4/16	4/16-5/10	5/10-6/4	6/4-6/28	6/28-7/23	7/23-8/17
1998	5/3-5/29	5/29-6/24	6/24-7/19	7/19-8/13	8/13-9/6	9/6-9/30
1999	2/21-3/18	3/18-4/12	4/12-5/8	5/8-6/5	6/5-7/12	7/12-8/15
					8/15-10/7	10/7-11/9
2000	4/6-5/1	5/1-5/25	5/25-6/13	6/13-7/13	7/13-8/6	8/6-8/31

Libra	Scorpio	Sagittarius	Capricorn	Aquarius	Pisces
9/1-9/26	9/26-10/20	1/1-1/26	1/26-2/19	2/19-3/15	3/15-4/8
		10/20-11/14	11/14-12/6	12/9-1/4	
10/17-11/10	11/10-12/4	12/4-12/27	12/27-1/20		1/4-2/2
8/6-9/7	9/7-1/7			1/20-2/13	2/13-3/9
9/17-10/11	10/11-11/4	1/7-2/5	2/5-3/3	3/3-3/29	3/29-4/23
		11/4-11/28	11/28-12/22	12/22-1/16	
10/30-11/24	11/24-12/18	12/18-1/11			1/16-2/9
8/18-9/12	9/12-10/9	10/9-11/5	1/11-2/4	2/4-2/28	2/28-3/24
			11/5-12/8	12/8-1/23	
10/2-10/26	10/26-11/18	11/18-12/12	1/23-3/2	3/2-4/6	4/6-5/4
			12/12-1/5		
11/9-12/6	12/6-1/1			1/5-1/29	1/29-2/22
9/1-9/25	9/25-10/20	1/1-1/25	1/25-2/19	2/19-3/14	3/14-4/7
		10/20-11/13	11/13-12/9		
10/16-11/9	11/9-12/3	12/3-12/27			1/4-2/2
8/7-9/7	9/7-1/7			1/20-3/13	2/13-3/9
9/16-10/10	10/10-11/3	1/7-2/5	2/5-3/3	3/3-3/28	3/28-4/22
		11/3-11/28	11/28-12/22	12/22-1/15	
10/29-11/23	11/23-12/17	12/17-1/10			1/15-2/9
8/18-9/12	9/12-10/8	10/8-11/5	1/10-2/3	2/3-2/27	2/27-3/23
			11/5-12/10	12/10-1/16	
10/1-10/25	10/25-11/18	11/18-12/12	1/16-3/3	3/3-4/6	4/6-5/4
			12/12-1/5		
8/21-12/6	12/6-12/31	12/21-1/25/92		1/5-1/29	1/29-2/22
8/31-9/25	9/25-10/19	10/19-11/13	1/25-2/18	2/18-3/13	3/13-4/7
			11/13-12/8	12/8-1/3	
10/16-11/9	11/9-12/2	12/2-12/26	12/26-1/19		1/3-2/2
8/7-9/7	9/7-1/7			1/19-2/12	2/12-3/8
9/16-10/10	10/10-11/13	1/7-2/4	2/4-3/2	3/2-3/28	3/28-4/22
		11/3-11/27	11/27-12/21	12/21-1/15	
10/29-11/23	11/23-12/17	12/17-1/10/97			1/15-2/9
8/17-9/12	9/12-10/8	10/8-11/5	1/10-2/3	2/3-2/27	2/27-3/23
			11/5-12/12	12/12-1/9	
9/30-10/24	10/24-11/17	11/17-12/11	1/9-3/4	3/4-4/6	4/6-5/3
11/9-12/5	12/5-12/31	12/31-1/24		1/4-1/28	1/28-2/21
8/31-9/24	9/24-10/19	10/19-11/13	1/24-2/18	2/18-3/12	3/13-4/6
			11/13-12/8	12/8	

1901	MAR	1	Leo		DEC	17	Scp
	MAY	11	Vir	1907	FEB	5	Sag
	JUL	13	Lib		APR	1	Cap
	AUG	31	Scp		OCT	13	Aqu
	OCT	14	Sag		NOV	29	Pic
	NOV	24	Cap	1908	JAN	11	Ari
1902	JAN	1	Aqu		FEB	23	Tau
	FEB	8	Pic		APR	7	Gem
	MAR	19	Ari		MAY	22	Can
	APR	27	Tau		JUL	8	Leo
	JUN	7	Gem		AUG	24	Vir
	JUL	20	Can		OCT	10	Lib
	SEP	4	Leo		NOV	25	Scp
	OCT	23	Vir	1909	JAN	10	Sag
	DEC	20	Lib		FEB	24	Cap
1903	APR	19	Vir		APR	9	Aqu
	MAY	30	Lib		MAY	25	Pic
	AUG	6	Scp		JUL	21	Ari
	SEP	22	Sag		SEP	26	Pic
	NOV	3	Cap		NOV	20	Ari
	DEC	12	Aqu	1910	JAN	23	Tau
1904	JAN	19	Pic		MAR	14	Gem
	FEB	27	Ari		MAY	1	Can
	APR	6	Tau		JUN	19	Leo
	MAY	18	Gem		AUG	6	Vir
	JUN	30	Can		SEP	22	Lib
	AUG	15	Leo		NOV	6	Scp
	OCT	1	Vir		DEC	20	Sag
	NOV	20	Lib	1911	JAN	31	Cap
1905	JAN	13	Scp		MAR	14	Aqu
	AUG	21	Sag		APR	23	Pic
	OCT	8	Cap		JUN	2	Ari
	NOV	18	Aqu		JUL	15	Tau
	DEC	27	Pic		SEP	5	Gem
1906	FEB	4	Ari		NOV	30	Tau
	MAR	17	Tau	1912	JAN	30	Gem
	APR	28	Gem		APR	5	Can
	JUN	11	Can		MAY	28	Leo
	JUL	27	Leo		JUL	17	Vir
	SEP	12	Vir		SEP	2	Lib
	OCT	30	Lib		OCT	18	Scp

	NOV	30	Sag		MAY	26	Gem
1913	JAN	10	Cap		JUL	8	Can
	FEB	19	Aqu		AUG	23	Leo
	MAR	30	Pic		OCT	10	Vir
	MAY	8	Ari		NOV	30	Lib
	JUN	17	Tau	1920	JAN	31	Scp
	JUL	29	Gem		APR	23	Lib
	SEP	15	Can		JUL	10	Scp
1914	MAY	1	Leo		SEP	4	Sag
	JUN	26	Vir		OCT	18	Cap
	AUG	14	Lib		NOV	27	Aqu
	SEP	29	Scp	1921	JAN	5	Pic
	NOV	11	Sag		FEB	13	Ari
	DEC	22	Cap		MAR	25	Tau
1915	JAN	30	Aqu		MAY	6	Gem
	MAR	9	Pic		JUN	18	Can
	APR	16	Ari		AUG	3	Leo
	MAY	26	Tau		SEP	19	Vir
	JUL	6	Gem		NOV	6	Lib
	AUG	19	Can		DEC	26	Scp
	OCT	7	Leo	1922	FEB	18	Sag
1916	MAY	28	Vir		SEP	13	Cap
	JUL	23	Lib		OCT	30	Aqu
	SEP	8	Scp		DEC	11	Pic
	OCT	22	Sag	1923	JAN	21	Ari
	DEC	1	Cap		MAR	4	Tau
1917	JAN	9	Aqu		APR	16	Gem
	FEB	16	Pic		MAY	30	Can
	MAR	26	Ari		JUL	16	Leo
	MAY	4	Tau		SEP	1	Vir
	JUN	14	Gem		OCT	18	Lib
	JUL	28	Can		DEC	4	Scp
	SEP	12	Leo	1924	JAN	19	Sag
	NOV	2	Vir		MAR	6	Cap
1918	JAN	11	Lib		APR	24	Aqu
	FEB	25	Vir		JUN	24	Pic
	JUN	23	Lib		AUG	24	Aqu
	AUG	17	Scp		OCT	19	Pic
	OCT	1	Sag		DEC	19	Ari
	NOV	11	Cap	1925	FEB	5	Tau
	DEC	20	Aqu		MAR	24	Gem
1919	JAN	27	Pic		MAY	9	Can
	MAR	6	Ari		JUN	26	Leo
	APR	15	Tau		AUG	12	Vir

	SEP	28	Lib	1932	JAN	18	Aqu
	NOV	13	Scp		FEB	25	Pic
	DEC	28	Sag		APR	3	Ari
1926	FEB	9	Cap		MAY	12	Tau
	MAR	23	Aqu		JUN	22	Gem
	MAY	3	Pic		AUG	4	Can
	JUN	15	Ari		SEP	20	Leo
	AUG	1	Tau		NOV	13	Vir
1927	FEB	22	Gem	1933	JUL	6	Lib
	APR	17	Can		AUG	26	Scp
	JUN	6	Leo		OCT	9	Sag
	JUL	25	Vir		NOV	19	Cap
	SEP	10	Lib		DEC	28	Aqu
	OCT	26	Scp	1934	FEB	4	Pic
	DEC	8	Sag		MAR	14	Ari
1928	JAN	19	Cap		APR	22	Tau
	FEB	28	Aqu		JUN	2	Gem
	APR	7	Pic		JUL	15	Can
	MAY	16	Ari		AUG	30	Leo
	JUN	26	Tau		OCT	18	Vir
	AUG	9	Gem		DEC	11	Lib
	OCT	3	Can	1935	JUL	29	Scp
	DEC	20	Gem		SEP	16	Sag
1929	MAR	10	Can		OCT	28	Cap
	MAY	13	Leo		DEC	7	Aqu
	JUL	4	Vir	1936	JAN	14	Pic
	AUG	21	Lib		FEB	22	Ari
	OCT	6	Scp		APR	1	Tau
	NOV	18	Sag		MAY	13	Gem
	DEC	29	Cap		JUN	25	Can
1930	FEB	6	Aqu		AUG	10	Leo
	MAR	17	Pic		SEP	26	Vir
	APR	24	Ari		NOV	14	Lib
	JUN	3	Tau	1937	JAN	5	Scp
	JUL	14	Gem		MAR	13	Sag
	AUG	28	Can		MAY	14	Scp
	OCT	20	Leo		AUG	8	Sag
1931	FEB	16	Can		SEP	30	Cap
	MAR	30	Leo		NOV	11	Aqu
	JUN	10	Vir		DEC	2	1Pic
	AUG	1	Lib	1938	JAN	30	Ari
	SEP	17	Scp		MAR	12	Tau
	OCT	30	Sag		APR	23	Gem
	DEC	10	Cap		JUN	7	Can

	JUL	22	Leo		FEB	14	Aqu
	SEP	7	Vir		MAR	25	Pic
	OCT	25	Lib		MAY	2	Ari
	DEC	11	Scp		JUN	11	Tau
1939	JAN	29	Sag		JUL	23	Gem
	MAR	21	Cap		SEP	7	Can
	MAY	25	Aqu		NOV	11	Leo
	JUL	21	Cap		DEC	26	Can
	SEP	24	Aqu	1946	APR	22	Leo
	NOV	19	Pic		JUN	20	Vir
1940	JAN	4	Ari		AUG	9	Lib
	FEB	17	Tau		SEP	24	Scp
	APR	1	Gem		NOV	6	Sag
	MAY	17	Can		DEC	17	Cap
	JUL	3	Leo	1947	JAN	25	Aqu
	AUG	19	Vir		MAR	4	Pic
	OCT	5	Lib		APR	11	Ari
	NOV	20	Scp		MAY	21	Tau
1941	JAN	4	Sag		JUL	1	Gem
	FEB	17	Cap		AUG	13	Can
	APR	2	Aqu		OCT	1	Leo
	MAY	16	Pic		DEC	1	Vir
	JUL	2	Ari	1948	FEB	12	Leo
1942	JAN	11	Tau		MAY	18	Vir
	MAR	7	Gem		JUL	17	Lib
	APR	26	Can		SEP	3	Scp
	JUN	14	Leo		OCT	17	Sag
	AUG	1	Vir		NOV	26	Cap
	SEP	17	Lib	1949	JAN	4	Aqu
	NOV	1	Scp		FEB	11	Pic
	DEC	15	Sag		MAR	21	Ari
1943	JAN	26	Cap		APR	30	Tau
	MAR	8	Aqu		JUN	10	Gem
	APR	17	Pic		JUL	23	Can
	MAY	27	Ari		SEP	7	Leo
	JUL	7	Tau		OCT	27	Vir
	AUG	23	Gem		DEC	26	Lib
1944	MAR	28	Can	1950	MAR	28	Vir
	MAY	22	Leo		JUN	11	Lib
	JUL	12	Vir		AUG	10	Scp
	AUG	29	Lib		SEP	25	Sag
	OCT	13	Scp		NOV	6	Cap
	NOV	25	Sag		DEC	15	Aqu
1945	JAN	5	Cap	1951	JAN	22	Pic

	MAR	1	Ari		SEP	24	Lib
	APR	10	Tau		NOV	8	Scp
	MAY	21	Gem		DEC	23	Sag
	JUL	3	Can	1958	FEB	3	Cap
	AUG	18	Leo		MAR	17	Aqu
	OCT	5	Vir		APR	27	Pic
	NOV	24	Lib		JUN	7	Ari
1952	JAN	20	Scp		JUL	21	Tau
	AUG	27	Sag		SEP	21	Gem
	OCT	12	Cap		OCT	29	Tau
	NOV	21	Aqu	1959	FEB	10	Gem
	DEC	30	Pic		APR	10	Can
1953	FEB	8	Ari		JUN	1	Leo
	MAR	20	Tau		JUL	20	Vir
	MAY	1	Gem		SEP	5	Lib
	JUN	14	Can		OCT	21	Scp
	JUL	29	Leo		DEC	3	Sag
	SEP	14	Vir	1960	JAN	14	Cap
	NOV	1	Lib		FEB	23	Aqu
	DEC	20	Scp		APR	2	Pic
1954	FEB	9	Sag		MAY	11	Ari
	APR	12	Cap		JUN	20	Tau
	JUL	3	Sag		AUG	2	Gem
	AUG	24	Cap		SEP	21	Can
	OCT	21	Aqu	1961	FEB	5	Gem
	DEC	4	Pic		FEB	7	Can
1955	JAN	15	Ari		MAY	6	Leo
	FEB	26	Tau		JUN	28	Vir
	APR	10	Gem		AUG	17	Lib
	MAY	26	Can		OCT	1	Scp
	JUL	11	Leo		NOV	13	Sag
	AUG	27	Vir		DEC	24	Cap
	OCT	13	Lib	1962	FEB	1	Aqu
	NOV	29	Scp		MAR	12	Pic
1956	JAN	14	Sag		APR	19	Ari
	FEB	28	Cap		MAY	28	Tau
	APR	14	Aqu		JUL	9	Gem
	JUN	3	Pic		AUG	22	Can
	DEC	6	Ari		OCT	11	Leo
1957	JAN	28	Tau	1963	JUN	3	Vir
	MAR	17	Gem		JUL	27	Lib
	MAY	4	Can		SEP	12	Scp
	JUN	21	Leo		OCT	25	Sag
	AUG	8	Vir		DEC	5	Cap

1964	JAN	13	Aqu		JUL	18	Leo
	FEB	20	Pic		SEP	3	Vir
	MAR	29	Ari		OCT	20	Lib
	MAY	7	Tau		DEC	6	Scp
	JUN	17	Gem	1971	JAN	23	Sag
	JUL	30	Can		MAR	12	Cap
	SEP	15	Leo		MAY	3	Aqu
	NOV	6	Vir		NOV	6	Pic
1965	JUN	29	Lib		DEC	26	Ari
	AUG	20	Scp	1972	FEB	10	Tau
	OCT	4	Sag		MAR	27	Gem
	NOV	14	Cap		MAY	12	Can
	DEC	23	Aqu		JUN	28	Leo
1966	JAN	30	Pic		AUG	15	Vir
	MAR	9	Ari		SEP	30	Lib
	APR	17	Tau		NOV	15	Scp
	MAY	28	Gem		DEC	30	Sag
	JUL	11	Can	1973	FEB	12	Cap
	AUG	25	Leo		MAR	26	Aqu
	OCT	12	Vir		MAY	8	Pic
	DEC	4	Lib		JUN	20	Ari
1967	FEB	12	Scp		AUG	12	Tau
	MAR	31	Lib		OCT	29	Ari
	JUL	19	Scp		DEC	24	Tau
	SEP	10	Sag	1974	FEB	27	Gem
	OCT	23	Cap		APR	20	Can
	DEC	1	Aqu		JUN	9	Leo
1968	JAN	9	Pic		JUL	27	Vir
	FEB	17	Ari		SEP	12	Lib
	MAR	27	Tau		OCT	28	Scp
	MAY	8	Gem		DEC	10	Sag
	JUN	21	Can	1975	JAN	21	Cap
	AUG	5	Leo		MAR	3	Aqu
	SEP	21	Vir		APR	11	Pic
	NOV	9	Lib		MAY	21	Ari
	DEC	29	Scp		JUL	1	Tau
1969	FEB	25	Sag		AUG	14	Gem
	SEP	21	Cap		OCT	17	Can
	NOV	4	Aqu		NOV	25	Gem
	DEC	15	Pic	1976	MAR	18	Can
1970	JAN	24	Ari		MAY	16	Leo
	MAR	7	Tau		JUL	6	Vir
	APR	18	Gem		AUG	24	Lib
	JUN	2	Can		OCT	8	Scp

Year	Mon	Day	Sign		Year	Mon	Day	Sign
	NOV	20	Sag			FEB	25	Ari
1977	JAN	1	Cap			APR	5	Tau
	FEB	9	Aqu			MAY	16	Gem
	MAR	20	Pic			JUN	29	Can
	APR	27	Ari			AUG	13	Leo
	JUN	6	Tau			SEP	30	Vir
	JUL	17	Gem			NOV	18	Lib
	SEP	1	Can		1984	JAN	11	Scp
	OCT	26	Leo			AUG	17	Sag
1978	JAN	26	Can			OCT	5	Cap
	APR	10	Leo			NOV	15	Aqu
	JUN	14	Vir			DEC	25	Pic
	AUG	4	Lib		1985	FEB	2	Ari
	SEP	19	Scp			MAR	15	Tau
	NOV	2	Sag			APR	26	Gem
	DEC	12	Cap			JUN	9	Can
1979	JAN	20	Aqu			JUL	25	Leo
	FEB	27	Pic			SEP	10	Vir
	APR	7	Ari			OCT	27	Lib
	MAY	16	Tau			DEC	14	Scp
	JUN	26	Gem		1986	FEB	2	Sag
	AUG	8	Can			MAR	28	Cap
	SEP	24	Leo			OCT	9	Aqu
	NOV	19	Vir			NOV	26	Pic
1980	MAR	11	Leo		1987	JAN	8	Ari
	MAY	4	Vir			FEB	20	Tau
	JUL	10	Lib			APR	5	Gem
	AUG	29	Scp			MAY	21	Can
	OCT	12	Sag			JUL	6	Leo
	NOV	22	Cap			AUG	22	Vir
	DEC	30	Aqu			OCT	8	Lib
1981	FEB	6	Pic			NOV	24	Scp
	MAR	17	Ari		1988	JAN	8	Sag
	APR	25	Tau			FEB	22	Cap
	JUN	5	Gem			APR	6	Aqu
	JUL	18	Can			MAY	22	Pic
	SEP	2	Leo			JUL	13	Ari
	OCT	21	Vir			OCT	23	Pic
	DEC	16	Lib			NOV	1	Ari
1982	AUG	3	Scp		1989	JAN	19	Tau
	SEP	20	Sag			MAR	11	Gem
	OCT	31	Cap			APR	29	Can
	DEC	10	Aqu			JUN	16	Leo
1983	JAN	17	Pic			AUG	3	Vir

	SEP	19	Lib	1996	JAN	8	Aqu
	NOV	4	Scp		FEB	15	Pic
	DEC	18	Sag		MAR	24	Ari
1990	JAN	29	Cap		MAY	2	Tau
	MAR	11	Aqu		JUN	12	Gem
	APR	20	Pic		JUL	25	Can
	MAY	31	Ari		SEP	9	Leo
	JUL	12	Tau		OCT	30	Vir
	AUG	31	Gem	1997	JAN	3	Lib
	DEC	14	Tau		MAR	8	Vir
1991	JAN	21	Gem		JUN	19	Lib
	APR	3	Can		AUG	14	Scp
	MAY	26	Leo		SEP	28	Sag
	JUL	15	Vir		NOV	9	Cap
	SEP	1	Lib		DEC	18	Aqu
	OCT	16	Scp	1998	JAN	25	Pic
	NOV	29	Sag		MAR	4	Ari
1992	JAN	9	Cap		APR	13	Tau
	FEB	18	Aqu		MAY	24	Gem
	MAR	28	Pic		JUL	6	Can
	MAY	5	Ari		AUG	20	Leo
	JUN	14	Tau		OCT	7	Vir
	JUL	26	Gem		NOV	27	Lib
	SEP	12	Can	1999	JAN	26	Scp
1993	APR	27	Leo		MAY	5	Lib
	JUN	23	Vir		JUL	5	Scp
	AUG	12	Lib		SEP	2	Sag
	SEP	27	Scp		OCT	17	Cap
	NOV	9	Sag		NOV	26	Aqu
	DEC	20	Cap	2000	JAN	4	Pic
1994	JAN	28	Aqu		FEB	12	Ari
	MAR	7	Pic		MAR	23	Tau
	APR	14	Ari		MAY	3	Gem
	MAY	23	Tau		JUN	16	Can
	JUL	3	Gem		AUG	1	Leo
	AUG	16	Can		SEP	17	Vir
	OCT	4	Leo		NOV	4	Lib
	DEC	12	Vir		DEC	23	Scp
1995	JAN	22	Leo				
	MAY	25	Vir				
	JUL	21	Lib				
	SEP	7	Scp				
	OCT	20	Sag				
	NOV	30	Cap				

1901	JAN	19	Cap	1933	SEP	10	Lib
1902	FEB	6	Aqu	1934	OCT	11	Scp
1903	FEB	20	Pic	1935	NOV	9	Sag
1904	MAR	1	Ari	1936	DEC	2	Cap
	AUG	8	Tau	1937	DEC	20	Aqu
	AUG	31	Ari	1938	MAY	14	Pic
1905	MAR	7	Tau		JUL	30	Aqu
	JUL	21	Gem		DEC	29	Pic
	DEC	4	Tau	1939	MAY	11	Ari
1906	MAR	9	Gem		OCT	30	Pic
	JUL	30	Can		DEC	20	Ari
1907	AUG	18	Leo	1940	MAY	16	Tau
1908	SEP	12	Vir	1941	MAY	26	Gem
1909	OCT	11	Lib	1942	JUN	10	Can
1910	NOV	11	Scp	1943	JUN	30	Leo
1911	DEC	10	Sag	1944	JUL	26	Vir
1913	JAN	2	Cap	1945	AUG	25	Lib
1914	JAN	21	Aqu	1946	SEP	25	Scp
1915	FEB	4	Pic	1947	OCT	24	Sag
1916	FEB	12	Ari	1948	NOV	15	Cap
	JUN	26	Tau	1949	APR	12	Aqu
	OCT	26	Ari		JUN	27	Cap
1917	FEB	12	Tau		NOV	30	Aqu
	JUN	29	Gem	1950	APR	15	Pic
1918	JUL	13	Can		SEP	15	Aqu
1919	AUG	2	Leo		DEC	1	Pic
1920	AUG	27	Vir	1951	APR	21	Ari
1921	SEP	25	Lib	1952	APR	28	Tau
1922	OCT	26	Scp	1953	MAY	9	Gem
1923	NOV	24	Sag	1954	MAY	24	Can
1924	DEC	18	Cap	1955	JUN	13	Leo
1926	JAN	6	Aqu		NOV	17	Vir
1927	JAN	18	Pic	1956	JAN	18	Leo
	JUN	6	Ari		JUL	7	Vir
	SEP	11	Pic		DEC	13	Lib
1928	JAN	23	Ari	1957	FEB	19	Vir
	JUN	4	Tau		AUG	7	Lib
1929	JUN	12	Gem	1958	JAN	13	Scp
1930	JUN	26	Can		MAR	20	Lib
1931	JUL	17	Leo		SEP	7	Scp
1932	AUG	11	Vir	1959	FEB	10	Sag

	APR	24	Scp	1979	FEB	28	Can
	OCT	5	Sag		APR	20	Leo
1960	MAR	1	Cap		SEP	29	Vir
	JUN	10	Sag	1980	OCT	27	Lib
	OCT	26	Cap	1981	NOV	27	Scp
1961	MAR	15	Aqu	1982	DEC	26	Sag
	AUG	12	Cap	1984	JAN	19	Cap
	NOV	4	Aqu	1985	FEB	6	Aqu
1962	MAR	25	Pic	1986	FEB	20	Pic
1963	APR	4	Ari	1987	MAR	2	Ari
1964	APR	12	Tau	1988	MAR	8	Tau
1965	APR	22	Gem		JUL	22	Gem
	SEP	21	Can		NOV	30	Tau
	NOV	17	Gem	1989	MAR	11	Gem
1966	MAY	5	Can		JUL	30	Can
	SEP	27	Leo	1990	AUG	18	Leo
1967	JAN	16	Can	1991	SEP	12	Vir
	MAY	23	Leo	1992	OCT	10	Lib
	OCT	19	Vir	1993	NOV	10	Scp
1968	FEB	27	Leo	1994	DEC	9	Sag
	JUN	15	Vir	1996	JAN	3	Cap
	NOV	15	Lib	1997	JAN	21	Aqu
1969	MAR	30	Vir	1998	FEB	4	Pic
	JUL	15	Lib	1999	FEB	13	Ari
	DEC	16	Scp		JUN	28	Tau
1970	APR	30	Lib		OCT	23	Ari
	AUG	15	Scp	2000	FEB	14	Tau
1971	JAN	14	Sag		JUN	30	Gem
	JUN	5	Sc				
	SEP	11	Sag				
1972	FEB	6	Cap				
	JUL	24	Sag				
	SEP	25	Cap				
1973	FEB	23	Aqu				
1974	MAR	8	Pic				
1975	MAR	18	Ari				
1976	MAR	26	Tau				
	AUG	23	Gem				
	OCT	16	Tau				
1977	APR	3	Gem				
	AUG	20	Can				
	DEC	30	Gem				
1978	APR	12	Can				
	SEP	5	Leo				

SATURN SIGN 1903–2000

1903	JAN	19	Aqu	1949	APR	3	Leo
1905	APR	13	Pic		MAY	29	Vir
	AUG	17	Aqu	1950	NOV	20	Lib
1906	JAN	8	Pic	1951	MAR	7	Vir
1908	MAR	19	Ari		AUG	13	Lib
1910	MAY	17	Tau	1953	OCT	22	Scp
	DEC	14	Ari	1956	JAN	12	Sag
1911	JAN	20	Tau		MAY	14	Scp
1912	JUL	7	Gem		OCT	10	Sag
	NOV	30	Tau	1959	JAN	5	Cap
1913	MAR	26	Gem	1962	JAN	3	Aqu
1914	AUG	24	Can	1964	MAR	24	Pic
	DEC	7	Gem		SEP	16	Aqu
1915	MAY	11	Can		DEC	16	Pic
1916	OCT	17	Leo	1967	MAR	3	Ari
	DEC	7	Can	1969	APR	29	Tau
1917	JUN	24	Leo	1971	JUN	18	Gem
1919	AUG	12	Vir	1972	JAN	10	Tau
1921	OCT	7	Lib		FEB	21	Gem
1923	DEC	20	Scp	1973	AUG	1	Can
1924	APR	6	Lib	1974	JAN	7	Gem
	SEP	13	Scp		APR	18	Can
1926	DEC	2	Sag	1975	SEP	17	Leo
1929	MAR	15	Cap	1976	JAN	14	Can
	MAY	5	Sag		JUN	5	Leo
	NOV	30	Cap	1977	NOV	17	Vir
1932	FEB	24	Aqu	1978	JAN	5	Leo
	AUG	13	Cap		JUL	26	Vir
	NOV	20	Aqu	1980	SEP	21	Lib
1935	FEB	14	Pic	1982	NOV	29	Scp
1937	APR	25	Ari	1983	MAY	6	Lib
	OCT	18	Pic		AUG	24	Scp
1938	JAN	14	Ari	1985	NOV	17	Sag
1939	JUL	6	Tau	1988	FEB	13	Cap
	SEP	22	Ari		JUN	10	Sag
1940	MAR	20	Tau		NOV	12	Cap
1942	MAY	8	Gem	1991	FEB	6	Aqu
1944	JUN	20	Can	1993	MAY	21	Pic
1946	AUG	2	Leo		JUN	30	Aqu
1948	SEP	19	Vir	1994	JAN	28	Pic

1996	APR	7	Ari		1999	MAR	1	Tau
1998	JUN	9	Tau		2000	AUG	10	Gem
	OCT	25	Ari				OCT	16	Tau

How to Use the Uranus, Neptune, and Pluto Tables

Find your birthday in the list following each sign.

Look up your Uranus placement by finding your birthday on the following lists.

URANUS IN ARIES BIRTH DATES

March 31–November 4, 1927
January 13, 1928–June 6, 1934
October 10, 1934–March 28, 1935

URANUS IN TAURUS BIRTH DATES

June 6, 1934–October 10, 1935
March 28, 1935–August 7, 1941
October 5, 1941–May 15, 1942

URANUS IN GEMINI BIRTH DATES

August 7–October 5, 1941
May 15, 1949–August 30, 1948
November 12, 1948–June 10, 1949

URANUS IN CANCER BIRTH DATES

August 30–November 12, 1948
June 10, 1942–August 24, 1955
January 28–June 10, 1956

URANUS IN LEO BIRTH DATES

August 24, 1955–January 28, 1956
June 10, 1956–November 1, 1961
January 10–August 10, 1962

URANUS IN VIRGO BIRTH DATES

November 1, 1961–January 10, 1962
August 10, 1962–September 28, 1968
May 20, 1969–June 24, 1969

URANUS IN LIBRA BIRTH DATES

September 28, 1968–May 20, 1969
June 24, 1969–November 21, 1974
May 1–September 8, 1975

URANUS IN SCORPIO BIRTH DATES

November 21, 1974–May 1, 1975
September 8, 1975–February 17, 1981
March 20–November 16, 1981

URANUS IN SAGITTARIUS BIRTH DATES

February 17–March 20, 1981
November 16, 1981–February 15, 1988
May 27, 1988–December 2, 1988

URANUS IN CAPRICORN BIRTH DATES

December 20, 1904–January 30, 1912
September 4–November 12, 1912
February 15–May 27, 1988
December 2, 1988–April 1, 1995
June 9, 1995–January 12, 1996

URANUS IN AQUARIUS BIRTH DATES

January 30–September 4, 1912
November 12, 1912–April 1, 1919
August 16, 1919–January 22, 1920

URANUS IN PISCES BIRTH DATES

April 1–August 16, 1919
January 22, 1920–March 31, 1927
November 4, 1927–January 13, 1928

Look up your Neptune placement by finding your birthday on the following lists.

NEPTUNE IN CANCER BIRTH DATES

July 19–December 25, 1901
May 21, 1902–September 23, 1914
December 14, 1914–July 19, 1915
March 19–May 2, 1916

NEPTUNE IN LEO BIRTH DATES

September 23–December 14, 1914
July 19, 1915–March 19, 1916
May 2, 1916–September 21, 1928
February 19, 1929–July 24, 1929

NEPTUNE IN VIRGO BIRTH DATES

September 21, 1928–February 19, 1929
July 24, 1929–October 3, 1942
April 17–August 2, 1943

NEPTUNE IN LIBRA BIRTH DATES

October 3, 1942–April 17, 1943
August 2, 1943–December 24, 1955
March 12–October 9, 1956
June 15–August 6, 1957

NEPTUNE IN SCORPIO BIRTH DATES

December 24, 1955–March 12, 1956
October 9, 1956–June 15, 1957
August 6, 1957–January 4, 1970
May 3–November 6, 1970

NEPTUNE IN SAGITTARIUS BIRTH DATES

January 4–May 3, 1970
November 6, 1970–January 19, 1984
June 23–November 21, 1984

NEPTUNE IN CAPRICORN BIRTH DATES

January 19, 1984–June 23, 1984
November 21, 1984–January 29, 1998

Find your Pluto placement in the following list:
Pluto in Gemini—Late 1800s until May 28, 1914
Pluto in Cancer—May 26, 1914–June 14, 1939
Pluto in Leo—June 14, 1939–August 19, 1957
Pluto in Virgo—August 19, 1957–October 5, 1971
              April 17, 1972–July 30, 1972
Pluto in Libra—October 5, 1971—April 17, 1972
              July 30, 1972–August 28, 1984
Pluto in Scorpio—August 28, 1984–January 17, 1995
Pluto in Sagittarius—starting January 17, 1995

CHAPTER 10

Your Rising Sign: A Link Between Heaven and Earth

How the Moment You Were Born Colors Your Horoscope

Have you ever wondered why you don't look or act like others of your sign? You're supposed to be an outgoing Leo, but you come across as a serious Capricorn. On the other hand, perhaps you're a typical version of your sun sign—very easy to categorize. The reason for this confusion (or lack of it) could be your rising sign (also known as your ascendant).

At the moment you were born, when you assumed a physical body and became an independent person, an astrological sign—that is, a specific 30-degree portion of the zodiac—was passing over the eastern horizon. Called your "rising sign" or ascendant, this sign is very important in your horoscope, because it sets your horoscope (or "astrological life") in motion. In effect, it says "Here I am!" as it announces your arrival in the world.

Your rising sign is your link between the celestial zodiac and the real world. It is "your moment in time" and it is what makes your horoscope unique. Many people were born on the same day as you were, but only you were born at that exact moment in your place of birth. Without a rising sign to link the horoscope to a moment on earth and a specific place, you would have a chart that could apply to anyone born at given time, regardless of location.

Rising signs change every two hours with the Earth's rotation. If you were born early in the morning when the sun was on the horizon (which makes your sun sign also your rising sign), you will appear to others as the prototype of your sun sign. That is also why we call those born at with their sun sign on the horizon a "double Aquarius" or a "double Virgo." You have twice as much input from that sign. If you were born with another sign on the horizon, you will "announce" yourself more like that other sign. This other sign will mask slightly—or completely disguise— your basic sun sign character. If people have difficulty guessing your sun sign, this is probably the reason, particularly if you have a very outgoing ascendant, such a Leo ascendant and a rather shy sun sign, like Virgo. On the other hand, a rather conservative Capricorn ascendant can tone down the intensity of a Scorpio or make a jovial Sagittarian seem far more serious than he or she really is. Your rising sign is your "cover" or mask. Often a person will project just one facet of a rising sign—for exmaple, one person with a Sagittarius rising would be a lover of horses and a world traveler, another with the same ascendant would be spiritual leader.

In your horoscope chart, the other signs follow the rising sign in sequence, rotating counterclockwise. Therefore, the rising sign sets up the tone of your chart. It rules the 1st house, which is the physical body—your appearance—and also influences your style, tastes, health, and physical environment (where you are most comfortable working and living).

It is also the starting point for all the planetary cycles. As the planets move around the chart, the rising sign marks the ending of one cycle and the beginning of another.

You'll find your rising sign on the chart on pages 118–19. Since rising signs move rapidly, you should know your birth time as close to the minute as possible. If you are unsure about the exact time, but know within a few hours, check the following descriptions to see which is most like the personality you project.

ARIES RISING. You come across as a go-getter—headed for the fast track; dynamic, energetic, and assertive. Billy Graham and Bette Midler show the sparkle and fire of this ascendant. But since you can also be somewhat impatient and combative, try to either consider where the other person is coming from or head for an area where your feistiness will be appreciated. With this ascendant, you may prefer the color red—or wear it a lot—instinctively reaching for the red sweater or tie. Many of you walk with your head thrust forward like the ram. You may also have prominent

113

eyebrows or a very wide browline. At some point in your life, you may acquire a facial scar or a head injury.

TAURUS RISING. There is nothing lightweight about the impression you give. You have a strong, steady presence, not easily dismissed. You are more sensual, patient, and pleasure oriented than others of your sign. You love good food and may be an excellent cook. Green thumbs are also common with this nature-loving ascendant. You may have an unusual or memorable voice and great concentration and stamina, like TV news anchor Dan Rather. Though your frame is often stocky, with a tendency to gain weight, some curvaceous beauty queens and sex goddesses are born with this placement.

GEMINI RISING. You're a great talker, in constant motion. You're a quick thinker and fast learner, like comedienne Phyllis Diller and rock star Bruce Springsteen. On the minus side, you could come across as nervous, scattered, a jack-of-all-trades. Play up your analytical mind and your ability to communicate and to adapt to different people and environments. This ascendant could also give you writing talent or an affinity for work that uses your hands, such as massage or piano playing. Learning a keyboard is second nature to you. You gesture often and probably have light coloring and fine features.

CANCER RISING. You may come across as sensitive and caring, one who enjoys taking care of others. You may seem a bit moodier than others of your sign and more self-protective, like actor John Travolta. You have very quick responses to emotional situations. You are also very astute in business, with a sharp sense of what will sell, like H. Ross Perot, a double Cancer. You may choose work dealing with hotels or shelter businesses, decorating or working with children. Physically, you may be a lunar type, with a large chest area, a round face, and delicate sensitive skin. Or you may be a "crab" type with wide-set eyes and prominent bone structure.

LEO RISING. You project a regal air of authority, which instills confidence in your abilities. You come across as someone who can take charge. You are very poised in the spotlight and know how to present yourself to play up your special star quality, like Ava Gardner, Marilyn Monroe, and ballerina Cynthia Gregory. You attract attention and take center stage graciously. In business, you're the epitome of executive style.

VIRGO RISING. Though your style may be rather conservative, restrained, and classic, your intelligence and analytical ability shine brightly. You seem well organized, with a no-nonsense air of knowing what you're doing. Never one to slack off, you're a hard worker who gets on with it. Your manner may be a bit aloof and you can be critical of others who don't share your sense of mastery of your craft, of doing it to perfection. But this critical quality serves as well as an editor, writer, or teacher. You may also be drawn to the health or service fields. A high-profile example: George Bush.

LIBRA RISING. You come across as charming, attractive, well-dressed and diplomatic. Like Nancy Reagan, the first impression you give is one of social ease and harmony. You enjoy working with others and it shows. Not a loner, you thrive in partnerships and relationship. You may have aesthetic interests, such as fashion or design, or you could gravitate to the diplomatic or legal fields. Physically, you'll have delicate, harmonious features: graceful gestures; and a lovely, often dimpled, smile.

SCORPIO RISING. Even if you don't say a word, your presence carries a charge of excitment and an air of mystery. Margaret Thatcher and Jacqueline Onassis are good examples of your kind of charisma, the kind that can make its presence felt with a penetrating gaze. Be careful not to come on too overwhelmingly strong. You might consider toning down your intensity, tempering it with a touch of humor. Less open than others of your sign, you can be quite manipulative when pursuing your goals. You project an air of subtle sexuality, of a secret agenda that could fascinate others. Sexual expression will be an important issue for you. You may wear a great deal of the Scorpio "noncolor," black.

SAGITTARIUS RISING. This ascendant can push normally home-loving signs to exotic locales. Always on the go, you have energy to burn. You're a bouncy, athletic version of your sign, like Ted Turner, with an upbeat personality that exudes cheerful optimism. You adore competitive sports that require lots of leg power. You may also be drawn to horses or horse-related activities. You are frank and direct in manner and don't hesitate to say what you think, even if it means stepping on some tender toes. Travel excites you—the more exotic the destination, the better. You may be attracted to idealistic or philosophical activities, or to teaching, publishing, or religious careers. Your sense of humor wins fans, but some of you may have to work on developing tact and diplomacy. Another famous example: Raquel Welch.

CAPRICORN RISING. You are the serious, hard-working type with a very keen business sense. (*Cosmopolitan* editor Helen Gurley Brown, who has this ascendant, has called herself a "mouseburger.") But you could also have the traditional flair of Fred Astaire. A great organizer, you function well in a structured or corporate environment. Not a frivolous type, you aim to be taken seriously, like Paul Newman. You'll easily adapt to present the classiest impression appropriate to your business. You understand how to delegate and to use the talents of others, which could land you a leadership position. You prefer a traditional atmosphere, antiques, and possessions of "quiet quality." Take special care of your knees, teeth, and bone structure, which are vulnerable areas.

AQUARIUS RISING. Like daredevil Evel Knievel, you're charismatic and individualistic—you know how to get attention, sometimes in a startling way that shakes everyone up. You'll dress to please yourself—never mind the dress code. Be sure to find a business that appreciates your eccentric side, one with a cause or principles you believe in. Your job should give you plenty of space and allow you to work independently. You'll make your own rules and probably won't adapt well to authority or outside discipline—you know what's best for you, anyway. You may be attracted to a high-tech career or to one that probes the depths of the mind in some way.

PISCES RISING. You'll express the most artistic, romantic, and imaginative side of your sun sign. Like Phil Donohue, you'll come across as empathetic, a good listener who is able to cue in to where others are coming from—a valuable interview asset. You may be quite dramatic, and present yourself as a "character," like baseball's Yogi Berra or author Norman Mailer. You are very happy on the water, or in a home that overlooks water. You might gravitate to the theater, dance, or film worlds, or to any creative environment. Or you could take another Pisces tack and show your more spiritual side, dedicating yourself to helping others. Beautiful eyes and talented dancing feet are frequent gifts of this ascendant. One of your most vulnerable points is your supersensitivity to drugs, chemicals, or alcohol. High-profile example: Richard Pryor.

RISING SIGNS—A.M. BIRTHS

	1 AM	2 AM	3 AM	4 AM	5 AM	6 AM	7 AM	8 AM	9 AM	10 AM	11 AM	12 NOON
Jan 1	Lib	Sc	Sc	Sc	Sag	Sag	Cap	Cap	Aq	Aq	Pis	Ar
Jan 9	Lib	Sc	Sc	Sag	Sag	Sag	Cap	Cap	Aq	Pis	Ar	Tau
Jan 17	Sc	Sc	Sc	Sag	Sag	Cap	Cap	Aq	Aq	Pis	Ar	Tau
Jan 25	Sc	Sc	Sag	Sag	Sag	Cap	Cap	Aq	Pis	Ar	Tau	Tau
Feb 2	Sc	Sc	Sag	Sag	Cap	Cap	Aq	Pis	Pis	Ar	Tau	Gem
Feb 10	Sc	Sag	Sag	Sag	Cap	Cap	Aq	Pis	Ar	Tau	Tau	Gem
Feb 18	Sc	Sag	Sag	Cap	Cap	Aq	Pis	Pis	Ar	Tau	Gem	Gem
Feb 26	Sag	Sag	Sag	Cap	Aq	Aq	Pis	Ar	Tau	Tau	Gem	Gem
Mar 6	Sag	Sag	Cap	Cap	Aq	Pis	Pis	Ar	Tau	Gem	Gem	Can
Mar 14	Sag	Cap	Cap	Aq	Aq	Pis	Ar	Tau	Tau	Gem	Gem	Can
Mar 22	Sag	Cap	Cap	Aq	Pis	Ar	Ar	Tau	Gem	Gem	Can	Can
Mar 30	Cap	Cap	Aq	Pis	Pis	Ar	Tau	Tau	Gem	Can	Can	Can
Apr 7	Cap	Cap	Aq	Pis	Ar	Ar	Tau	Gem	Gem	Can	Can	Leo
Apr 14	Cap	Aq	Aq	Pis	Ar	Tau	Tau	Gem	Gem	Can	Can	Leo
Apr 22	Cap	Aq	Pis	Ar	Ar	Tau	Gem	Gem	Gem	Can	Leo	Leo
Apr 30	Aq	Aq	Pis	Ar	Tau	Tau	Gem	Can	Can	Can	Leo	Leo
May 8	Aq	Pis	Ar	Ar	Tau	Gem	Gem	Can	Can	Leo	Leo	Leo
May 16	Aq	Pis	Ar	Tau	Gem	Gem	Can	Can	Can	Leo	Leo	Vir
May 24	Pis	Ar	Ar	Tau	Gem	Gem	Can	Can	Leo	Leo	Leo	Vir
June 1	Pis	Ar	Tau	Gem	Gem	Can	Can	Can	Leo	Leo	Vir	Vir
June 9	Ar	Ar	Tau	Gem	Gem	Can	Can	Leo	Leo	Leo	Vir	Vir
June 17	Ar	Tau	Gem	Gem	Can	Can	Can	Leo	Leo	Vir	Vir	Vir
June 25	Tau	Tau	Gem	Gem	Can	Can	Leo	Leo	Leo	Vir	Vir	Lib
July 3	Tau	Gem	Gem	Can	Can	Can	Leo	Leo	Vir	Vir	Vir	Lib
July 11	Tau	Gem	Gem	Can	Can	Leo	Leo	Leo	Vir	Vir	Lib	Lib
July 18	Gem	Gem	Can	Can	Can	Leo	Leo	Vir	Vir	Vir	Lib	Lib
July 26	Gem	Gem	Can	Can	Leo	Leo	Vir	Vir	Vir	Lib	Lib	Lib
Aug 3	Gem	Can	Can	Can	Leo	Leo	Vir	Vir	Vir	Lib	Lib	Sc
Aug 11	Gem	Can	Can	Leo	Leo	Leo	Vir	Vir	Lib	Lib	Lib	Sc
Aug 18	Can	Can	Can	Leo	Leo	Vir	Vir	Vir	Lib	Lib	Sc	Sc
Aug 27	Can	Can	Leo	Leo	Leo	Vir	Vir	Lib	Lib	Lib	Sc	Sc
Sept 4	Can	Can	Leo	Leo	Leo	Vir	Vir	Vir	Lib	Lib	Sc	Sc
Sept 12	Can	Leo	Leo	Leo	Vir	Vir	Lib	Lib	Lib	Sc	Sc	Sag
Sept 20	Leo	Leo	Leo	Vir	Vir	Vir	Lib	Lib	Sc	Sc	Sc	Sag
Sept 28	Leo	Leo	Leo	Vir	Vir	Lib	Lib	Lib	Sc	Sc	Sag	Sag
Oct 6	Leo	Leo	Vir	Vir	Vir	Lib	Lib	Sc	Sc	Sc	Sag	Sag
Oct 14	Leo	Vir	Vir	Vir	Lib	Lib	Lib	Sc	Sc	Sag	Sag	Cap
Oct 22	Leo	Vir	Vir	Vir	Lib	Lib	Lib	Sc	Sc	Sc	Sag	Cap
Oct 30	Vir	Vir	Vir	Lib	Lib	Lib	Sc	Sc	Sag	Sag	Cap	Cap
Nov 7	Vir	Vir	Lib	Lib	Lib	Sc	Sc	Sc	Sag	Sag	Cap	Cap
Nov 15	Vir	Vir	Lib	Lib	Sc	Sc	Sc	Sag	Sag	Cap	Cap	Aq
Nov 23	Vir	Lib	Lib	Lib	Sc	Sc	Sag	Sag	Sag	Cap	Cap	Aq
Dec 1	Vir	Lib	Lib	Sc	Sc	Sc	Sag	Sag	Cap	Cap	Aq	Aq
Dec 9	Lib	Lib	Lib	Sc	Sc	Sag	Sag	Sag	Cap	Cap	Aq	Pis
Dec 18	Lib	Lib	Sc	Sc	Sc	Sag	Sag	Cap	Cap	Aq	Aq	Pis
Dec 28	Lib	Lib	Sc	Sc	Sag	Sag	Sag	Cap	Aq	Aq	Pis	Ar

RISING SIGNS—P.M. BIRTHS

	1 PM	2 PM	3 PM	4 PM	5 PM	6 PM	7 PM	8 PM	9 PM	10 PM	11 PM	12 MID-NIGHT
Jan 1	Tau	Gem	Gem	Can	Can	Can	Leo	Leo	Vir	Vir	Vir	Lib
Jan 9	Tau	Gem	Gem	Can	Can	Leo	Leo	Leo	Vir	Vir	Vir	Lib
Jan 17	Gem	Gem	Can	Can	Can	Leo	Leo	Vir	Vir	Vir	Lib	Lib
Jan 25	Gem	Gem	Can	Can	Leo	Leo	Leo	Vir	Vir	Lib	Lib	Lib
Feb 2	Gem	Can	Can	Can	Leo	Leo	Vir	Vir	Vir	Lib	Lib	Sc
Feb 10	Gem	Can	Can	Leo	Leo	Leo	Vir	Vir	Lib	Lib	Lib	Sc
Feb 18	Can	Can	Can	Leo	Leo	Vir	Vir	Vir	Lib	Lib	Sc	Sc
Feb 26	Can	Can	Leo	Leo	Leo	Vir	Vir	Lib	Lib	Lib	Sc	Sc
Mar 6	Can	Leo	Leo	Leo	Vir	Vir	Vir	Lib	Lib	Sc	Sc	Sc
Mar 14	Can	Leo	Leo	Vir	Vir	Vir	Lib	Lib	Lib	Sc	Sc	Sag
Mar 22	Leo	Leo	Leo	Vir	Vir	Lib	Lib	Lib	Sc	Sc	Sc	Sag
Mar 30	Leo	Leo	Vir	Vir	Vir	Lib	Lib	Sc	Sc	Sc	Sag	Sag
Apr 7	Leo	Leo	Vir	Vir	Lib	Lib	Lib	Sc	Sc	Sc	Sag	Sag
Apr 14	Leo	Vir	Vir	Vir	Lib	Lib	Sc	Sc	Sc	Sag	Sag	Cap
Apr 22	Leo	Vir	Vir	Lib	Lib	Lib	Sc	Sc	Sc	Sag	Sag	Cap
Apr 30	Vir	Vir	Vir	Lib	Lib	Sc	Sc	Sc	Sag	Sag	Cap	Cap
May 8	Vir	Vir	Lib	Lib	Lib	Sc	Sc	Sag	Sag	Sag	Cap	Cap
May 16	Vir	Vir	Lib	Lib	Sc	Sc	Sc	Sag	Sag	Cap	Cap	Aq
May 24	Vir	Lib	Lib	Lib	Sc	Sc	Sag	Sag	Sag	Cap	Cap	Aq
June 1	Vir	Lib	Lib	Sc	Sc	Sc	Sag	Sag	Cap	Cap	Aq	Aq
June 9	Lib	Lib	Lib	Sc	Sc	Sag	Sag	Sag	Cap	Cap	Aq	Pis
June 17	Lib	Lib	Sc	Sc	Sc	Sag	Sag	Cap	Cap	Aq	Aq	Pis
June 25	Lib	Lib	Sc	Sc	Sag	Sag	Sag	Cap	Cap	Aq	Aq	Ar
July 3	Lib	Sc	Sc	Sc	Sag	Sag	Cap	Cap	Aq	Aq	Pis	Ar
July 11	Lib	Sc	Sc	Sag	Sag	Sag	Cap	Cap	Aq	Pis	Ar	Tau
July 18	Sc	Sc	Sc	Sag	Sag	Cap	Cap	Aq	Aq	Pis	Ar	Tau
July 26	Sc	Sc	Sag	Sag	Sag	Cap	Cap	Aq	Pis	Ar	Tau	Tau
Aug 3	Sc	Sc	Sag	Sag	Cap	Cap	Aq	Aq	Pis	Ar	Tau	Gem
Aug 11	Sc	Sag	Sag	Sag	Cap	Cap	Aq	Pis	Ar	Tau	Tau	Gem
Aug 18	Sc	Sag	Sag	Cap	Cap	Aq	Pis	Pis	Ar	Tau	Gem	Gem
Aug 27	Sag	Sag	Sag	Cap	Cap	Aq	Pis	Ar	Tau	Tau	Gem	Gem
Sept 4	Sag	Sag	Cap	Cap	Aq	Pis	Pis	Ar	Tau	Gem	Gem	Can
Sept 12	Sag	Sag	Cap	Cap	Aq	Aq	Pis	Ar	Tau	Tau	Gem	Can
Sept 20	Sag	Sag	Cap	Cap	Aq	Pis	Pis	Ar	Tau	Gem	Gem	Can
Sept 28	Cap	Cap	Aq	Aq	Pis	Ar	Tau	Tau	Gem	Gem	Can	Can
Oct 6	Cap	Cap	Aq	Aq	Pis	Ar	Ar	Tau	Gem	Gem	Can	Leo
Oct 14	Cap	Aq	Aq	Pis	Ar	Tau	Tau	Gem	Gem	Can	Can	Leo
Oct 22	Cap	Aq	Pis	Ar	Ar	Tau	Gem	Gem	Can	Can	Leo	Leo
Oct 30	Aq	Aq	Pis	Ar	Tau	Tau	Gem	Can	Can	Can	Leo	Leo
Nov 7	Aq	Aq	Pis	Ar	Tau	Tau	Gem	Can	Can	Can	Leo	Leo
Nov 15	Aq	Pis	Ar	Tau	Gem	Gem	Can	Can	Can	Leo	Leo	Vir
Nov 23	Pis	Ar	Ar	Tau	Gem	Gem	Can	Can	Leo	Leo	Leo	Vir
Dec 1	Pis	Ar	Tau	Gem	Gem	Can	Can	Can	Leo	Leo	Vir	Vir
Dec 9	Ar	Tau	Tau	Gem	Gem	Can	Can	Leo	Leo	Leo	Vir	Vir
Dec 18	Ar	Tau	Gem	Gem	Can	Can	Can	Leo	Leo	Vir	Vir	Vir
Dec 28	Tau	Tau	Gem	Gem	Can	Can	Leo	Leo	Vir	Vir	Vir	Lib

CHAPTER 11

How Astrology Can Help You Stay Healthy and Fit

Over the past few years, changes involving our health care may have the most effect on our future well-being. We'll be asked to take on more responsibility for our own health, beginning with adopting a healthier lifestyle. Astrology can help you sort out your health priorities and put your life on a positive course by getting in step with these times of health care reform. Since astrology began, different parts of the body, and their potential illnesses, have been associated with specific signs of the zodiac. Today's astrologers will work with these ancient associations, using them not only to locate potential health problems, but also to help clients harmonize their activities with those favored by each sign.

Why not use some of these time-tested techniques yourself? Using the stars as a guide, you can create your own master plan for a healthier lifestyle by paying special attention to that part of your body ruled by your sun sign and the activities most likely to promote physical fitness.

If you are dieting, there are times when you should find it easier to lose weight, because your body will be less likely to retain fluid and you'll have more discipline to stick to a diet. The months of Virgo and Capricorn, both practical, disciplined earth signs, should be especially good times to begin a diet and fitness program. Perhaps that's why the busiest time of year for health clubs and spas is in Capricorn-ruled January, when we have the resolve to put New Year's resolutions into action. Another good time might be during a fire sign (Aries, Sagittarius, and Leo), when the energies favor athletic activities and there is good motivation to burn calories. On the other hand, the time ruled by water signs (Cancer, Scorpio, and Pisces) is notorious for retaining fluid in the body, and it may be difficult to shed "water weight." Pleasure-loving, Venus-ruled signs, Taurus and Libra, are times when you might be more susceptible to high-calorie, sweet temptations, which does not bode well for dieters.

There are other times when weight loss could be especially difficult. When Jupiter (the planet of expansion) is stimulating your ascendant (rising sign) or sun sign, your body is also likely to expand. This year, that will be those who have Capricorn sun or rising signs. The prevailing energies are to "blow up," like a balloon, and you may find yourself doing just that. Try adding extra exercise or taking up a new sport at this time. But be sure it's an enjoyable activity—Jupiter does not favor those that require concentration and discipline.

The planet of discipline and contractive forces, Saturn, can be your ally when dieting. If this planet is aspecting your sun sign or rising sign, you will be in situations requiring more discipline—and this might be an ideal time to curb your appetite and start on a serious fitness program. This year, Saturn will be ending its transit through Pisces in April and then will move into Aries, where it will remain until 1998.

Moon-time Dieting

The prevailing lunar wisdom advises starting a diet to lose weight on a waning moon in a favorable sign, such as one of the fire signs, Virgo or Capricorn. To gain weight, start on a waxing moon, and choose a water sign.

Aries

YOUR HEALTH.

Aries naturally has one of the strongest constitutions in the zodiac. Mars-ruled, you have energy to burn and love to challenge yourself physically. However, that same Aries go-power can engender the desire to push yourself to the limits, which can eventually cause burnout. Healthwise, if you've been burning the candle at both ends or repressing anger, this may show up as headaches. Work off steam by scheduling extra time at the gym, taking up a racket sport,

Ping-Pong, anything that lets you hit an object hard! Participate in spring training with your local baseball team!

YOUR DIET.

Active Arians are usually not overweight. However, when you have to wait for something or when your big plans are frustrated, you may then decide to raid the refrigerator. Arians can be so busy that they ignore food altogether. Guard against eating too quickly or impulsively.

EXERCISE TIPS.

You need exercise that is challenging and allows you to push yourself to the limit safely. Aerobics, competitive sports, any activities that burn calories are favored. Try a new sport that has plenty of action and challenge, like soccer or bike racing. Be sure you have the proper headgear for your sport, since Aries rules the head and is prone to head injuries.

Celebrity Role Models: Steven Seagal, Ali MacGraw

Taurus

YOUR HEALTH.

Taurus is a hardy sign with great stamina and endurance. Taurus rules the neck and throat area, which includes the thyroid glands and vocal cords. If you are becoming lethargic, your thyroid might be sluggish. Get a pillow specially designed to support your neck area, for a more restful sleep. Neck massages are a sybaritic way to release tension in the neck area—try one!

YOUR DIET.

Yours is one of the signs that finds it extremely difficult to diet. The enjoyment of food is a major pleasure, and you don't like to be deprived of delicious sensations of any kind—and you tend to like sweet, rich foods. Though some Taureans, like Cher or the late Audrey Hepburn, remain slim, they usually do so with great effort and determination. You're sure to know the best bakery in your area. Shift your pleasure to finding the freshest, most perfect produce. Shop at the local farmers' markets and add more fresh vegetables to your diet. And be sure there are always plenty of low-calorie treats available when you feel the urge to raid the refirgerator.

EXERCISE TIPS.

You need a pleasant place to work out, and what could be more pleasant than a scenic natural park. Explore the woodlands and seashore in your area with long nature hikes. Or plant an extensive garden that requires lots of maintenance. Working with animals can also be a joy for Taurus. Try to combine your exercise with pleasurable activities. Walk or bicycle to work, dance or rock climb, work out to your favorite music.

Celebrity Role Models: Cher, Shirley MacLaine.

Gemini

YOUR HEALTH.

One of the most social signs, Gemini rules the nerves, our body's lines of communication. If your nerves are frazzled, you may need more fun and laughter in your life. Getting together with friends, going to parties, doing things in groups, brings more perspective into your life. Investigate natural ways to relieve tension such as yoga or meditation. Doing things with your hands, playing the piano, typing, doing craftwork—are also helpful. Since Gemini also rules the lungs, yours are especially sensitive, so, if you smoke, consider quitting.

YOUR DIET.

Restless, sociable Geminis are usually one of the skinnier signs. However, lots of parties and restaurant meals can pile on the pounds if you hang around the buffet table instead of the dance floor. Your desire to sample a bit of everything could also add up calories before you realize it. Your challenge is to find a diet with plenty of variety, so you won't get bored. Develop a strategy for eating in restaurants and coping with buffets (pile the plate with salad and veggies).

EXERCISE TIPS.

Doing things with others is most therapeutic for you. Include friends in your exercise routines. Join a friendly exercise class or jogging group. Gemini-type sports require good timing and manual dexterity as well as interaction with others, like tennis or golf. Those of you who jog may want to add hand weights or upper-body exercises to your daily routine, for benefits to the Gemini-ruled arms and hands. Celebrity Role Models: Elle MacPherson, Marky Mark

Cancer

YOUR HEALTH.

Cancer rules digestive difficulties, especially gastric ulcers. Emotionally caused digestive problems—those stomach-knotting insecurities—can crop up under Cancer. Console yourself with some extra pampering if you're feeling blue. Being with loved ones, old friends, and family could give the support you need. Plan some special family activities that bring everyone close together. The breast area is ruled by Cancer, a reminder to have regular checkups, according to your age and family health history of breast-related illness.

YOUR DIET.

For this sign that loves good food, dieting is especially difficult and can be laden with problems. Cancer can be conflicted about food: you may want to be fashionably thin or thin to appeal to a loved one, but yours is a sign that loves to eat and often becomes the family cook. Princess Di of England is a good example of a Cancer who is facing an eating disorder. It is important in any diet you choose not to have a feeling of deprivation. Focus on a food lifestyle plan that is low in fat, high in vegetables and fruits. Remember to nurture yourself by airing problems and finding emotional support, perhaps through a food-oriented therapy group.

EXERCISE TIPS.

Boating and water sports are ideal Cancer-time activities. Sometimes, just a walk by a nearby pond or sitting for a few moments by a fountain can do wonders to relieve emotional stress and tension that can lead to overeating. Make exercise a family activity by creating a family gym, playing sports, or going to exercise classes with loved ones.

Celebrity Role Models: Princess Di, Sylvester Stallone.

Leo

YOUR HEALTH.

Leo rules the upper back and heart, two important areas to protect throughout your life. Be sure you have a good mattress to support the vulnerable Leo spine. Ruled by the sun, you're one sign that usually loves to tan, like Leo George Hamilton. Considering the permanent damage sun exposure can cause, however, you may elect to remain porcelain white, like Madonna or ageless beauty Arlene Dahl. So don't leave home without a big hat, umbrella, and sunblock formulated for your skin type.

YOUR DIET.

Leos are proud of their bodies and usually take excellent care of them. Your sign summons up great discipline and determination to maintain your public image. That includes staying with a healthy diet. The Leo downfall could be your preference for the finer things in life, which might include dining at the best restaurants and indulging in gourmet foods. Indulge yourself now and then, but balance this with exercise. And a Lion that is not getting the love and attention you need can easily turn to food for consolation. Learn to give yourself the royal treatment in non-food ways, such as an extra trip to the beauty salon for pampering.

EXERCISE TIPS.

Leos love showing off a beautiful body and looking great in a swimsuit. You'll go to great lengths to maintain a fabulous physique. To glorify the body beautiful, why not consider what a body-building regime could do for you? Exercises to strengthen your back and develop your aerobic capacity are also necessary to protect your vulnerable areas, the heart and spine.

Celebrity Role Models: The list of Leo beauty queens and kings is long. For starters, how about Arnold Schwarzenegger, Madonna, Mae West, Linda Carter, Stephanie Seymour, and Iman.

Virgo

YOUR HEALTH.

Virgo rules the care of the body in general and the maintenance of the abdomen, digestive tract, liver, and intestines in particular. This is a troubleshooting sign, one that is constantly checking (and worrying about) your progress. Schedule regular medical exams and diagnostic tests and generally evaluate your health. If you need a change of diet, supplements, or special care, consult the appropriate advisers. You have probably learned that running your life efficiently does much to eliminate health-robbing stress. It's a great comfort to know you've got a smooth health-maintenance routine organized.

YOUR DIET.

Virgos are naturally concerned about nutrition—and can make quite an issue out of food quality and preparation. Many of you will devise a special diet to promote health and you'll have the discipline to stick with it. Postassium-rich vegetables are especially important for your sign, and macrobiotic diets appeal to many Virgos. If you become overweight, it is usually because you are easing worries and frayed nerves with comfort foods. To counteract this tendency, be sure to include activities in your life that promote tranquillity and peace of mind. Meditation, crafts, and detail work seem to be especially soothing to Virgo and could draw your attention away from food.

EXERCISE TIPS.

Virgos greatly benefit from exercises that stress the relationship of mind and body, such as yoga and tai chi. Sports

that require a certain technical skill to master can also challenge Virgo. The key factor is that any exercise routine should involve self-improvement on several levels.
Celebrity Role Model: Raquel Welch

Libra

YOUR HEALTH.

Overdoing in any area of your life can send your personal scales swinging. Restoring balance is your key to health. Since Libra rules the kidneys and lower back, consider yoga, spinal adjustments, or a detoxification program. If you have been working too hard or taking life too seriously, what you may need is a dose of culture, art, music, or perhaps some social activity. Make time to entertain friends. Be romantic with the one you love.

YOUR DIET.

When Libras put on too much weight, it is usually because they're overindulging their famous sweet tooth. It's important for this sign to do everything in moderation—and that includes dieting. Avoid extreme eating regimes and opt for losing weight slowly, as you incorporate healthier eating habits into your life. Because your sign rules the kidneys, it is important to drink plenty of water, to cleanse this area as you reduce weight. Since you are one of the most social signs, you tend to eat in restaurants, entertain, or be entertained more often than others. Make an eating plan before you go out, so you face the menu or buffet prepared. Indecision can be your worst enemy here, so making your healthy choices in advance and sticking to them could be your best strategy when faced with a beautiful, tempting buffet.

EXERCISE TIPS.

Since this is the sign of relationships, you may enjoy working out with a partner or with loved ones. Make morning walks or weekend hikes family affairs. Take a romantic bicycle tour and picnic in the autumn countryside. Put more beauty in all areas of your life. Libra is also the sign of grace, and what's more graceful than dancing or ice skating? If ballet is not your thing, why not swing to a Latin or African beat? Dancing combines art, music, romance, relaxation, graceful movement, social contact, and exercise. What more can you ask?

Celebrity Role Models: Cheryl Tiegs, Heather Locklear, Martina Navratilova, Nancy Kerrigan.

Scorpio

YOUR HEALTH.

This sign rules the regenerative and eliminative organs, so sexual activity can be a source of good or ill health for Scorpio. It is important to examine your attitudes about sex, and to follow safe sexual practices. Though you have a strong constitution that can literally rise from the ashes of extreme illness or injury, it is important not to take this for granted or abuse it with self-destructive habits. Try to curb excessive tendencies in any area of your life, since going to extremes is one of the Scorpio's health pitfalls. You are often challenged by testing that famous Scorpio willpower by living too close to the edge.

YOUR DIET.

Scorpios should guard against yo-yo dieting, which can do more harm than remaining overweight. This sign often works transformation on yourself, by going from extreme obesity to thinness and back again. Since you can obsess about food and diet, try to diffuse this energy into other areas of your life.

EXERCISE TIPS.

It's no accident that this passionate time is football season, which reminds us that sports are a very healthy way to diffuse emotions. If you enjoy winter sports, why not prepare for the ski slopes or ice skating? Scorpio loves intense life-or-death competition, so be sure your muscles are warmed up before going all out.

Celebrity Role Models: Lauren Hutton, Demi Moore, Oksana Baiul

Sagittarius

YOUR HEALTH.

In maintaining health, Sagittarians would do well to remember that yours is a goal-setting sign. So aim for the best you can be, then set a plan to achieve it. Good health for you is often a matter of staying motivated. Once you've decided on a course of action, get going. Being on the move and physically active keeps you in the best of health, improves your circulation, and protects your arteries. Your difficulties could arise from injuries to the hip or thigh area and arterial problems. So be sure to protect yourself with the proper equipment for your activity and don't push yourself beyond your capacity.

YOUR DIET.

Since your sign is naturally expansive, you may have difficulty staying with a diet; one that is part of a spiritually oriented lifestyle, such as vegetarianism, might have the most lasting appeal. Beware of fad diets that promise instant results and come with a high-pressure sales pitch. Avoid gimmicks, pills, or anything "instant." Since patience is not a Sagittarian strong point, aim for long-range benefits and balance a sane, practical eating plan with plenty of exercise.

EXERCISE TIPS.

Your sign loves working out in classes or groups, so combine socializing with athletic activities. Touch football games, bike riding, hikes, and long walks with your dog are fun as well as healthy. Let others know that you'd like a health-promoting gift—sports equipment, a gym membership, or an exercise video for Christmas. In your workouts, concentrate on Sagittarius-ruled areas—the hips, legs, and thighs. Yours is a sports-loving sign, ideal for downhill or cross-country skating or roller blading and basketball. Since you're likely to travel a lot, plan an exercise routine that can be done anywhere. Isometric-type exercises, which work one muscle group against another, can be done in a car or plane seat. If you travel often, investigate equipment that fits easily in your suitcase, such as water-filled weights, home gym devices, elastic exercise bands.

Celebrity Role Models: Jane Fonda, Katarina Witt, JFK, Jr.

Capricorn

YOUR HEALTH.

Capricorn, the sign of Father Time, brings up the subject of aging. If sags and wrinkles are keeping you from looking as young as you feel, you may want to investigate plastic surgery. Teeth are also ruled by this sign, a reminder to have regular cleanings and dental checkups. Capricorn is also the sign of the workaholic, so be sure not to overdo in your quest for health. Keep a steady, even pace for lasting results. Remember to include pleasurable activities in your self-care program. Grim determination can be counterproductive if you're also trying to relieve tension. Take up a sport for pure enjoyment, not necessarily to become a champion. Check your office environment for hidden health saboteurs, like air quality, lighting, and comfort. Get an ergonomically designed chair to protect your back, or buy a specially designed back-support cushion, if your chair is uncomfortable. If you work at a computer, check your keyboard and the height of the computer screen for ergonomic comfort.

YOUR DIET.

Most Capricorns are gifted with great self-discipline, so it is a rare Capricorn who gets too overweight. However, if you give in to pessimism or melancholy, and console yourself with food, then even this strong-willed sign can pile on pounds. So lighten up your life with cheerful people and kick up your heels a bit—you'll be sure to lighten your weight as well.

EXERCISE TIPS.

Capricorn rules the skeletal structure, so pay special attention to your posture, bones, and joints with proper exercise. It's never too early to counteract osteoporosis by adding weight-bearing exercise to your routine. If your knees or joints are showing early signs of arthritis, you may need to add calcium supplements to your diet. Check your posture, which affects your looks and your health. Remember to protect your knees, perhaps doing special exercises to strengthen this area.

Celebrity Role Models: Diane Sawyer, Marlene Dietrich, Victoria Principal

Aquarius

YOUR HEALTH.

Since Aquarius rules the circulatory system, you might benefit from a therapeutic massage, a relaxing whirlpool, or one of the new electronic massage machines. Calves and ankles are also Aquarius territory and should be emphasized in your exercise program. Be sure your ankles are well supported and guard against sprains. Consider the air quality around you—Aquarians are often vulnerable to airborne allergies and are highly sensitive to air pollution. Do some air-quality control on your environment with an air purifer, ionizer, or humidifer. During flu season, read up on ways to strengthen your immune system.

YOUR DIET.

This sign of sharing loves to diet in a group. Aquarius enjoys the support of others in the same situation, like Oprah Winfrey, whose weight-loss ups and downs became media events. You should do well by finding your own support system of fellow-dieters, either through an organized program or informally. Try to find a flexible group which adapts to unique personalities, rather than one that imposes a rigid structure.

EXERCISE TIPS.

Make your own fitness rules, adapting the latest high-tech gadgets and techniques. If your schedule makes it difficult to get to the gym and take regular exercise classes, look at the vast selection of exercise videos available and take class anytime you want. Or set up a home gym with portable home exercise equipment. New Age treatments are favored by Aquarius, so consider alternative approaches to health and fitness. Aquarius is a sign of reaching out to others, a cue to make your health regime more social—doing your exercises with friends could make staying fit more fun.

Celebrity Role Models: Oprah Winfrey, Christie Brinkley

Pisces

YOUR HEALTH.

Perhaps it's no accident that we often do spring cleaning during Pisces. The last sign of the zodiac, which rules the lymphatic system, is supersensitive to toxins, and spring is an ideal time to detox your system with a liquid diet or supervised fast. This may also help you get rid of water retention, a common Pisces problem. Feet are Pisces territory. Consider how often you take your feet for granted and how miserable life can be when your feet hurt. Since our feet reflect and affect the health of the entire body, devote some time to pampering them. Check your walking shoes or buy new ones tailored for your kind of exercise. Investigate orthotics, especially if you walk or run a lot. These custom-molded inserts could make a big difference in your comfort and performance. The soles of our feet connect with all other parts of our body, just as the sign of Pisces embodies all the previous signs. This is the theory behind reflexology, a therapeutic foot massage that treats all areas of the body via the nerve endings on the soles of the feet. For the sake of your feet, as well as your entire body, consider treating yourself to a session with a local practitioner of this technique.

YOUR DIET.

Since your sign tends to hold water, it is very easy to gain or lose weight depending on your fluid retention level. You are also an emotional eater who can turn to food for comfort under stress, which can sabotage your self-discipline. A good diet strategy for Pisces is to take it slow and easy, avoiding any sense of deprivation, which can make you feel depressed, and to surround yourself with a positive support system. Encouraging friends and loved ones, a diet or nutrition coach, and a loving, upbeat atmosphere can help you stay on your diet program. Avoid negative people and stressful situations, wherever possible.

EXERCISE TIPS.

Pisces may find it difficult to stick to a rigid routine. Instead, look for exercise that releases your feelings, such as dance or ice skating. Since water is your element, find a water aerobics class or swim laps at your local pool. A good exercise instructor can also make a difference in your motivation. Walking is a perfect exercise for Pisces, since it releases tension, gets you outdoors, and can be a positive way to socialize with friends—away from the temptation of food and drink. Try doing local errands on foot, if you live in a city, or find a nearby park where you can take a daily hike. Invite someone you love or would like to get to know better to share it with you.

Celebrity Role Models: Cindy Crawford, Sharon Stone, Elizabeth Taylor

CHAPTER 12

Do You Love the One You *Want* . . . or the One You *Need?*

Make Your Own Compatibility Chart and Find Out!

How many people turn to astrology for the light it can shed on their love life? Probably the question astrologers hear most is: What sign is best for me in love? Or: I'm a Taurus and my lover is a Gemini, what are our prospects? Each sun sign does have certain predictable characteristics in love and, by comparing the sun signs, you can reach a better understanding of the dynamics of the relationship. However, it it very easy to oversimplify. Just because someone is in a so-called incompatible sign is no reason why the relationship can't work out. A true in-depth comparison involves far more than just the sun sign. An astrologer considers the interrelationships of all the planets and houses (where they fall in your respective horoscopes). There are several bonds between planets that can offset any difficulties between sun signs. It's worthwhile to analyze them to learn more about your relationship. You can do this by making a very simple chart that compares the moon, Mars, and Venus, as well as the sun signs of the partners in a relationship. You can find the signs of Mars and Venus in the tables in this book. Unfortunately, the moon tables are too long for a book of this size, so it might be worthwhile to consult an astrological ephemeris (a book of planetary tables) in your local library or to have a computer chart cast to determine the moon placement.

Simply look up the signs of Mars and Venus (and the moon, if possible) for each person and list them, together with the sun sign, next to each other, then add the element of each sign. The earth signs are Taurus, Virgo, Capricorn.

The air signs are Gemini, Libra, Aquarius. The fire signs are Aries, Leo, Sagittarius. The water signs are Cancer, Scorpio, Pisces.

Example:

	SUN	MOON	MARS	VENUS
Romeo	Aries/Fire	Leo/Fire	Scorpio/Water	Taurus/Earth
Juliet	Pisces/Water	Leo/Fire	Aries/Fire	Aquarius/Air

As a rule of thumb, signs of the same element or complementary elements (fire with air and earth with water) get along best. So you can see that this particular Romeo and Juliet could have some challenges ahead.

The Lunar Link—Here's the person you *need*.

The planet in your chart that governs your emotions is the moon (although the moon is not technically a planet, it is usually referred to as one by astrologers), so you would naturally take this into consideration when evaluating a potential romantic partnership. If a person's moon is in a good relationship to your sun, moon, Venus, or Mars, preferably in the same sign or element, you should relate well on some emotional level. Your needs will be compatible: you'll understand each other's feelings without much effort. If the moon is in a compatible element, such as earth with water or fire with air, you may have to make a few adjustments, but you will be able to make them easily. With a water-fire or earth-air combination, you'll have to make a considerable effort to understand where the other is coming from emotionally.

It's worth having a computer chart done, just to find the position of your moon. Because the moon changes signs every two days, the tables are too long to include in this book.

The Venus Attraction—Here's the one you *want*.

Venus is what you respond to, so if you and your partner have a good Venus aspect, you should have much in common. You'll enjoy doing things together. The same type of lovemaking will turn you both on. You'll have no trouble pleasing each other.

Look up both partners' Venus placements in the charts on pages 88–95. Your lover's Venus in the same sign or a sign of the same element as your own Venus, Mars, moon, or sun is best. Second best is a sign of a compatible element (earth with water, air with fire). Venus in water with air, or earth with fire means that you may have to make a special effort to understand what appeals to each other. And you'll have to give each other plenty of space to enjoy activities that don't particularly appeal to you. Note: This chart can work not only for lovers, but for any relationship where compatibility of tastes is important to you.

The Mars Connection—This one lights your fire!

The positions of Mars reveal your sexual energy—how often you like to make love, for instance. They also show your temper—do you explode or do a slow burn? Here you'll find out if your partner is direct, aggressive, and hot-blooded or more likely to take a cool, objective approach. Mutually supportive partners have their Mars working together in the same or complementary elements. But *any* contacts between Mars and Venus in two charts can strike sexy sparks. Even the difficult aspects—your partner's Mars three or six signs away from your sun, Mars, or Venus—can offer sexual stimulation. Who doesn't get turned on by a challenge, from time to time? Sometimes the easy Mars relationships can drift into dullness.

The Solar Bond

The sun is the focus of our personality and therefore the most powerful component involved. Each pair of sun signs has special lessons to teach and learn from each other. As you'll discover, there is a negative side to the most ideal couple and a positive side to the most unlikely match. Each has an up- and a downside.

Here is a lineup of sun-sign combinations for all signs. Remember that most successful relationships have a balance of harmonious points and challenges, which stimulate you to grow and which sustain lively interest over time. So, if the forecast for you and your beloved (or business associate) seems like an uphill struggle, take heart! Such legendary lovers as Juan and Eva Peron, Ronald and Nancy Reagan, Harry and Bess Truman, Julius Caesar and Cleopatra, Billy and Ruth Graham, and George and Martha Washington are among the many who have made successful partnerships between supposedly incompatible sun signs.

Aries–Aries

The Upside: Here's someone who can keep up with you! And has red-hot enthusiasm to match yours. You encourage each other, find new projects together. The romantic sparks fly, especially in the beginning.

The Downside: Who's going to be boss? Who's got patience to stick it out in tough times? And who is going to get those wonderful projects completed? Better find the answers before you take this one seriously.

Aries–Taurus

The Upside: Here's the backup you need to follow through on your ideas. Taurus keeps plugging when you run out of steam. You finally get things done with this partner. And they'll bring sensual pleasure, real comfort into your life.

The Downside: They're too slow for you. Will they *ever* get going? You may well ask. By the time they get started you could be off on a new venture, or bored with the old one. You like quick results and instant satisfaction. They go for the long haul. And bossing them around is like bashing an immovable object.

Aries–Gemini

The Upside: You have a lively time together. Gemini is never boring. They lead you on a merry chase. And once captured, they keep you interested. There is plenty of talk and action here!

The Downside: You like to come first in your loved one's affections; with Gemini, the "grass is always greener." Better curb your jealousy or this one will burn out fast.

Aries–Cancer

The Upside: Cancer has a shrewd intuitive sense that understands what you like and how you like it. They spell you out, sensing the many things you miss while rushing about. With their business ability and your enthusiasm, you could make a great team.

The Downside: Are they ever possessive and sensitive! One thoughtless word and they sulk for days and remember the slight always. Do you really want to live your life with kid gloves on? As for moods—you'll never know what to expect from day to day. You may not want to bother catering to this one. They'd love to fence you in, stay home and sulk, while you'd rather go out adventuring.

Aries–Leo

The Upside: You two steal the show. You're both romantic and theatrical, radiate warmth alone together or in a crowd. For sheer star power, you'll light up each other's life with excitement.

The Downside: Better stake out your territory here. Leos like to run the show and so do you! And both of you hate to give in. Ego problems could dynamite this affair of passion.

Aries–Virgo

The Upside: This odd combination often works out beautifully. You thrill conservative Virgos, sweep them off their feet. In return, they'll tie up your loose ends, check the details you rush past, keep the motor running. You both have lots of energy to give each other—and you get things done!

The Downside: Virgo's put-downs could deflate your enthusiasm. Somehow they can't resist picking your ideas apart, trying to plant your high-flying feet on the ground. You have a difficult time living up to their standards, so why try?

Aries–Libra

The Upside: Opposites attract and you're drawn to Libra's charm, style, and sheer class. This is a very elegant partner, who smooths out your rough edges. They love your decisiveness and you love—and need—their diplomacy.

The Downside: You like competition, they hate to make waves. Arguments with Librans go nowhere; they will tune you out completely. When you want some action, their hesitancy and constant debating can drive you mad.

Aries–Scorpio

The Upside: This is a powerful combination. You really challenge each other. You both love competition and playing hard to get. Like Katharine Hepburn and Spencer Tracy, you could turn the battle of the sexes into a lasting love affair.

The Downside: You're an upfront type, with cards on the table, while Scorpio plays them close to the vest. You can get mighty suspicious of this sign—you never know what they're up to. You're both jealous and like to control the situation; it can work, if you don't square off or play around on the side.

Aries–Sagittarius

The Upside: You're two outgoing adventurers. You can travel well together in mind and body. Here's a great buddy as well as a lover. This duo works particularly well if you share the same life goals and spiritual ideals. Religious ties are a very important bond.

The Downside: You are both very self-involved, and put your own interests first. If you don't share common goals, prepare for a struggle. And if you need a lot of handholding or emotional and financial backup, Sagittarius just won't be available. Your joint ventures may sizzle, then fizzle.

Aries–Capricorn

The Upside: You're both workaholics who like plenty of

action. Neither of you has trouble making decisions or getting started. You give Capricorn fresh new ideas; they give you follow-through and organization. Not a bad exchange.

The Downside: Capricorn's melancholy moods rain on your parade. They want status; you want stardom. They can be old fogies, while you can be a real baby.

Aries–Aquarius

The Upside: If you both share common goals or work for the same worthy causes, this can be a winner. You push their ideas, are stimulated by their mind. And you love their surprises!

The Downside: You need attention and Aquarius has so many other interests. When are they going to have time for you? Their detachment could send you looking elsewhere.

Aries–Pisces

The Upside: Your next-door neighbor in the zodiac makes a very good buddy. You love their creativity and how anxious they are to please you. No problem getting attention here. They're thrilled when you dazzle them with new ideas or sweep them off their feet!

The Downside: Again, you're dealing with a hypersensitive water sign. They get hurt easily and these fish can turn into sharks! They have a way of drowning your enthusiasm, while your inconsideration and bossiness could drive them to drink.

Taurus–Aries

The Upside: Here is someone who really needs your organization and follow-through—not to mention your patience and stamina. You need Aries to get you up and moving, provide you with great new ideas. You two can move mountains together.

The Downside: This sign often jumps in without testing the water. You're the cautious type who focuses on long-term goals. And when they get pushy, you won't budge. They want freedom; you want a cozy, secure lifestyle. There will be lots of compromises here.

Taurus–Taurus

The Upside: You are so comfortable together that it's tempting never to move. Here is someone who loves acquiring beautiful things as much as you do. And they'll be just as faithful, passionate, and sentimental as you are. Sound perfect?

The Downside: They are also just as stubborn as you are. Neither do they tend to forgive and forget. You could get bogged down and look for other stimulation to get out of your rut.

Taurus–Gemini

The Upside: Here is the sparkle you need to inspire you to get out and about. Gemini's quick mind and charm are a turn-on for you. You share many laughs together. And you bring order to their life.

The Downside: Gemini is not a sign to stay home by the fire for long. They love being busy, doing two things at once, having friends over. You may long for peace and tranquility. Gemini flirts; you're the faithful possessive type. Let's hope you can communicate on other levels.

Taurus–Cancer

The Upside: You do great things for each other. Cancer gives you tenderness, a lovely home. You give this moody sign comfort and support. You're a dynamite team in business and in pleasure.

The Downside: Cancer operates from an emotional, intuitive level. You like to make solid, sensible plans. You both tend to brood and withdraw. Could be a Mexican standoff.

Taurus–Leo

The Upside: Here is someone who thinks big and loves beautiful things, as you do. And who better to show them

141

off? You love Leo's glamour and style and know how to make them purrrr.

The Downside: You keep an eye on the budget at all times—accumulation is the idea. Leo believes that living well is a divine right, even if the bills aren't paid yet. Taurus is very possessive; the lion won't be caged. And both of you hate to give in. But something's got to give here.

Taurus–Virgo

The Upside: Virgo relaxes under your calm steady hand. You bring out their sensual side. They take care of all those details you hate and make sure you stay healthy and wise as well as wealthy.

The Downside: Virgo's worrying, nagging, and constant criticizing disrupt your tranquility. Little things seem to irritate them in a big way. When their nit-picking tries your patience, it's hard to keep the peace. If this is allowed to escalate, you could have a very uncomfortable situation.

Taurus–Libra

The Upside: This seems to be your perfect match, at first. You could be dazzled by Libra's beauty, charm, and finesse, and by their talent for creating a lovely environment. You take over the burdensome decision making and financial matters. Both of you delight in acquiring the finer things in life together.

The Downside: Libra is a social being, while Taurus is a homebody. Taurus is possessive; Libra is flirtatious. Taurus likes to save; Libra likes to spend. And just when Taurus thinks a decision has been made, Libra changes its mind.

Taurus–Scorpio

The Upside: From opposite sides of the zodiac, you seem to be the perfect complements. You love those intense Scorpio passions. They can make the total commitment you so desire. Your calm, steady nature is a tranquil oasis for Scorpio.

The Downside: Control and power can be devisive issues here. Both of you are stubborn and like to hold the reins. And neither likes to give in. To stay in control, either may resort to manipulative tricks. Better stake out your territory early in the relationship.

Taurus–Sagittarius

The Upside: You admire their honesty and directness, and enjoy their love of the outdoors and terrific sense of humor. And they really need the organization and solid base of operations you provide.

The Downside: Sagittarius is a wanderer who can't be tied down. They often have a roving eye, too. You won't have many cozy nights at home with this one. Better curb your jealousy and possessiveness.

Taurus–Capricorn

The Upside: This is an extremely comfortable situation where both of you share similar tastes and goals. You're hard workers who love beauty, quality, and tradition. You're both responsible and mature—what you see is what you get.

The Downside: Climbing to the top in the business and social world is a priority to Capricorn. You'd better fit into their plans, otherwise forget it. Let's hope you can deal with their ambitions and late nights at the office or the club.

Taurus–Aquarius

The Upside: You two could go far with your practical know-how and their originality. You give them solid grounding, and they give you inspiration. You'll do things you'd never dreamed of trying before—and enjoy yourself. Aquarius jolts you out of a rut, encourages you to expand your mind, think beyond your comfortable little world.

The Downside: You like the predicable; Aquarians love surprises. They are not security-minded and will give their all—and yours—to a worthy cause. You like a close intimate relationship, which Aquarius could find confining. Bear all this in mind.

Taurus–Pisces

The Upside: You respond happily to their deep emotional needs. In turn, they give you all the adoration and attention you want. You both love taking care of each other. And you help them market those creative ideas and bring in profits.

The Downside: You may think you have control of the situation, but it is only an illusion. The fish is very difficult to hook. You'll be continually frustrated if you try to tie this one down. Better get used to constant fluctuations—or swim away.

Gemini–Aries

The Upside: This romance gets off to a brilliant beginning. Aries loves your constant flow of ideas. You make life interesting for them. They sweep you off your feet, thrilling you with daring maneuvers. You never bore each other.

The Downside: You like a constant change of scene, jobs, and partners. Though Aries' energy keeps you hopping, they won't tolerate any flirtatious games. They like being number one. To you, the more, the merrier. Aries' jealousy could be a drag. So could their tendency to bully and use strong-arm tactics. You like a light touch.

Gemini–Taurus

The Upside: The contrast of Taurus' steady, reliable, orderly nature sets off your vivacious sparkle. You're a play of opposites with much to give each other. You particularly like the way they follow through on your bright ideas, making them happen! You can count on them to be there when you need them most, and to soothe your jangled nerves with creative comforts.

The Downside: When someone holds you too tight, you feel suffocated and slip through their fingers. The possessive Taurus clutches could leave you gasping for air and space. And who wants to stay home all the time? Not a "people person" like you!

Gemini–Gemini

The Upside: You have so many sides to your personality that, the odds are, many of them will get along beautifully. One thing's for sure, you can always change. You have much to share and explore together.

The Downside: Sometimes you have to stop talking and do something. Then who takes responsibility? And who does the nitty-gritty work? Someone with two feet on the ground and you'd better decide which one—or two—of you will make things happen. Otherwise you'll float away.

Gemini–Cancer

The Upside: You show Cancer how to laugh away those bleak moods. Then Cancer tenderly soothes your nerves. You'll be a pair who entertains at home, with Cancer mothering the guests and you adding the sparkle and charm.

The Downside: Working out the right balance of power is your biggest chore. If Cancer feels secure, it has a chance. Otherwise, their moods will really get on your nerves. You'll have to curb your flirting. Cancer takes infidelity of any sort very much to heart.

Gemini–Leo

The Upside: Socially you are a stellar couple. Your charm and Leo's glamour are a winning combination. And Leo's confidence makes you sparkle even brighter. You both love to move in high style with high society.

The Downside: Leos take your flirting as a personal affront. They take themselves very seriously and will roar with displeasure if you make fun of them in any way. Be careful about leading a double life, and use your genius for saying the right thing at the right time. You may get bored providing their quota of adoration.

Gemini–Virgo

The Upside: You've got so much to talk about and you enjoy each other's different point of view. Virgo's practical approach gives you balance, while you bring humor and social sparkle into the serious Virgo life. This can be a good, stimulating companionship on all levels.

The Downside: Virgo's negative fault-finding, worrying, and nit-picking dampens your enthusiasm, while your constant activity gets on Virgo's nerves. You'll go off in a mental realm to escape, while Virgo gets an upset stomach. You may need outside medicine to make this one work.

Gemini–Libra

The Upside: You both have a meeting of minds—and bodies. You love social life, elegant surroundings, interesting conversation, and beautiful things. There is so much to share here. And you're both born flirts who won't get overly possessive.

The Downside: Everything's fine while the sun shines, but you both get seasick when the going gets rough. When Libran scales sway, you become a bundle of nerves. You need many other stabilizing factors in your charts to keep your balance. It helps if you can give Libra the attention and flattery they need. A compliment goes a long way with this sign.

Gemini–Scorpio

The Upside: You're the challenging one Scorpio can't figure out. And you can laugh away their black moods. Meanwhile, intense Scorpio keeps your mind on track and supplies the focus and direction you need—a good bargain.

The Downside: Power and control are what Scorpio is all about, which might be enough to scare you off. They're always manipulating behind the scenes, but if you bat an eyelash at anyone else, watch out for the Scorpio sting. Your gadding about may seem a bit out of control to them. Get ready for some heavy going, emotionally.

Gemini–Sagittarius

The Upside: Life's a party to you two fun-lovers. This is the ideal person to enjoy games of all kinds with, as long as you play by the rules. You're both outgoing types who love to be on the move and won't fence each other in.

The Downside: Neither one stays in one place for long, so when will you get together? Better get some definite goals to aim for, or you'll be traveling in different directions.

Gemini–Capricorn

The Upside: If your communicating talents dovetail with Capricorn's ambition, you're in business! You lighten up their life, and bring them out into the social whirl. Your charm is a great foil for their aristocratic manner.

The Downside: Capricorn can be all work and no play, particularly if their eye is fixed on a goal. It had better be your goal, too, or you'll be spending evenings alone! Their dour moods can be a drag—they take everything too seriously.

Gemini–Aquarius

The Upside: You are people collectors who never get lost in the crowd. You give each other all the space you both need to explore and experiment. You love their surprises; they love your many facets. This is a high-flying combination.

The Downside: Aquarius has such fixed ideas, while you find it hard to commit yourself to any one cause or concept. Neither of you gets too involved on a personal level, so where's the chemistry, the grand passion? It's fine, if you're content to stay buddies, but if you need a few sparks, don't look here!

Gemini–Pisces

The Upside: You're both dual, mutable signs, which means there's enough action on every level to keep you both fasci-nated. Here is someone who will give you all the variety you need and add real romance to your life. You'll never get tired of playing different roles together.

The Downside: Neither of you likes to be bored, so a lot of mundane practical matters go unattended. Your mental games get taken seriously by sensitive Pisces, who then might retaliate with underhanded maneuvers. You're just not on the same wavelength. Better get a good translator.

Cancer–Aries

The Upside: You make Aries feel like number one in your life. In return, they support you with warmth, enthusiasm, and loyalty. You understand how to make their schemes and dreams pay off. Your sensitivity and intuition see nuances and opportunities that headstrong Aries misses. This is great, when it works.

The Downside: A frustrated Aries doesn't care whose toes are stepped on—including yours! Your complaints fall on deaf ears—or absent ones! They have no understanding of or patience with your moods. You seem like a crybaby to them, while they seem infantile and immature to you. There will be few cozy evenings at home for you two.

Cancer–Taurus

The Upside: Here's a solid support that won't let you down. There are lots of sexy cuddles when you need them. And you'll coddle Taurus in return. A very cozy duo of happy homebodies.

The Downside: Taurus likes a smooth steady road, and won't be sympathetic to lunar ups and downs. They may be too slow-moving for you. You do like to get going and when you push, Taurus balks.

Cancer–Gemini

The Upside: Here's a fascinator who makes you forget the blues. Gemini takes you out in the world, exposes you to new ideas. Together you could profit from them. Gemini really appreciates your shrewd insights and your clever ability to accumulate funds. Your tender attention soothes their frazzled nerves. Socially, the Gemini charm and your maternal caring draw others to you as a pair.

The Downside: You need a faithful partner, not one who rocks your boat. It may be tough getting freedom-loving Gemini to take any commitment seriously, and Gemini head games can hurt your sensitive feelings. Better learn to talk things out. You'll both have to make many compromises.

Cancer–Cancer

The Upside: This is a comforting combination. You both enjoy having a lovely home. You are very tender and tolerant of each other's moods. There is great emotional understanding.

The Downside: Brooding, complaining, and guilt trips are Cancer's unlovely qualities which double up here. You could smother each other with possessiveness. Or, if you have territorial disputes, you both cling fiercely to your turf. Neither one lets go easily. You could resent each others' demands.

Cancer–Leo

The Upside: Sun-ruled Leo can light up your day with confidence and charisma. And do they ever respond to your adoring attention! You'll shine together in business or socially, and you're both natural parents.

The Downside: Your negative moods are a real downer to Leo, who can't bear complaining. They simply will not deal with you at the full moon. You may find this lack of understanding unbearable and look for solace elsewhere. This combination just seems to lack the depth and emotional communication you need.

Cancer–Virgo

The Upside: You'll have the neatest home on the block. You are two people who take care of others in different ways—Virgo gives practical support, you provide for emotional needs. You are both beautifully organized and really care. You can count on each other.

The Downside: Cancer's moods can provoke Virgo criticism, which start a vicious circle. When both of you turn negative, it's a contest of complaints, incessant nagging, and guilt trips. You must realize that Virgo is a natural faultfinder and stop taking this personally. Virgo must learn to give you praise and emotional coddling.

Cancer–Libra

The Upside: Two very creative, beauty-loving signs have much in common. You appreciate a happy, secure, and beautiful home environment. And you'll never create messy scenes. You instinctively understand Libra's delicate balance, and they in turn would never deliberately disturb your sensitive feelings. Cancer's decisiveness and need for action can work to motivate Libra.

The Downside: This could be a case of swinging moods versus swaying scales. Rational Libra can never fathom your feelings. Nor have you much patience for their endless debates of pros and cons. You may also disagree on how mutual moneys are spent. Libra goes for beauty and luxury regardless of price; you're budget-conscious, intent on maintaining security at all costs.

Cancer–Scorpio

The Upside: Here is all the depth you want in a relationship. You both live on a "feeling" level. It's easy to communicate, even without words. Your mutual possessiveness works well here, making you both feel secure and protected.

The Downside: Both of you have dark moody spells, which, if they coincide, can be hard to shake. Scorpio's reserve and your self-protectiveness can create ill will. Neither gives their all; both want control and are likely to use some underhanded manipulative tricks.

Cancer–Sagittarius

The Upside: You are both ambitious. Cancer will decide which of Sag's bright ideas have potential, and which are shots in the dark. Sag's sense of humor and outgoing energy can be just the right tonic for your moods. They'll show you how to laugh your troubles away!

The Downside: Sag's gambling instincts are no laughing matter to Cancer, who likes to play it safe. Security is critical to Cancer, whereas freedom gets top priority from Sagittarius. Sag's roving eye and Cancer's clinging claws could send you both scurrying in opposite directions.

Cancer–Capricorn

The Upside: You're two achievers who enjoy getting results and making a profit. You both have traditional values—Capricorn's fatherly and Cancer's mothering instincts complement each other.

The Downside: Cancer's emotional needs can take up too much of Capricorn's time. You have to balance your energies between work and home life and learn to use, not abuse, each other's talents. And bring your sense of humor to the rescue when melancholy moods hit.

Cancer–Aquarius

The Upside: You could be the happy odd couple. Aquarius needs the personal touch, which you naturally provide. And you respect their strong convictions and loyalty to their ideals. They seem so trustworthy and idealistic, while you're the practical one who takes care of business.

The Downside: Is this person going to give you the emotional satisfaction you need? Forget hearth and home when Aquarius has a meeting or a rally to attend. If you want priority in Aquarius' life, better share their causes and interests.

Cancer–Pisces

The Upside: At last, here is someone who understands how to soothe you out of your moods, or just leave you alone until they pass. You encourage each other creatively, and have no trouble communicating on most levels.

The Downside: Cancer's possessiveness is the weak link. Pisces must swim freely; too much clinging or subtle hooks makes them want to slip away. You are both changeable, so it is difficult to find real security here on either side. And when Pisces plays the martyr and Cancer the victim of circumstances, beware! You two sensitive souls know how to wound each other deeply.

Leo–Aries

The Upside: You two steal the show. You're both romantic and theatrical, radiate warmth alone together or in a crowd. For sheer star power, you'll light up each other's life with excitement.

The Downside: Better stake out your territory here. Aries likes to run the show and so do you! And both of you hate to give in. Pride problems could dynamite this affair of passion.

Leo–Taurus

The Upside: Here is someone who thinks big and loves beautiful things as much as you do. And who better to show them off? Taurus adores your glamour and style, and they know how to give just the right strokes to make you purr.

The Downside: Taurus keeps an eye on the budget at all times—accumulation is the name of their game—while you believe that living well is your divine right, even if the bills aren't paid yet. Taurus is very possessive; you won't be caged. And both of you hate to give in. But something's got to give, here.

Leo–Gemini

The Upside: Socially, you are a stellar couple. Gemini's charm and your glamour are a winning combination. Gemini's wit and humor make you sparkle even brighter. You both love to move in high style with high society.

The Downside: You'll take Gemini's flirting as a personal affront. You do take yourself very seriously and will roar with displeasure if Gemini makes fun of you in any way. Gemini often leads a double life, which really hurts your pride. You must be the one and only. This romance starts hot but could blow cold.

Leo–Cancer

The Upside: You light up Cancer's dark moods and take them out into the social world. In return, they'll give you tender loving care and the benefit of their shrewd insights and sharp business sense. You're both natural protective parents who value a secure home territory. There is much to be gained here.

The Downside: You are a born optimist who has no patience with negative moods and constant complainers. When Cancer gets weepy and too emotional, you'll turn a deaf ear or shine your light elsewhere, while Cancer withdraws.

Leo–Leo

The Upside: Here is someone to share the limelight. You're both corulers, who give and get first-class treatment. You'll revel in each other's success and share the wealth, generously.

The Downside: It's especially important for each of you to have your own territory, where you are the acknowledged star. You are not a couple who likes to share the spotlight or, heaven forbid, to take orders. You need to have some areas where you can be boss. Fighting for the same turf can cause serious arguments.

Leo–Virgo

The Upside: Here is the perfect partner to back you up, taking care of the details and organization, while you provide the sales expertise and public relations. Virgo will give you the attention you need, never competing with you. While your confidence is contagious, you can make this shy sign shine!

The Downside: Virgo will tend to bog you down with details and insist you stick to a budget. You just can't think small. Unless you curb your extravagant tendencies, you're in for a constant critique. Virgo won't recognize your divine rights.

Leo–Libra

The Upside: Elegant Libra and radiant Leo make a stunning couple. You'll spare no expense to create an atmosphere of beauty and luxury. And Libran diplomacy plus Leo graciousness and dignity make formidable social assets. Those sweet Libran words make you feel like royalty, while you make their decisions with regal assurance.

The Downside: Runaway extravagance could curb your luxurious lifestyle. You may need a third party to handle finances. You both love attention and flattery, and may succumb to other enticements, if you feel you're not getting proper appreciation.

Leo–Scorpio

The Upside: You sense the powerful chemistry at work and approach each other with mutual respect. This is no combination to trifle with! You'll get all the attention you need and more! You bring out Scorpio's finer points. While you direct, Scorpio produces!

The Downside: You both go about controlling the situation in different ways. Leo is openly demanding and bossy, while Scorpio is the power behind the throne. Their manipulative technique could find Leo caught in a trap, with your spending habits curtailed. You're not easily tamed, so watch out!

Leo–Sagittarius

The Upside: You're two optimists who shoot for the stars. You'll inspire each other and share adventures together. Their jovial good humor and your sunny outgoing nature draw others to you. Together, you can sell anything!

The Downside: This combination is fine, as long as you're both on a high roll. But when financial troubles cause a crash, better find a net. Sagittarius is a rover, whereas Leo demands loyalty: another thorny issue. And the Leo ego could deflate under Sagittarius' barbs.

Leo–Capricorn

The Upside: You have found a fellow aristocrat who values power and status as you do. What's more, Capricorn has the organizational know-how to compliment your sales ability. Together you can move mountains.

The Downside: Capricorn is a tough, well-disciplined loner who can live without posh perks, if it means achieving a goal. Leo must have luxury at all costs and won't tolerate stinginess or spartan living. Leo also needs social contacts, which Cap may find frivolous.

Leo–Aquarius

The Upside: Here are two opposites, who both love to be onstage, surrounded by people. Leo's warmth and graciousness complement Aquarian objectivity and concern for humanity. You attract attention, a great costarring team.

The Downside: All goes well as long as there's a meeting of minds. But Leo wants wholehearted commitment, and this may rub Aquarius the wrong way. Common interests are needed to focus your energies. And Leo must learn to curb any jealous or competitive tendencies.

Leo–Pisces

The Upside: The Piscean flair for fantasy is fine foil for your theatrical talent. They have wonderful romantic ideas, perfect for sizzling love scenes. They know how to shower you with adoration and appreciation. And you boost their often-fragile egos, giving them the confidence to shine. These talented people can thrine under your supervision.

The Downside: The fish is hard to catch and even harder to hold on to. They may not give you the commitment or loyalty you want. Pisces seems easy to control, but the tighter you grab, the more they slip away. And their soggy emotions, and fondness for liquid substances, could dampen your party spirit.

Virgo–Aries

The Upside: Uninhibited Aries loves to bring out those Virgo fantasies. You're a real challenge. You'll have fun and thrills together. You'll provide the stability and financial acumen, while Aries does the selling and go-getting. This is one of those odd earth and fire attractions that often makes wonderful chemistry.

The Downside: Virgo likes things wholesome and conservative, while Aries is always first with the newest trend. You could have serious differences in taste and style. Virgo's desire for perfection is read by Aries as a dull and definite downer, while Aries' tendency to start things and leave you to finish could drive you mad. Virgo likes mental activities, and subtle perfect phrasing. Aries would rather get physical fast and blurts out feelings before thinking about the consequences. This duo is not very appealing.

Virgo–Taurus

The Upside: You relax under Taurus' calm, steady hand. They bring out your sensual side. If you clean up all those details they hate and make sure they are healthy and wise, they'll make sure *you* are wealthy.

The Downside: Your worrying, nagging, and constant criticizing jangle the placid Taurus system. Those little things that irritate you seem to roll off their backs. And when you try the Taurus' patience, the bull will charge. Then, watch out!

Virgo–Gemini

The Upside: You two have much to talk about and enjoy each other's differing point of view. Your practical approach gives Gemini balance, while they bring humor and social sparkle into your serious life. This can be a good, stimulating companionship on all levels.

The Downside: Your negative fault-finding, worrying, and nitpicking dampens Gemini enthusiasm, while their constant flighty activity gets on your nerves. Gemini goes off in a mental realm to escape, while you get an upset stomach. To make this one work, you may need outside medicine.

Virgo–Cancer

The Upside: You'll have the neatest home on the block. You are two people who take care of others in different ways. Virgo gives practical support, whereas Cancer provides for emotional needs. You are both beautifully organized and very caring people. You can count on each other.

The Downside: Cancer's moods can provoke Virgo criticism, which starts a vicious circle. When both of you turn negative, it becomes a contest of complaints, incessant nagging, and guilt trips. You must realize that Cancer takes everything personally and learn to provide praise and emotional coddling. These folks need stroking, not poking!

Virgo–Leo

The Upside: You provide the backup, managing the details and organization, while Leo handles the sales and public relations. You give Leo the attention they need, never the competition. And Leo makes you shine!

The Downside: You tend to get bogged down with details, one of which is the budget. Leo can't think small, has extravagant tendencies, and feels a divine right to go first class all the way. Your constant reminders will cause roars of displeasure.

Virgo–Virgo

The Upside: You are both dedicated perfectionists who understand each other's needs. You'll make every effort to live up to those high standards, and cater to each other. With every detail in order, you'll keep this relationship running smoothly.

The Downside: You might fight over trivial details, such as who gets the crossword puzzle. And you may try too hard to satisfy each other, and lack inspiration or passion. This pairing could be too prim and pristine to have any fun.

Virgo–Libra

The Upside: Libra's refined good looks and perfect sense of style are awesome. And their sweet talk boosts your confidence. You'll also respect the intelligent way they weigh every situation before making a balanced decision.

The Downside: Virgo criticism can set Libran scales swaying. So can their preoccupation with reality when Libra would rather concentrate on ideas. Libra wants compliments and flattery, and may turn a deaf ear when you tell them something they *need* to hear. And their constant spending on clothes and social activities is nerve-racking.

Virgo–Scorpio

The Upside: You are both cool on the surface, but have a turbulent inner life. Scorpio will psych-out your fantasies and help you live them. You don't mind them taking control and letting you handle the details. With Scorpio stamina and Virgo discipline, you'll go far.

The Downside: Scorpio's emotional manipulations seem just too underhanded to you. And when you nag, Scorpio will retaliate with a stinging barb that penetrates all your defenses. You'll like them to be more on the level, but Scorpio will never give up that icy control.

Virgo–Sagittarius

The Upside: Sagittarius badly needs your follow-through, while you could use their sense of humor and optimistic outlook, as well as their superb energy and salesmanship. This is a fire-earth combo that could go far.

The Downside: Sagittarius seems just too irresponsible for the conventional, conservative Virgo. And Virgo's realism and eye for detail may seem narrow-minded and confining to Sagittarius. You'll get very tired of cleaning up after this one, so don't gamble on it.

Virgo–Capricorn

The Upside: You are two realists, high achievers with conservative values. This is a super-organized pair who expect and deliver a great deal. You'll watch the profits mount and shore each other up in tough times.

The Downside: This is a serious pair who may badly need to lighten up and take a vacation. What do you do together when you're not working? It's up to Virgo to supply the nurturing and Capricorn to spend a little or a lot on pure pleasure.

Virgo–Aquarius

The Upside: This can be an interesting odd couple. Both of you are highly intelligent, and enjoy exploring your many interests together. Aquarius is happy to let you organize, while they handle the public. There is no jealousy here to deflect your affections.

The Downside: Aquarius has many activities going at once and you may have to fight for attention, never mind top priority. It's tough competing with a worthy cause. Virgo seems too practical and earthbound for Aquarius, who hates details, including a budget. Are the compromises going to be worthwhile?

Virgo–Pisces

The Upside: Under your cool Virgo exterior, you long for romance. Pisces senses your need for affection, and their delightful fantasies add a new romantic dimension to your life. You encourage their creativity and give them solid practical support.

The Downside: The way Pisces operates can drive orderly Virgo mad. These people seem to live by intuition, whereas you know that poetry won't pay the rent. If you're prepared to provide substance, this can last. But if you resent the Pisces modus operandi, nag them too much, or try to reform them, they'll swim away.

Libra–Aries

The Upside: Opposites attract, and you're drawn to dynamic energy and decisiveness. Aries is happy to make your mind for you. And you'll smooth out their rough edges by teaching them the social arts of charm, good manners, and diplomacy.

The Downside: They like competition; you hate to make waves. When Aries wants some action, your deliberations could drive him mad. They want instant results, while you will only settle for the perfect solution. This romance may put you in a quandary.

Libra–Taurus

The Upside: At first you're relieved to be with someone who has a definite direction and some clear-cut goals. They seem so sure, solid, and reliable. And they're impressed by your finesse, your elegant taste, and your good looks. There are many merits to this couple.

The Downside: Your vacillations could drive them crazy. Taurus is after concrete, tangible results. Your goals are more idealistic. And while you allow yourself to change your mind, they stick stubbornly with their original plan. Taurus' possessiveness is another no-no with you—what's the harm in an occasional lively flirtation?

Libra–Gemini

The Upside: You have a meeting of minds and bodies. You both love social life, elegant surroundings, interesting conversation, and beautiful things. There is so much to share. And you're both born flirts who won't get too possessive.

The Downside: Everything's fine while the sun shines, but you both get seasick when the going gets rough. When Libran scales sway, Gemini becomes a bundle of nerves. You need many other stabilizing factors in your charts to keep your balance.

Libra–Cancer

The Upside: You're both very creative, beauty-loving signs with much in common. You appreciate a happy, secure, and beautiful home environment. You'd never wound Cancer's sensitive feelings, while this sign instinctively understands your need for balance and harmony.

The Downside: You can never fathom Cancerian mood swings. Nor do they have patience for your indecision. You may also disagree on how mutual moneys are spent. You like beauty and luxury; Cancer budgets for security.

Libra–Leo

The Upside: Elegant Libra and radiant Leo make a stunning couple. You'll spare no expense to create an atmosphere of beauty and luxury. And Libran diplomacy plus Leo graciousness and dignity are formidable social assets. You make Leo feel like royalty, letting them make the decisions with regal assurance.

The Downside: You may need a third party to handle finances. Runaway extravagance could curb your luxurious lifestyle. You both love attention and flattery, and may succumb to other enticers if you feel you're getting proper appreciation.

Libra–Virgo

The Upside: Virgo appreciates your good looks and sense of style. You boost their confidence, while they take care of the messy clean-up chores. There is much likely talk here and communication on a mental level. Their attention to detail frees you for more creative chores.

The Downside: You don't appreciate Virgo's critical mind when they encroach on your territory. They seem too preoccupied with the practical, while you're concerned with matters of taste and aesthetics. Form doesn't always follow function with you; it does, with Virgo. How to spend money is another subject for debate, especially when you've bought a smashing new wardrobe.

Libra–Libra

The Upside: Here is someone to share everything with. You both love an elegant lifestyle and a full social calendar. And you look so well together! You give each other the affectionate reassurance you both need.

The Downside: Since neither of you wants to upset the balance, who will make the decisions? There is much mutual debate, but no real conclusions. Often, everything is left up in the air. You need some substance here, for anything to get accomplished, or strong outside influences may take over.

Libra–Scorpio

The Upside: The intensity of Scorpio is fascinating at first. You love the total attention they give as they try to figure you out. Since you understand the game of playing hard to get, you could lead them on a merry chase. They also adore the power of your good looks and social graces.

The Downside: When Scorpio closes in and tries to take over, Libra may exit diplomatically. And if Libra exercises charm on others, Scorpio will upset the balance, willfully. Scorpio demands total commitment (though they may not always give it), while you Librans are never quite sure.

Libra–Sagittarius

The Upside: You are an attractive couple, socially. Sagittarius is everyone's buddy, while you major in finesse. Their energy will light your fire and fan the flame. Neither of you takes it all too seriously.

The Downside: The Sagittarian style is open and confrontational, whereas you avoid nasty scenes at all cost. And their barbs of truth come at the most awkward moments. They don't think before they speak, while your words are carefully considered. Both of you are spenders, so better get an outside party to manage the funds.

Libra–Capricorn

The Upside: You are each other's best social asset. Capricorn's taste for quality and yours for elegance dovetail perfectly. They'll provide the substance for the lifestyle you both love. You'll lighten their life and get them out of the office and into the social whirl.

The Downside: Capricorn is a disciplined spender who watches the pennies. Libra will splurge on beautiful objects or clothes without considering the cost. Libra likes togetherness at all times; Capricorn can be a lone wolf. For Capricorn, social life is a reward, but for Libra, it's a necessity.

Libra–Aquarius

The Upside: Here's a good mental mate. You are two idealists who love to discuss and debate your cause. And you both enjoy group activities. Aquarians applaud your good judgment, while you uphold their worthy causes. And you both dislike sticky emotional scenes.

The Downside: You need to be surrounded by beautiful objects and a harmonious atmosphere. Aquarius likes to shake people up. Their shock tactics can jolt your equilibrium. They may also be too opinionated for you. And if their cause is rebellious and their crowd becomes raucous, you'd make a quick getaway. Aquarius may be too busy to satisfy your need for reassurance, flattery, and companionship.

Libra–Pisces

The Upside: On a creative level, this is an inspired partnership where the Pisces spiritual, intuitive approach is balanced by your critical, intellectual style. You encourage each other; Pisces gives you affectionate reassurance while you reason them out of dark moods. And you both enjoy pampering each other with beautiful sentimental gifts.

The Downside: You need lots of give and take to satisfy Pisces' emotionally and avoid murky waters. And 24-hour-a-day romance may not be enough for you. After all, someone has to finance your spending sprees. You could find yourself swimming away in your search for direction and decisiveness.

Scorpio–Aries

The Upside: This is a powerful combination. You love to challenge each other. Competition and playing hard to get are part of the game. You turn the battle of the sexes into a lasting love affair.

The Downside: You're forever deciding who's really boss. Aries is an upfront type with all cards on the table, while you play them close to the vest. This does not engender trust. You're both jealous and like to control the situation. Someone has to give in or give up.

Scorpio–Taurus

The Upside: From opposite sides of the zodiac, you seem to complement each other. Taurus loves your intensely passionate nature, and they can make the total commitment you desire. You'll find a calm and beautiful oasis here.

The Downside: Control and power are the devisive issues here. You are both stubborn and like to hold the reins. And neither of you will give in. To stay in control, you may resort to manipulative tricks. Better stake out your territory early in the relationship.

Scorpio–Gemini

The Upside: Gemini's an intriguing challenge. You love the way they laugh away your dark moods. In return, you keep their mind on track and give them much-needed direction. Not a bad deal.

The Downside: Your need for power could scare Gemini off. You're always manipulating behind the scenes, which makes Gemini nervous. And Gemini's a fickle flirt, a definite lightweight emotionally. If you're looking for depth, move on!

Scorpio–Cancer

The Upside: Here's all the depth you want in a relationship. You both live on a "feeling" level. It's easy to communicate, even without words. Your mutual possessiveness works well here, making you both feel secure and protected.

The Downside: Both of you have dark moody spells which, if they coincide, can be difficult to shake. Scorpio's reserve and Cancer's self-protectiveness can create ill will. Neither gives their all; both want control and are given to some underhanded maneuvering.

Scorpio–Leo

The Upside: You sense the powerful chemistry at work and approach each other with mutual respect. This is no combination to trifle with! Leo gets all the attention they need and more while they bring out your finer points. Let Leo direct—you produce!

The Downside: You both go about controlling the situation in different ways. Leo is openly demanding and bossy, while Scorpio is the power behind the throne. Your manipulative techniques could have Leo roaring in the cage. They are not easily tamed, so watch out for claws and jaws.

Scorpio–Virgo

The Upside: You're both cool and reserved on the surface, with fascinating interior lives. You'll enjoy psyching-out the "virgin's" fantasies and helping them explore the depths and heights of passion. They'll let you wield the power if you let them manage and organize. You'll both keep an eagle eye on the budget.

The Downside: Your emotional tactics could leave Virgo cold. And when they criticize, you'll retaliate with stinging barbs that penetrate Virgo's cool reserve. For this to work you both have to keep the faith.

Scorpio–Libra

The Upside: Your intensity is fascinating to Libra at first. They love the total attention you give as you try to figure them out. Since Libra understands the game of hard-to-get, they'll lead you on a merry chase. But you adore the power of their good looks and social graces.

The Downside: When Scorpio closes in and tries to take over, Libra exits, diplomatically. And if Libra exercises charm on others, Scorpio will upset their balance willfully. Scorpio wants commitment, while Librans are never quite sure—with good reason.

Scorpio–Scorpio

The Upside: You are both fascinators attuned to each other's powerful needs. You'll guess each other's secrets, explore the mysteries of life together. And you'll give each other the security of true intimacy, loyalty, and loving.

The Downside: Control is always an issue with Scorpio, especially with an equal partner. You take everything too seriously and if one of you transgresses, the other will never forget. In an all-or-nothing situation, there's no room to grow. You need outside contacts in order not to feel smothered. Allow each other some breathing space.

Scorpio–Sagittarius

The Upside: The archer and the Scorpio eagle are meant to explore the heights together. Sagittarius is a good sport who admires your stamina, discipline, and competitive spirit. Their humor will send your dark moods soaring, and their philosophical point of view gives you a new dimension.

The Downside: Sagittarius would rather love 'em and leave 'em than probe any emotional depths. Scorpio is the jealous type who has no patience with happy wanderers. This love affair is no laughing matter if you arouse each other in the wrong way. Sagittarian barbs and Scorpio stings will fly.

Scorpio–Capricorn

The Upside: You both have a healthy respect for work, power, and achievement. And your ambitions know no bounds. Neither of you needs the company of others, but you'll both enjoy the results you get together. You'll find you get ahead faster when you help each other up the mountain.

The Downside: Scorpio's murky moods and Capricorn's melancholy could make for some grim going. You may be so intent on the climb that you have little time for your partner. Better make some room in your busy schedules or there will be no one to share your success.

Scorpio–Aquarius

The Upside: Aquarius has some original ideas you'll love, while you'll give them unique experiences even they could not imagine. Scorpio loves being the power behind the scenes and cheerfully gives Aquarius center stage. And Aquarius is the perfect partner to live out your fondest fantasies. You'll probe the depths of matters while Aquarius flies high, giving each other plenty of space and respectful distance.

The Downside: Both of you have strong opinions and a need for control. But Aquarius demands independence, while you need someone who really needs *you.* If you're looking for deep emotions, long nights at home, and total commitment, look elsewhere!

Scorpio–Pisces

The Upside: You both live in emotional territory, and revel in tides of passion. This can be a storybook romance. Pisces creates the fantasies, Scorpio makes them happen. They love your intensity—it makes them feel secure—and know just how to soothe your turbulent inner waters.

The Downside: Pisces is the sign of illusion and mystery. And you'll never be able to guess their secret of survival. They seem like cute goldfish sometimes, vicious sharks at others. Be careful not to get in too deep or you'll be drowning your sorrows in liquids stronger than seawater.

Sagittarius–Aries

The Upside: You are two outgoing adventurers who travel well together in mind and body. This is a great match for Sagittarius, who needs a buddy as well as a lover. And you can keep up with the energetic Aries.

The Downside: You are both very self-involved and put your own interests first. If you don't share common goals, prepare for a struggle. And if you need some hand-holding or financial backup, Aries won't be available. Your joint ventures may sizzle, then fizzle.

Sagittarius–Taurus

The Upside: You are both direct, honest people who love the outdoors. Taurus gives you the backup and organization you need. They can help you make your dreams happen.

The Downside: You're an adventurer who can't be tied down. And you often have a roving eye. Taurus loves those cozy nights at home, while you'd rather be off and running. Their jealousy and possessiveness cramps your style.

Sagittarius–Gemini

The Upside: Life's a party to you two fun-lovers. This is the ideal person to share games of all kinds, as long as you establish the rules in the beginning. You're both outgoing optimists who love to be on the move and won't fence each other in.

The Downside: Neither one stays in place for long, so when will you get together? Better set some definite goals to aim for, or you'll be traveling in different directions.

Sagittarius–Cancer

The Upside: You are both ambitious. Cancer will see which of your bright ideas have potential and which are shots in the dark. Cancer's sense of humor and outgoing energy can be just the right tonic for your moods. They'll show you how to laugh your troubles away!

The Downside: Your gambling instincts are no laughing matter to Cancer, who likes to play it safe. Security is critical to Cancer, while freedom gets top priority from Sagittarius. Your roving eye and the crab's clinging claws could send you both scurrying in opposite directions.

Sagittarius–Leo

The Upside: You're two optimists who shoot for the stars. You'll inspire each other and share adventures together. Their jovial good humor and your sunny outgoing nature draws others to you. When you join forces, you can sell anything!

The Downside: This combination is fine as long as you're both on a high roll. But when financial troubles cause a crash, better find a net. Sag is a rover, while Leo demands loyalty—another thorny issue. And the Leo ego could deflate under Sag's barbs.

Sagittarius–Virgo

The Upside: You badly need Virgo's follow-through, while Virgo could use your sense of humor and optimistic outlook, as well as your superb energy and salesmanship. This is a fire-earth combination that could go far.

The Downside: You just seem a bit too irresponsible for the conventional, conservative Virgo. And Virgo's realistic eye for detail may seem narrow-minded and confining to you. Don't gamble too much on this one getting off the ground.

Sagittarius–Libra

The Upside: You are an attractive couple socially. You are everyone's buddy, while Libra majors in finesse. Their energy will light your fire and fan the flame. Neither of you takes it all too seriously.

The Downside: Your style is open and confrontational, while Libra avoids nasty scenes at all cost. And when your barbs of truth come at an awkward moment, Libra makes a diplomatic exit. Both of you are big spenders, so better get an outside party to manage the funds.

Sagittarius–Scorpio

The Upside: The archer and the Scorpio eagle are meant to fly high together. You admire the Scorpio stamina, discipline, and competitive spirit. And your humor sends their dark moods soaring. You'll have many long philosophical discussions, as you explore the mysteries of life together.

The Downside: You'd rather love 'em and leave 'em than get in too deep. Scorpio is the jealous type who has no patience for happy wanderers. This love affair will be no laughing matter if you arouse each other the wrong way. Sagittarian barbs and Scorpio stings will fly.

Sagittarius–Sagittarius

The Upside: Here's a best friend as well as a lover. You'll search for adventure together, share the same goals, and shore each other up. Yours is a relationship with deep spiritual roots that grows more committed with time and travel together.

The Downside: You have a spiritual twin, not a complement here. There are many practical matters left unattended. Be sure you arrange a backup squad or you'll squabble over who gets the dirty work. You are best off traveling together. Absence may make the heart grow fonder of someone nearby.

Sagittarius–Capricorn

The Upside: Capricorns give your arrows a solid target. Here is someone who can make your ideas happen—and who will appreciate your super salesmanship. Your blunt honesty and their realism go well together. Here's someone who listens, does not wound easily.

The Downside: It's optimist versus pessimist. You may get tired of dispersing Capricorn's melancholy moods. You like to be spontaneous, Capricorn plans ahead—for years. And forget taking a gamble; Capricorn is after a sure thing. You could high-roll away from this one.

Sagittarius–Aquarius

The Upside: Aquarius is as independent as you are. And you're both unpredictable and original. Sounds like a great match. You light their fire, they fan the flame. And your frankness and idealism could dovetail with theirs. This duo is a winner if you have a worthy cause in common.

The Downside: You are both fast talkers who need listening ears. Trouble is, you're often in love with your own voice. And you may never be in the same place together long enough to make a good connection.

Sagittarius–Pisces

The Upside: You've both got a case of wanderlust and a strong spirit of adventure. Pisces' fantasies can spark some exotic goings-on. And your optimism gives them confidence. You'll do the selling that makes Pisces' dreams come true. While they take you on an exciting mental and physical trip.

The Downside: You are two drifters who need a good strong raft. You need an outside party to provide the financial backup and the follow-through. Both of you are big spenders—another case for finding a watchdog. And watch out for Pisces' sensitive feelings. When stroked the wrong way, they bite!

Capricorn–Aries

The Upside: You're both workaholics who like to take charge. Neither has trouble making decisions or getting started. Aries gives Capricorn fresh new ideas; you give them follow-through and discipline. Not a bad exchange.

The Downside: Your melancholy moods rain on Aries' parade. You want status; they want stardom. You can become an old fogy, if they act immature and headstrong. It becomes a case of optimism versus pessimism, with neither listening to the other. You have to work on communication.

Capricorn–Taurus

The Upside: This is a comfortable situation where both share similar tastes and goals. You're hard workers who love rich rewards—beauty, quality, and tradition. You're both responsible and mature; what you see is what you get. And it's usually good value.

The Downside: Ascending to the top in the business and social world is your priority. But Taurus may have other plans. And they may want you to stay home at night when there's work to do at the office. Ambition versus family obligations could be the bone of contention here.

Capricorn–Gemini

The Upside: You can use Gemini's communications talents. Socially your classy aristocratic manner is a great foil for Gemini wit and charm. And they need you to organize their life, help them achieve solid results.

The Downside: You can be all work and no play, particularly if your goal is in sight. But Gemini needs to be out and about, and can easily attract other companions. They never take anything too seriously, either. They may be just too frivolous and flighty for you. And their finances may be no laughing matter!

Capricorn–Cancer

The Upside: You are two achievers who enjoy getting results and making a profit. You both have traditional values—Capricorn's fatherly and Cancer's mothering instincts complement each other well. Cancer will create a gracious haven for you to come home to, and give you food for body and soul.

The Downside: Cancer's emotional needs can take up too much of Capricorn's time. You have to balance your energies between work and home life, and learn to use, not abuse each other's talents. Bring your sense of humor to the rescue when melancholy moods strike.

Capricorn–Leo

The Upside: You have found a fellow aristocrat who values power and status as you do. What's more, Capricorn has the organizational know-how to complement the Leo sales ability. Together you can move mountains.

The Downside: Capricorn is a tough, well-disciplined loner who can live without posh perks, if it means achieving a goal. Leo must have luxury at all costs and won't tolerate stinginess or spartan living. Leo also needs social contacts which Capricorn may find frivolous.

Capricorn–Virgo

The Upside: You are two realists, high achievers with conservative values. This is a super-organized pair who expect and deliver a great deal. You'll watch the profits mount and shore each other up in tough times.

The Downside: This is a serious pair that may badly need to lighten up and take a vacation. What do you do together when you're not working? It's up to Virgo to supply the nurturing and Capricorn to spend a little or a lot on pure pleasure, for a change.

Capricorn–Libra

The Upside: You are each other's best social asset. Your taste for quality and Libra's taste for elegance blend perfectly. You'll provide the substance for the lifestyle Libra loves. They'll lighten your life and get you out of the workplace and into the social whirl.

The Downside: Capricorn is a sign that keeps close tabs on the cash flow. Libra will splurge on beautiful objects or clothes without counting the cost. You can be a lone wolf; Libra likes togetherness at all times. For you, social life is a reward, for Libra, it's a necessity. Lots of compromises needed here.

Capricorn–Scorpio

The Upside: You both have a healthy respect for work, power, and achievement. And your ambitions know no bounds. Neither of you needs the company of others, but you'll both enjoy the results you get together. You'll climb higher, faster if you help each other up the slopes.

The Downside: Scorpio's murky moods and the Capricorn melancholy could make for grim going. You may be so intent on the climb that you have no time for your partner. Better make some room in your busy schedules or there will be no one home to share your success.

Capricorn–Sagittarius

The Upside: You can focus the wandering Sagittarius energy right on the target of success. You are both realists and you'll particularly appreciate the blunt Sagittarian truthfulness. They'll inspire you to greater heights.

The Downside: When an optimist (Sag) and a pessimist get together, there's bound to be a constant drain of emotion. Sag will eventually get tired of laughing off your melancholy moods. And you'll be annoyed by their lack of discrimination in associates, not to mention how they can fritter away funds. There is much negotiating here.

Capricorn–Capricorn

The Upside: You make an earthy team that forges upward until you reach your goals. This is someone who understands you, sympathizes, and will never complain that you work too much. They won't spend all your money, either.

The Downside: The problem is one of stimulation. There's an earthy attraction at first, but you can easily get distracted. Or you both may expend all your energy in the workplace. In which case, those home fires grow cold.

Capricorn–Aquarius

The Upside: When the lone wolf and the maverick get together for a cause, you're a great team. Aquarius will raise the funds, while you organize. Their electricity sparks some novel ideas in your head, while you give them the earthy backup they need.

The Downside: You're a traditionalist who wants a quality home life. Fame is the name of the game for Aquarius. They are rather detached when it comes to paying attention to you—it seems as though they always have more important things to do or think about.

Capricorn–Pisces

The Upside: Pisces puts romance in your life, while you give these sensitive souls the protection and security they need. And you know just how to put their creative talents to good use.

The Downside: You are a realist; Pisces lives in fantasy. That's what fuels their terrific imagination. You'll have to live with a dreamy attitude toward the practical things in life. You may prefer terra firma to the ever-changing tides.

Aquarius–Aries

The Upside: If you both share common goals or work for the same worthy causes, this relationship can be a winner. Aries pushes your ideas and is stimulated by your mind. And they love your surprises! You can have a stimulating companionship, especially when your originality fans their fire!

The Downside: Aries needs attention, but you have too many other interests to put them first all the time. Your detachment could send them looking elsewhere for ego gratification.

Aquarius–Taurus

The Upside: You could go far, with your original ideas and their practical know-how. You inspire Taurus, while they put you on solid ground. You share many of the same enthusiasms for bettering the environment. And you shake them up now and then, which does them a world of good.

The Downside: Taurus is predictable; Aquarius is full of surprises. You are not security-minded; in fact, you find budgets or any restrictions too limiting. And the Taurus possessiveness can really be suffocating. They often think your ideas are far out and don't understand your need for so much independence. Think this one out, first.

Aquarius–Gemini

The Upside: You are two people collectors who never get lost in the crowd. You give each other all the space you both need to explore and experiment. You love Gemini's many-faceted personality—and you give them ideas even *they* never imagined.

The Downside: Gemini finds it hard to commit to one idea or cause, while you carry your banner high. And though you are not a possessive type, the idea of two-timing turns you off. There's a certain lack of conviction here.

Aquarius–Cancer

The Upside: Success depends on whether Cancer can identify emotionally with your goals. They can complement you very well, providing the intimacy and one-on-one warmth while you handle the crowds. You can count on their devotion to back you up and their shrewd business sense to make a profit.

The Downside: Home-loving Cancers have very strong emotional needs, which may not interest Aquarius. And their possessiveness can be smothering. You'll have to spend some time at home and do a lot of hand-holding to make this work. It's helpful if you work at home, or your partner works in the same place with you.

Aquarius–Leo

The Upside: Here are two opposites, who both love to be onstage, surrounded by people. Leo's warmth and graciousness complement Aquarian objectivity and concern for humanity. You attract attention, a great costarring team.

The Downside: All goes well as long as there's a meeting of minds. But Leo wants wholehearted commitment, which may rub Aquarius the wrong way. And Leo needs so much continual attention, while you have other things to do. Common interests are needed to focus your energies. And Leo must learn to curb jealous or competitive urges.

Aquarius–Virgo

The Upside: This pair is an interesting odd couple. Both are highly intelligent and could stimulate each other mentally. Aquarius is happy to let Virgo organize, while they handle the public. And neither needs constant attention from the other. There is no jealousy here to deflect your affections.

The Downside: Aquarius has many outside interests, and Virgo may have to fight for time, never mind top priority. This could take the form of incessant nagging. Virgo seems too practical and earthbound for Aquarius, who hates to bother with detail, including the budget. Can you tolerate Virgo constantly reminding you to get organized or tidying up after you? Are the compromises going to be worthwhile?

Aquarius–Libra

The Upside: Here's a good mental mate. You are two idealists who love to discuss and debate your cause endlessly. And you both enjoy group activities. You applaud Libra's good judgment, while they uphold your worthy causes. And you both dislike sticky emotional scenes.

The Downside: Libra needs to be surrounded by beautiful objects and a harmonious atmosphere. Aquarius likes to shake people up—your shock tactics can jolt their equilibrium. You may also be too opinionated for them. And if your cause is rebellious and your crowd becomes raucous, count on Libra to make a quick getaway. You may be too busy to satisfy their need for reassurance, flattery, and companionship.

Aquarius–Scorpio

The Upside: Scorpio loves your original ideas, while they give you deep experiences and passion you've never even dreamed possible. Scorpio loves being the power behind your throne, letting you please the crowds, while they pull the strings. You'll give each other plenty of space to take your power trips—then you'll have a rapturous rendezvous.

The Downside: Both of you have strong opinions and a need to control. But Aquarius demands independence, while Scorpio needs to be needed. The problems arise when you both feel unsatisfied on a deep level. If you want this one to last, better give Scorpio some powerful reasons.

Aquarius–Sagittarius

The Upside: Sagittarius is just as independent as you are. And you're both unpredictable. Sounds like a great match when your electricity plus the Sagittarius fire sparks great ideas. You give each other plenty of space to wander, and you'll rendezvous to compare travel notes. You'll never object to each other's outside interests.

The Downside: Someone has to tend the home fires if they are to stay aflame. And neither of you is the domestic type. And someone has to manage the money. You may well ask what you *need* each other for. Well, you *want* each other, that's enough—or is it?

Aquarius–Capricorn

The Upside: When the lone wolf and the maverick get together for a cause, you're a great team. Practical earthy Capricorn will organize, while you raise funds and give speeches. Capricorn respects your idealism and commitment and you know you can count on them.

The Downside: You are both more involved in work and ideas than in personal life. But Capricorn is a traditionalist who likes a solid home environment. You prefer to expend your energies elsewhere. Can a rule maker (Capricorn) and a rule breaker (Aquarius) coexist peacefully? When Capricorn pushes for more structure, you push for more freedom. You'll need some strategy sessions to make this one last.

Aquarius–Aquarius

The Upside: Nothing shocks either of you, so you'll love surprising each other! You know when to give each other space, and when your presence is needed. You both understand the concept of equal partnership and are best friends as well as lovers.

The Downside: You may stay best friends without a real romantic spark. Or you could float off in other directions. You both look for ways to expand your mind and may not find them in a mirror image. However, shared causes and mutual interests may be enough to hold you together.

Aquarius–Pisces

The Upside: The impersonal Aquarius and the emotional Pisces are next-door neighbors who mean much to each other. Pisces gives you emotional depth and creative fantasies. You give them good friendship and objectivity—and they appreciate your original ideas and electric charisma.

The Downside: Pisces needs 24-hour-a-day romance, which could bore you after a while. And their more soggy emotions leave you cold. Better find another outlet where you can help the needy—or better yet, find one together!

Pisces–Aries

The Upside: Your next-door neighbor in the zodiac makes a very good companion. You love the energy and enthusiastic way they get your projects started. Here's the one to dazzle you and sweep you off your feet. As a best friend or romantic lead, Aries plays the role to perfection.

The Downside: When you get hurt, you either get weepy or turn into a shark. Then Aries goes bounding off without a backward glance or even a Band-Aid for your bruised feelings. Inconsiderate and bossy, they get their way by bashing through barriers. Your hypersensitivity is not understood or appreciated.

Pisces–Taurus

The Upside: Taurus responds happily to your deep emotional needs. In turn, you give them all the adoration and attention they want. This works very well on a sensual level. You both love taking care of each other. And professionally, Taurus can help you market those creative ideas and bring in profits.

The Downside: Taurus likes everything under control, which seems too predictable to you. You're not one to be fenced in, no matter how lovely the pasture. Taurus can get continually frustrated trying to hook you—and an angry bull is no fun to live with.

Pisces–Gemini

The Upside: You're both dual, mutable signs, which means there's enough action on every level to keep you both fascinated. Here is someone who will give you all the variety you need and add real romance to your life. You'll never get tired of playing different roles together.

The Downside: Neither of you likes to be bored, so a lot of mundane practical matters go unattended. You take Gemini's mental games seriously, while they laugh off your silly moods. You then retaliate with underhanded maneuvering. Face it, on many important matters, you're just not on the same wavelength.

Pisces–Cancer

The Upside: At last, here is someone who understands how to soothe you out of your moods, or just leave you alone until they pass. You encourage each other creatively. And you have no trouble communicating on every level.

The Downside: Cancer's possessiveness is the weak link. Pisces must swim freely; too much clinging or subtle hooks make them slip away. You are both changeable, so it is difficult to find security here on either side. And when Pisces plays the martyr and Cancer the victim of circumstances, beware! You two sensitive souls know how to wound each other deeply.

Pisces–Leo

The Upside: The Piscean love of fantasy sets the stage for Leo's theatrical talent, while Leo's romantic nature is perfect for sizzling love scenes. You know how to show appreciation, and their warm encouragement gives you the confidence to shine.

The Downside: The fish is difficult to catch and you are even harder to hold on to. You may not give Leo the commitment or loyalty they demand. And when they try to boss you, you tune them out—or come on suddenly powerful, like a shark.

Pisces–Virgo

The Upside: Under Virgo's cool exterior, they long for romance. Pisces senses Virgo's need for affection, and your delightful fantasies add a new romantic dimension to their life. In return, they encourage your creativity and give you practical support. You are opposites who can help each other very much.

The Downside: The way you operate can drive orderly Virgo mad. You live by intuition, while Virgo never believes that poetry can pay the rent. If Virgo is prepared to provide the substance, this can last. But if they resent your modus operandi or nag you too much, you'll swim away.

Pisces–Libra

The Upside: On a creative level, this is an inspired partnership where the Pisces spiritual, intuitive approach is balanced by Libra's critical, intellectual style. You encourage each other, giving Libra affectionate reassurance, while they reason you out of dark moods. And you both enjoy pampering each other with beautiful sentimental gifts.

The Downside: You need lots of give and take to satisfy Libra's need for constant reassurance. And someone has to finance their spending sprees. You could find yourself swimming away in your search for direction and focus.

Pisces–Scorpio

The Upside: You both live in emotional territory, and revel in tides of passion. This can be a storybook romance. Pisces creates the fantasies, Scorpio makes them happen. You are one sign who loves Scorpio's intensity—it makes you feel so secure—and you know just how to soothe their turbulent inner waters.

The Downside: Pisces is the sign of illusion and mystery. You need freedom and a nurturing atmosphere to develop your marvelous creative ideas. Scorpio needs to control and possess, and will undermine your confidence if necessary to do so. To protect yourself, you could turn from a goldfish into a shark.

Pisces–Sagittarius

The Upside: You both have a case of wanderlust and a strong spirit of adventure. Pisces' fantasies can spark some exotic goings-on. And Sagittarius' optimism gives you confidence, laughs away your tears. They'll do the selling that makes your dreams come true.

The Downside: You are two drifters who need a good strong raft. Both are big spenders; neither has a taste for practical matters. And Sag's blunt barbs hurt tender Pisces' feelings. It could be touch and go here.

Pisces–Capricorn

The Upside: You put romance in this workaholic's life. They give you the protection and security you need—and help you put your creative talents to good use. It's a bargain!

The Downside: Capricorn is a realist; Pisces lives in a world of dreams and fantasies. That's what fuels your terrific talent. But your dreamy attitude toward the practical things in life and your unorthodox style may leave Capricorn searching for firmer ground.

Pisces–Aquarius

The Upside: You and Aquarius care about the same things. You both value freedom, friendship, and working to make the world a better place. And you bring Aquarius the personal touch. You can get close without being possessive, a revelation!

The Downside: Pisces' emotional drama finds no audience in Aquarius—they prefer head games or humor. This can work if you have many common interests. Otherwise, Aquarius will just make you one of the buddies.

Pisces–Pisces

The Upside: You start out as soul mates, who are mutually tender and protective. You are each others' romantic hero or heroine, playing every love story known. You don't need words to communicate those powerful feelings.

The Downside: This could be too much of a good thing. You need stimulation and variety to balance your emotions—and solid backing to develop your talent and increase your confidence. Alas, off-screen, you are not likely to give this support to each other.

What's the Cosmic Chemistry Between These Celebrity Couples?

Some of the lovers on the following list are still steaming, others have cooled their passions. Using Mars and Venus signs, and the chart you've just learned to do, find out why some celebrity pairs still sizzle and others have fizzled.

Maria Shriver (Scorpio: 11/6/55) and Arnold Schwarzenegger (Leo: 7/30/47)

Julia Roberts (Scorpio: 10/25/67) and Lyle Lovett (Scorpio: 11/1/57)

Cindy Crawford (Pisces: 2/10/66) and Richard Gere (Virgo: 8/31/49)

Iman (Leo: 7/25/55) and David Bowie (Capricorn: 1/2/47)

Naomi Campbell (Taurus: 5/20/70) and Robert de Niro (Leo: 8/17/43)

Meg Ryan (Scorpio: 11/19/62) and Dennis Quaid (Aries 4/9/54)

Delta Burke (Leo: 7/30/56) and Gerald McRaney (Leo: 8/19/47)

Candice Bergen (Taurus: 5/9/46) and Louis Malle (Scorpio: 10/30/32)

Roseanne (Scorpio: 11/3/52) and Tom Arnold (Pisces: 3/6/59)

Christie Brinkley (Aquarius: 2/2/54) and Billy Joel (Taurus: 5/9/49)

Marla Maples (Scorpio: 10/27/63) and Donald Trump (Gemini: 6/14/46)

Jill Eikenberry (Pisces: 2/21/42) and Michael Tucker (Aquarius: 2/6/44)

Mia Farrow (Aquarius: 2/9/45) and Woody Allen (Sagittarius: 12/1/35)

Kim Basinger (Sagittarius: 12/8/53) and Alec Baldwin (Aries: 4/3/58)

Tatum O'Neal (Scorpio: 11/5/63) and John McEnroe (Aquarius: 12/16/59)

Jane Fonda (Sagittarius: 12/21/37) and Ted Turner (Scorpio: 11/19/38)

Prince Andrew (Aquarius/Pisces: 2/19/60) and "Fergie" (Libra: 10/15/59)

Prince Charles (Scorpio: 11/14/48) and Princess Di (Cancer: 7/1/61)

Prince Charles (Scorpio: 11/14/48) and Camilla Parker-Bowles (also Cancer: 7/17/47)

Linda Evans (Scorpio: 11/18/42) and Yanni (Scorpio: 11/14/54)

Frank Gifford (Leo: 8/16/30) and Kathie Lee Gifford (Leo: 8/16/53)

Phil Donohue (Sagittarius: 12/21/35) and Marlo Thomas (Scorpio: 11/21/38)

Steve Martin (Leo: 8/14/45) and Victoria Tennant (Libra: 9/30/50)

Golden Hawn (Scorpio: 11/21/45) and Kurt Russell (Pisces: 3/17/51)

Demi Moore (Scorpio: 11/11/62) and Bruce Willis (Pisces: 3/19/55)

Mick Jagger (Leo: 7/26/43) and Jerry Hall (Cancer: 7/2/56)

Diane Sawyer (Capricorn: 12/22/45) and Mike Nichols (Scorpio: 11/6/31)

Tom Cruise (Cancer: 7/3/62) and Nichole Kidman (Gemini/Cancer cusp: 6/21/67)

Bonnie Raitt (Scorpio: 11/8/49) and Michael O'Keefe (Taurus: 4/24/55)

Mikhail (Pisces: 3/2/31) and Raisa (Capricorn: 1/5/32) Gorbachev

Connie Selleca (Gemini: 5/25/55) and John Tesh (Cancer: 7/9/52)

Kirk Cameron (Libra: 10/12/70) and Chelsea Noble (Sagittarius: 12/4/64)

Paula Abdul (Gemini: 6/19/63) and Emilio Estevez (Taurus: 5/2/62)

Elizabeth Taylor (Pisces: 2/27/32) and Larry Fortensky (Capricorn: 1/17/52)

John Travolta (Aquarius: 2/18/54) and Kelly Preston (Libra: 10/13/62)

Annette Bening (Gemini: 5/29/58) and Warren Beatty (Aries: 3/30/37)

Danny De Vito (Scorpio: 11/17/44) and Rhea Perlman (Aries: 3/31/48)

Daryl Hannah (Sagittarius: 12/3/60) and JFK, Jr. (Sagittarius: 11/25/60)

Whitney Houston (Leo: 8/9/63) and Bobby Brown (Aquarius: 2/5/69)

Michael Jackson (Virgo: 8/29/58) and Lisa Marie Presley (Aquarius: 2/1/68)

Oprah Winfrey (Aquarius: 1/29/54) and Stedman Graham (Pisces: 3/6/51)

Hillary (Scorpio: 10/26/47) and Bill Clinton (Leo: 8/19/46)

CHAPTER 13

Hot Tips: How Astrology Can Make Your Life Better Every Day!

- When Venus transmits your sun sign, you'll be especially attractive to others. Use this time to socialize and network with potential clients and flirt up a storm with someone who hasn't been giving you the time of day.
- For fast regrowth, cut your hair when the moon is in a water sign (Cancer, Scorpio, Pisces).
- When Mars is in your sign, your energy gets a big boost. Go for it!
- If your partner's moon is in the same sign as your sun, or vice versa, you're likely to be compatible.
- Good fortune—and big money—is associated with Jupiter, the planet of expansion. To find out where you'll have the best chance at hitting the jackpot this year, find the Capricorn-ruled house in your chart. Use the rising sign chart in this book and consult the following list:

Aries rising: Build up your image, career, public activities.

Taurus rising: Aim high, get more education, travel aboard.

Gemini rising: Watch the cash flow. Practice the art of the deal with banks, creditors, loan companies, and tax collectors. Be careful with credit cards—you could easily run up your debts.

Cancer rising: Partnerships are favored, and those with whom you have committed relationships can be fortunate for you. Many of you will be walking down the aisle this year.

Leo rising: The care and maintenance part of your life should be top priority. This includes health, diet, and exercise as well as getting organized.

Virgo rising: For anyone involved in the creative fields, this is bonanza time, as inspiration flows. Love affairs, recreation, and activities shared with children should brighten your life.

Libra rising: Success is tied to your domestic life. This can often mean a relocation. Establish your personal base, strengthen family ties.

Scorpio rising: Luck is just around the corner in your local area. Communications, local social life, short-distance travel can bring fortunate contacts.

Sagittarius rising: Money should be flowing in this year. You could find a higher-paying job.

Capricorn rising: You look like a winner—sell yourself!

Aquarius rising: Warm up for the big time. Use what you've learned in the past 12 years to make plans for the future.

Pisces rising: Your popularity soars. Get the support of groups. Join clubs, run for office.

- Use lunar timing for best results. Begin on the new moon, go public during the full moon, wind down on the waning moon.
- Can't decide where to go for a vacation? Look in the sun sign chapters and chose a place favored by your sign. You're sure to have a great time.
- Take action during the days when the moon is in a fire sign (Aries, Sagittarius, Leo). Everyone will be motivated to get going! (Look in the daily forecasts for moon signs.)
- Days when the moon is in a water sign (Cancer, Scorpio, Pisces) are great for getting close to someone, so plan your big seduction scenes for then.
- Got some heavy thinking to do, need to work the phones, make sales contacts? Plan your power telephoning for times when the moon is in an air sign (Gemini, Libra, Aquarius). Moon in Aquarius is great for concentrated brain work. Sales pitches should go well when the moon is in Leo or Sagittarius.
- Need a loan or a raise? Time it for when the moon is in a generous sign, like Leo or Sagittarius. Avoid times when moon is in critical Virgo or thrifty Capricorn.

- Start a diet under the sun or moon influence of Virgo or Capricorn, when you'll have self-discipline and determination to stick with it. The waning moon is the best moon timing for weight loss.

CHAPTER 14

All About Gemini

Your Gemini Appeal

The Gemini way of life is a state of constant activity. You juggle several irons in the fire, often do two or more things at once, thrive on variety and change. Your mind is always clicking, and you can talk a blue streak, so it is especially important that you be around people, or at least a telephone or two. Living with you can be either stimulating or nerve-racking, depending on the needs of others in your life. You want to know and experience everything, have a variety of people in your life—all happening at once! Possessive mates, complainers, or those who need a great deal of attention are going to feel neglected or rejected—you will only aggravate their negative qualities. On the other hand, some of these same people are likely to be the more solid, earthbound types who will have just the talents you need to follow through on your projects (you'll have several in various stages of completion), provide backup organization, or do the detail work. In relationships, you do best when you are mentally stimulated yet not so much that you have lost touch with practical reality. It's your challenge to find the right blend of your partner's qualities and yours that will materialize your bright ideas and create a mutually fulfilling life.

The Gemini Man: Fast on His Feet

The Gemini man's mind is always seeking out new interests, new moves, and new ways to play the game of life. As a mutable air sign, you tap into the undercurrents of life, sensing that the "here and now" is not "all there is."

You have the gift of communicating with virtually any other type without intruding, always keeping the proper distance with a touch of wit—never getting in too deeply. Frequent social contacts are important to you, because even though you love to read, you learn most from direct experience, where you have immediate feedback. You usually slip away from anyone who would tie you down or isolate you from others. (The key to keeping you around is to make you feel you'll be missing out on an exciting experience—Gemini can't bear to miss out!)

Many Gemini men thrived and rose to power during the 1980s when, thanks to their flair for communications, they became the masters of financial deal making. The list of Gemini mega-millionaires of the decade included Donald Trump (who wrote *The Art of the Deal* before losing much of his fortune), Mort Zuckerman, Robert Maxwell, Maurice Saatchi, and Armand Hammer. As the decade closed, several of the most dazzling financial wizards became overextended and lost their luster, if not their entire fortunes. Those who remained in power were able to expand their deal-making talents and financial sleight of hand into creative problem solving and make a comeback.

In a Relationship

Since predictable routines and emotional demands can feel confining to a natural freelancer like Gemini, you may be far more comfortable in the changing whirl of business and social life than in any intense one-on-one relationship. You tend to walk away from difficult situations involving emotions, especially romantic ones. One reason depth of feeling may be difficult for you to understand is that you are primarily mental, rather than emotional. You'd rather turn to whatever or whoever is new and different, than work through long-standing or deep-rooted problems. As former President George Bush said: "I'm not an emotional kind of guy." Some Geminis avoid emotional responsibilities by refusing to grow up—they become the Peter Pans of the zodiac—and lose their grip on reality if they have to handle serious matters or crises. In the entertainment world, Gemini rock signers Boy George and Prince choose to embody this public image.

The Gemini man is not averse to beauty when you search for your life partner, but what you really look and long for is a "twin soul," a partner who will be a best friend and companion, as well as a lover. Providing stability, security, or physical amenities is not as high priority with Gemini as with other signs, even though your bright mind can devise ways to earn a steady, sometimes spectacular, income. Many of your sign often juggle two jobs or careers simultaneously. You're best suited to a free-thinking woman, who can adapt to changes and will not object too strenuously to your being constantly on the move. She should also enjoy contact with many different people and be willing to live with many projects in various stages of completion. (Barbara Bush fills this bill perfectly!) You keep a youthful fun-loving view throughout your life, and are one of the most amusing, interesting companions. Though you may not give a woman emotional reassurance as often as she would like (please work on this!), she'll never be bored.

The Gemini Woman: A Talent to Amuse

The Gemini women can't be typecast. She's a seller of illusions, like Marilyn Monroe, whose little-girl voice, sensuous walk, and vulnerability disguised a restless, intelligent, inquiring mind. You Geminis are always interesting—and interested. You may not have a college education, but you've probably done an excellent job of educating yourself. You learn from everyone you encounter and have a remarkable, retentive memory (you are the proverbial "quick study"). An excellent mimic, you pick up manners, mannerisms, and speech patterns faster than Eliza Doolittle. You can change your image to suit the job or the man. Your mind races so fast that you often know the answers before the question is asked!

For good examples of Gemini "quick studies" (fast learners who can match wits with anyone and "spin on a dime"), look no further than talk-show hostess and comedienne Joan Rivers, or soap star Joan Collins, who have adapted their careers to suit every audience. Since you rarely get too attached to anything or anyone, and you are so attuned to what's going on, you can make changes easily and quickly.

Face it, you'd be miserable in a life of routine. Often you'll do two things at once—hold down two jobs, combine a job with a personal interest, talk on two telephones, have two love affairs simultaneously, just to keep life interesting. But you always manage to keep from getting tied down. Isn't it more fun to keep your options open? After all, something or someone more exciting might appear.

"Can we talk?" At some point, you've got to figure out where you're going, get some "grounding" and focus in your life. Otherwise you could become like those lost Gemini girls, looking somewhere "Over the Rainbow," as Judy Garland and Marilyn Monroe, both Geminis, strayed. It is important for you to reconcile the twins within—that is, your feminine emotions with your detached "masculine" intelligence. When you're using your excellent mind correctly and have a clear sense of direction, you can find the right balance of stimulation and security that is your real "pot of gold."

In a Relationship

The Gemini woman usually prefers to keep working after marriage, so she can delegate the more mundane chores to someone else. And an interesting job gives her the change of scene and social contact she needs to keep from getting bored. Geminis often marry more than once, because it's not easy to find a man who can match your wit and intelligence, give you the space you need, yet provide solid support. You may find this person later in life, when the men you meet have mellowed and have more inner security and self-esteem. The type who responds well to your sparkle and joie de vivre is a man who longs to feel young and lively again, one who loves to dance, socialize, and travel. Gemini is rarely the sentimental stay-at-home type. You'd much rather have a full social schedule, with some games, frivolity, and style—a bit of madness now and then. You love to flirt and need a mate who won't get too jealous. If there is room in your relationship for personal freedom, however, Gemini provides a life of sparkle and variety.

Gemini at Home

As a Parent

Gemini is rarely a traditional parent. In fact, you're more likely to be a pal to your children and share an active companionship with them throughout life, especially if you have common interests. Gemini usually finds child rearing more satisfying and fulfilling after the child is old enough to communicate verbally. You take a great interest in the various stages of development; however, you may suffer though the early phases, when the child demands much emotional attention and routine care—and takes so much time away from your other activities.

As the child grows older, you may take on the role of teacher, exposing him or her to the world of ideas and mental pursuits. You are a fascinating playmate and a superb storyteller. You know how to make difficult or complex problems easy to understand when you help with homework. Unlike more possessive parents, Geminis encourage their children to be self-reliant and help them explore and develop any glimmer of talent or ability.

As a Stepparent

Gemini's sense of humor and lack of possessiveness are tools for forging a good relationship with stepchildren. Your lighthearted, breezy manner can smooth over rough spots in the initial phases, and you'll think of fun things to do together. You'll allow them as much time as they need with your mate, since you have many other activities to pursue. And when emotional problems crop up, you'll use your analytical mind to find an intelligent, workable solution, without getting personally drawn into the situation. Your new family will soon accept you as a nonthreatening companion and friend, who is an extra bonus in their lives.

As a Grandparent

You're the young-at-heart, sexy senior citizen, who is spry and sociable, the life of the party. You love company, especially young people, and are up on the latest trends. Or you'll regale them for hours with stories of your past adventures (and there will be many).

You'll be the most companionable grandparent, never interfering with the house rules, but encouraging them to be as independent, adventurous, and exciting as you are! Your curiosity about the world at large makes you an interesting companion. And your positive, optimistic outlook and hard-won wisdom makes you a valuable adviser.

Living the Gemini Way

Here's how to use astrology's cues to create the perfect environment to express yourself, decorate your home, energize, or unwind!

The Gemini Way to Decorate

Flexible is the word for the perfect Gemini environment. You need a place that accommodates all your different interests with plenty of storage space, so you can sweep your projects quickly out of sight when friends drop in. A light, neutral background would allow you to switch accessories and change the color accents with your mood. Lots of bookcases, a telephone or three, and furniture you can rearrange in many different ways should provide you with enough variety. You're the sign with a telephone on both sides of the bed and alongside the bathtub. Have a separate room or corner with a desk where you can organize all your lists, Roladexes, and appointment books, so you won't waste time looking for them. Many Geminis enjoy having houses in more than one place (you're often bicoastal) and keep residences in different cities or a country house, so they can switch enviroments when bored.

The Sounds of Gemini

To Gemini, the words are as important as the music. The witty lyrics of Cole Porter, the poetry of Bob Dylan have Gemini appeal; so does abstract classical music, nothing too heavy or loud that might distract from conversation or bring on the blues. Mix a variety of music so you can change moods frequently, perhaps mixing Johnny Depp with Paula Abdul, some rap music, Winona Judd, opera, and Cole Porter, Judy Garland, Mahler, and Aznavour.

Gemini R & R

Stay away from desert islands—unless you need some peace and quiet to write your novel. Stick to places where there's a lively social scene, some interesting exotica and good conversation. You might improve your language skills by visiting a foreign country—you'll have no trouble communicating in sign language, if necessary.

Dare to travel with an empty suitcase—and get some interesting clothes and supplies at your destination (think of how fast you'll speed through the airport!). Lightness is the key to Gemini travel—don't weigh yourself down with luggage.

Keep a separate tiny address book for each city, so the right numbers are always handy. Look for beautifully designed travel cases and briefcases. Since you're on the go so much, spend some time looking for the perfect luggage, portable notebook computers (with a modem), and fold-up cellular telephones.

The Gemini Spectrum

Soft gray, pale yellow, and Windsor blue are Gemini colors. Sound bland? That's because these are great background colors, the ones you can live with over a period of time. You can change the look of these colors at will, accenting them with brights or blending with other pastels.

Gemini Haberdashery

You have fun with fashion and never take your fashion image too seriously. Some real fashion legends, like the Duchess of Windsor, were born under your sign! We remember Wallis Windsor for her witty way with accessories, like those fabulous jewels she wore with casual aplomb (some engraved with secret messages from the duke). Yet she never varied her "signature" hairdo or her elegantly simple style of dressing.

You always do something interesting with your clothes. Sometimes, like Cyndi Lauper, you can be downright outrageous! Play up your expressive hands with a perfect manicure and beautiful rings. A hairstyle that you can wear several different ways could satisfy your need for variety (Joan Rivers transforms her classic style into a tumble of curls with a few hot rollers).

Since you have such a changeable personality, you'll probably experiment with every kind of look before you settle on the style that becomes you best. Usually you're up to the minute, however, with a touch of the newest trend coming down the runway. The fashion team of Dolce and Grabbana, the with-it looks of Anna Sui, or the androgynous menswear styles would be fun for you to experiment with.

Gemini Career Counselor

Gemini is a juggler whose greatest asset in business is the ability to deal with many complicated projects at once. You need constant contact with people—even if they are at the end of a telephone line (or several lines simultaneously). You are one of the most adaptable signs, who finds it a challenge to adjust to many changing environments, quickly sizing up each new situation. Some might call you restless, others an opportunist, still others a jack-of-all trades. You do project an air of brilliance, a wonderful ability to communicate with many different kinds of people (sometimes in several languages), and a quicksilver charm. Find a permissive job with constant variety and movement, to challenge your lively mind, provide a flow of interesting people—one that won't tie you down with rigid rules.

Study the careers of these Gemini millionaires for tips on what to do and what *not* to do to make the most of your sign's money-making potential.

Donald Trump
Robert Maxwell
Mortimer Zuckerman
Sam Wanamaker
Katherine Graham of *The Washington Post*
Baron Heinrich von Thurn und Taxis
Advertising's Charles and Maurice Saatchi
John Diebold
Edgar Bronfman of Seagrams
Laurence Rockefeller
Baron Guy de Rothschild

To Get Ahead Fast

Pick a job with variety and mental stimulation. Play up your:

- Verbal and written communications skills
- Ability to handle pressure

- Charm and sociability
- Manual dexterity
- Ability to learn quickly
- Analytical ability

The Best Jobs for Gemini

Gemini has many winning cards to play in the career game. Your quick mind works best in a career where there is enough mental stimulation to keep you from getting bored. High-pressure situations which would be stressful to others are stimulating to you. Many things happening simultaneously, phones ringing off the hook, daily client meetings, constant changes are all exciting to you. Your ability to communicate with a variety of people works well in sales, journalism, public relations, agent or broker work, personnel, consulting, literally any job that requires verbal or writing skills. You who learn languages easily could be a language teacher or interpreter. Manual dexterity is another Gemini gift which can find craft, musical, or medical expression (especially surgery or chiropractic). What to avoid: a job that is too isolated, routine, detail-oriented, or confining. Stay away from companies that are hidebound, with rigid rules. Instead, look for a place that gives you strong backup but also gives you free rein. Gemini often works well in a freelance position, provided they have a solid support system.

Gemini in Command

Gemini can be fun to work for, if your organization is one where there is fast movement and flexibility. Your office will be a beehive of activity, with telephone lines busy, clients and coworkers coming and going. You operate best as a deal maker, an entrepreneur rather than an operations manager. You often change your mind, so you should hire underlings who are adaptable enough to keep up with you, yet who are organized to provide direction and structure. You will change course rapidly if a project gets bogged down, rather than stick it through. Sometimes you have so many projects going on at once that others are confused, yet you are known for innovative ideas and cool analysis of problems. You are especially gifted in making a deal, coordinating many diverse aspects of a project. Working for you brings a chance to experiment, develop flexibility and growth. And you're never boring.

The Gemini Team Player

The Gemini worker shines in a job full of variety and quick changes. The key: you must be stimulated mentally. Financial security alone rarely motivates you. You can learn a job quickly, but leave it just as quickly, once it becomes routine. You work beautifully in a team, where your light-hearted sense of humor and friendliness and ability to express yourself clearly are appreciated. Your spot should be dealing with the public, in a sales or communications position. You are also skilled at office politics; it's all part of the game to you. You rarely get emotionally involved. (Let someone else do the record keeping, financial management, or accounting.) Or you can handle a position where you report to several different people or juggle several different assignments, though you may do less well if the job requires intense concentration, patience, and perseverance. Go where the action is!

CHAPTER 15

Gemini Astro-Outlook 1996

Throughout this year, optimism prevails, because you finally are rid of burdens, obligations you carried as result of misguided altruism. Put succinctly, you are now free to make a fresh start in a new direction, to be original and dynamic, to be vulnerable to love. It is especially important to study your Day-by-Day astrological guides. During 1996, you will find that Leo and Aquarius persons will play significant roles in your life, and are likely to have these letters or initials in their names: A, S, J.

Each month, your daily forecast blends both astrological and numerical cycles, which enables you to take greater charge of your own destiny.

During January, the spotlight will be on hidden values, the occult, tax and license requirements, the financial status of some one who would be your partner or mate. It is a time for you to learn more about the financial side of your life.

The focus will be on deadline pressure and meeting your responsibilities. It will be evident that Capricorn and Cancer will play significant roles. In matters of speculation, stick with number 8.

In February, you could gain weight! The accent will be on your body image, popularity, and social activity. You'll look just grand, feel fit, if you stick to a recent exercise, diet or nutrition plan. You could be consulting travel agencies in preparation for a possible journey. The focus is also on advertising, publishing, and communicating. Take charge of fund-raising entertainment for a charitable or political organization. Your lucky number throughout this month will be 3.

The new moon will be at the top part of your chart, the 10th House, in March. This means a leadership role. The emphasis is on your standing in the community. You'll be tearing down in order to rebuild on a more secure foundation. A special note: Check references and signatures, read between lines, correct mechanical defects in your automobile and other machinery. Taurus, Leo, and Scorpio play significant roles.

You might be terming April "my magic month!" The Aries new moon relates to your 11th House; this, in turn, dominates hopes, wishes, desires, popularity, the ability to win friends and influence people as a result of your powers of persuasion. Wishes are fulfilled in a seemingly mysterious way. Here's the catch-22: It is necessary for you to know what you want or desire, to separate wishes from necessities. The scenario features change, travel, variety, gain via words—verbal or written. You could become engaged. If you're married, a decision is reached about where to go for vacations, and also the size of your family. In matters of speculation, stick to number 5.

In May, be aware of your high- and low-cycle days. When your cycle is high, take the initiative, because circumstances turn in your favor. Conversely, when your cycle is low, lie low. Play the waiting game. Your high-cycle days will be the 17th, 18th, 19th, and 20th. Your low-cycle days will be the 4th, 5th, 6th, 7th, and 31st.

The most memorable days are the 2nd, 11th, and 20th. Mark the 20th on your calendar; all stops are out, push forward your policies and "take a chance on love."

The lunation falls in your own sign in June. The astrological and numerical cycle is number 7. You'll be attractive, dynamic, and sensual. Define terms, find out what others expect from you and what you, in return, can expect as a result of your efforts. Almost as if by some supernatural force, events will transpire to bring you closer to your ultimate goal. Spiritual values surface, psychic capabilities surge forward. Make personal appearances, assert your views, and wear Gemini colors as often as practical—silver, bright green, and yellow.

July could be your most significant and memorable month of 1996. You'll be dealing with executive types, so-called higher-ups, people who spin the wheels that make the world go round. These are likely to be Cancer and Capricorn individuals, with these letters or initials in their names: H, Q, Z. The spotlight is on money, payments, collections, promotion, production—intense emotional reactions and responses. Your marital status figures prominently and you might be anticipating either a long-term visitor or an addition to your family.

In August, the emphasis is on communication, trips, visits, ideas that can be developed into viable concepts. Focus on universal appeal, the ability to overcome distance and language problems. An overseas journey is not out of the question. You'll learn more about import-export activities. You'll gain knowledge about nations and of foreign cuisine. You'll be contemplating the existence of your soul mate. Aries and Libra play major roles, and are likely to have these letters or initials in their names: I and R.

Where previously you felt "closed-in," during September you'll now have more space, independence of thought and action. A new love could be on the horizon. Stress originality, innovativeness, and inventiveness. Have the courage of your convictions. Leo and Aquarius play major roles. Attention revolves around the home, security, basic issues, and property value. Take the initiative during your high-cycle Days for September: 3rd, 4th, 5th, 6th, 7th, 30th.

Romance, creative juices stir up a variety of sensations in October, especially on the 6th, 15th, and 24th. The emphasis is on the sale or purchase of property, your marital status, the tendency or opportunity to fall madly in love. You'll have luck in matters of speculation, especially by sticking with number 2. You regain your sense of direction and motivation. Capricorn and Cancer play outstanding roles, will have these letters or initials in their names: B, K, T. It will be in conjunction with a Cancer native that you could hit the financial jackpot. A side issue in this relationship will be the ability to locate lost articles.

In November, the key is to diversify, to play up your sense of humor and your intellectual curiosity. Tasks that begin as routine can become creative adventures. Scorpio, Sagittarius, and another Gemini figure prominently, and will have these letters or initials in their names: C, L, U. Be direct in getting to the heart of matters on your high-cycle days, which will be the 24th, 25th, 26th, 27th, and 28th. During Thanksgiving, joy will replace boredom. A relative or close friend arrives from a distance, to share this special holiday.

Your low-cycle days will be the 9th, 10th, 11th, and 12th. Your most memorable days are the 4th, 13th, 22nd, and 31st.

During the high-cycle days, take the initiative, be independent, express your own style, and let the chips fall where they may. Conversely, when your cycle is low, keep a low profile. On your most memorable days, accept challenges, focus on promotion, production, and intense relationships. These are the days which you'll remember when the month is reviewed. The new moon relates to areas of partnership, legal affairs, contracts, public appearances, and marriage. Taurus, Leo, and Scorpio figure prominently, and are likely to have these letters or initials in their names: D, M, V. You did the right thing in making a fresh start in a new direction this year. Celebrate that fact on New Year's Eve.

Happy New Year and remember to study the daily guides on the following pages.

CHAPTER 16

Eighteen Months of Day-by-Day Predictions: July 1995 to December 1996

JULY 1995

Saturday, July 1 (Moon in Leo) Prepare for a holiday—check the list of relatives you plan to invite or to send Fourth of July greetings to. The emphasis is on responsibility and deadline pressure. Plan entertainment with flair and showmanship. This day will be memorable! Relationships intensify and affect the future. Your lucky number is 8.

Sunday, July 2 (Moon in Leo to Virgo 7:35 a.m.) Relatives gather in connection with the lifting of a burden. Accent your versatility, humor, and willingness to experiment. Discuss a possible journey. Realize that your influence can be felt far and wide. An Aries or Libra could become your soul mate.

Monday, July 3 (Moon in Virgo) Although it is Monday, it might feel more like Saturday night. Plainly, this will be much more exciting than your usual Monday. A love relationship reignites. Stress independence, daring, and a pioneering spirit. But also emphasize your willingness to be vulnerable to emotions. You'll have luck with the number 1.

Tuesday, July 4 (Moon in Virgo to Libra 3:55 p.m.) Your sense of direction is featured. A family member says, "Let's do something to bring us all together on this holiday." The spotlight also falls on property values, motivation, and dealings with an older, female member of the family. Attention revolves around long-term negotiations involving your future security.

Wednesday, July 5 (Moon in Libra)   Lucky lottery: 3, 7, 27, 5, 4, 19. You'll read and write, distribute information relating to direction and safety. A flirtation or chance meeting, mild in manner at the beginning, could lead to something more serious than you anticipated. A Libra, in a romantic mood, indicates, "I can't keep my hands off you!"

Thursday, July 6 (Moon in Libra to Scorpio 9:19 p.m.) At the track: post position special—number 4 P.P. in the fourth race. Pick six: 8, 5, 1, 4, 3, 3. In selecting names or potential winning horses or jockeys, watch for these letters: D, M, V. Taurus, Libra, and Scorpio figure in today's exciting scenario.

Friday, July 7 (Moon in Scorpio)   The spotlight falls on style, panache, creative endeavor, sensuality, and sex appeal. You won't be standing still. Activity is featured, both mental and physical. Another Gemini companion is likely to have a name with these letters or initials: E, N, W. Be analytical; insist on reasons why things happen.

Saturday, July 8 (Moon in Scorpio to Sagittarius 11:38 p.m.)   Attention revolves around basic issues, romance, style, and your ability to win friends and influence people. A domestic adjustment could prove beneficial—beautify your surroundings. Emphasize harmony and music. Taurus plays an outstanding role, providing the incentive to continue your search for a soul mate. Your lucky number is 6.

Sunday, July 9 (Moon in Sagittarius)   Spiritual values are featured—suddenly you feel, "After all, it is worthwhile!" You're referring to a recent episode in your life involving a Libra who is likely to have a name with these letters: G, P, Y. Terms will be defined. You'll learn where you stand with a temperamental person who keeps you guessing.

Monday, July 10 (Moon in Sagittarius to Capricorn 11:44 p.m.)   The spotlight falls on power, authority, and responsibility. An intense relationship becomes controversial. Today's scenario highlights commitment, dedication, a legal agreement, and a major decision relating to marriage.

You're in the driver's seat, steering your own fate and destiny. Capricorn plays a role.

Tuesday, July 11 (Moon in Capricorn)   At the track: post position special—number 8 P.P. in the first race. Pick six: 8, 5, 1, 3, 7, 7. In selecting names of potential winning horses or jockeys, look for these letters: I and R. You'll reach more people today. Love will not be a stranger. You'll exude a subtle kind of sex appeal.

Wednesday, July 12 (Moon in Capricorn to Aquarius 11:21 p.m.)   Lucky lottery: 10, 12, 22, 1, 20, 7. The full moon highlights hidden resources, and the completion of a financial statement. A strong love relationship dominates. You'll make a fresh start in a new direction. You'll no longer be taken for granted. You are special, so let us hear the music of you blowing your own horn.

Thursday, July 13 (Moon in Aquarius)   Focus on your marital status. There could be family conflicts relating to who did what for whom, who should get the money. You'll deal successfully with women, or products for women, because you'll sense the pulse of public. A lost article is located. You almost literally get a new lease on life. Your lucky number is 2.

Friday, July 14 (Moon in Aquarius)   You were not unlucky yesterday, despite the date—today you advance, you celebrate, an emotional-financial weight is lifted. The astrological and numerical cycles highlight variety, fun, humor, correspondence, and a possible journey. You'll be oh so romantic!

Saturday, July 15 (Moon in Aquarius to Pisces 12:37 a.m.) Look beyond the immediate. You'll have luck in dealings with Taurus, Leo, and Scorpio—especially those with these letters in their names: D, M, V. Double check references, do some research, take nothing for granted in connection with payments or collections. Lucky lottery: 4, 40, 13, 8, 9, 10.

Sunday, July 16 (Moon in Pisces)   Be ready for change, travel, and variety. Put requests in writing. The Pisces moon relates to promotion, production, and your standing in church and community. Someone you admire, a member of the opposite sex, boosts your morale.

Monday, July 17 (Moon in Pisces to Aries 5:23 a.m.)
Attention revolves around the evaluation of property, and
the possible sale or purchase of a home. The emphasis is on
movement, sound, color, decoration, architecture, and your
marital status. You'll be told, "You seem to know without
knowing that you are something else!" Taurus is involved.

Tuesday, July 18 (Moon in Aries)   The Aries moon
touches your eleventh house, which means you will aggres-
sively take a stand, seize a goal. Don't waste this day! The
spotlight falls on your ability to win friends, to influence,
to make your own luck in connection with your career,
business, or romance. Virgo plays a significant role.

*Wednesday, July 19 (Moon in Aries to Taurus 2:20
p.m.)*   Lucky lottery: 8, 10, 9, 1, 35, 4. The emphasis is
on structure, design, organization, and the ability to extri-
cate yourself from a losing proposition. An older person
whom you admire will say, "I'll not only lend the benefit
of experience, but help you obtain funding, if needed." A
Cancer is represented.

Thursday, July 20 (Moon in Taurus)   Someone who attempts to give you the runaround will be caught red-
handed, will be embarrassed, and will offer an abject apol-
ogy. Don't settle for second best—strive for universal appeal. Deal gingerly with an Aries whose name has these
letters: I and R.

Friday, July 21 (Moon in Taurus)   Make a fresh start
in a new direction. The money picture brightens; dark corners of your life receive more light. Chase fear, superstition,
ignorance, and prejudice—you get a second chance for
love. Leo and Aquarius figure in this outstanding scenario.

*Saturday, July 22 (Moon in Taurus to Gemini 2:23
a.m.)*   The emphasis is on partnership, public relations,
credibility, and marital status. A clandestine relationship
lends spice, but realize it soon must be out in the open.
Protect your finances and emotions—it's okay to take a
risk, but don't be a glutton for punishment. Lucky lottery:
2, 20, 22, 5, 11, 33.

Sunday, July 23 (Moon in Gemini)   Your judgment and intuition hit the bull's-eye—events transpire to bring you closer to your ultimate goal. Timing and luck ride with you; circumstances take a dramatic turn in your favor. Wear shades of silver, green, and yellow—make personal appearances, take the initiative in getting to the heart of matters.

Monday, July 24 (Moon in Gemini to Cancer 3:16 p.m.)   Accent personality, initiative, and originality. Be willing to take a risk. Your timing is honed to razor-sharpness. You'll bring your product up to the state of the art. You'll be tearing down for the ultimate purpose of rebuilding on a more suitable base. Taurus, Leo, and Scorpio figure in today's dynamic scenario.

Tuesday, July 25 (Moon in Cancer)   The financial picture is more than merely promising. You locate a missing link or ingredient—you're on your way. You overcome obstacles that might include distance and language. A lack of experience will not prevent you from advancing—don't let others discourage you with their negativity.

Wednesday, July 26 (Moon in Cancer)   Lucky lottery: 20, 6, 2, 40, 5, 9. Attention revolves around family relationships, property value, and antiques. Emphasize diplomacy, make an intelligent concession, but don't water down your principles. You'll receive a gift representing a token of esteem and affection—it could be silver in color.

Thursday, July 27 (Moon in Cancer to Leo 3:07 a.m.) The new moon in Leo highlights showmanship, a reunion with a long-lost relative, and a pleasure trip. Romance could be part of today's exciting scenario, but don't give up something of value for a mere temporary thrill. Ideas are activated, and so are creative juices. Pisces plays a dynamic role.

Friday, July 28 (Moon in Leo)   This is a power day— nothing happens halfway; you'll be in the thick of things. The key word is intensity—focus on organization, responsibility, and awareness of a time limitation. You could be inextricably involved with someone who wants to dominate you. Don't let it go too far!

Saturday, July 29 (Moon in Leo to Virgo 1:12 a.m.)
Finish what you start, reaching beyond previous expectations. Aries, Leo, and Libra play outstanding roles and are likely to have these letters in their names: I and R. The emphasis is on universal appeal, import-export activities, a possible journey, and publishing, writing, or advertising.

Sunday, July 30 (Moon in Virgo)   Make a fresh start, imprint your style. Today's scenario will feature children, change, travel, and variety. A new arrival lends sunshine—your home environment is brighter as a result. You'll have luck in speculation, especially if you stick with these numbers: 1, 10, 19, 28. Leo is represented.

Monday, July 31 (Moon in Virgo to Libra 9:23 p.m.)   As July comes to an end, you might be asking, "Is this déjà vu?" Many events and experiences seem to be repeating. The focus is on home, family relationships, security, and marital status. You'll settle a question of whether to go into business for yourself, possibly an enterprise involving food or a restaurant.

AUGUST 1995

Tuesday, August 1 (Moon in Libra)   On this first day of August, your stars and numbers favor money, travel, and love. A burden is lifted, drawing more people to your talent or product. You're on a solid base. You could also be flirting with fame and fortune. A love relationship is the opposite of tepid—it's best described as hot and heavy.

Wednesday, August 2 (Moon in Libra)   Lucky lottery: 7, 17, 1, 6, 40, 50. Make a fresh start. Let go of the status quo. The Libra moon coincides with stirring up your creative juices. Focus on sensuality, your personality, personal magnetism, and sex appeal. A Leo who plays a magnificent role could have a name with these letters: A, S, J.

Thursday, August 3 (Moon in Libra to Scorpio 3:29 a.m.)
Focus on real estate, property values, family relationships, and your marital status. You regain a sense of fitness, direction, and motivation—you might be considering a long-term visitor or a possible addition to your family. Your marital status

figures prominently—you'll be exploring new universes, and you could also admit that you are madly in love.

Friday, August 4 (Moon in Scorpio)   You need more room for a special program or entertainment. Somehow, when there seemed no additional space, you managed to find it. Focus on versatility, humor, diversity, and intellectual curiosity. The Scorpio moon highlights your home, property, and basic values. You finish long-term negotiations. Your lucky number is 3.

Saturday, August 5 (Moon in Scorpio to Sagittarius 7:14 a.m.)   Lucky lottery: 4, 8, 12, 22, 33, 5. Correct mechanical defects, review and revise, rebuild, choose quality material. Attend to basic issues. Focus on employment, pet ownership, receipt of a unique honor. Taurus, Leo, and Scorpio play significant roles. Reinforce the structures in your life.

Sunday, August 6 (Moon in Scorpio)   The emphasis is on your reputation, credibility, and public image, as well as your legal affairs and marital status. You'll gain via the written word. Getting away from the status quo could be beneficial. Analyze character, imprint your style, express your views. Virgo, Sagittarius, and another Gemini figure prominently.

Monday, August 7 (Moon in Sagittarius to Capricorn 8:52 a.m.)   Attention revolves around your lifestyle and your ability to beautify your surroundings. A domestic adjustment could include location, partnership, or marital status. Be diplomatic but don't dilute your principles. A surprise gift includes flowers. There will be music in your life. Libra is involved.

Tuesday, August 8 (Moon in Capricorn)   Check facts and figures, become more familiar with accounting procedures. An element of deception could be present—get behind the scenes, be aware of a magic formula. Create an aura of glamour—show that you can keep a secret. Pisces and Virgo can help you today.

Wednesday, August 9 (Moon in Capricorn to Aquarius 9:29 a.m.)   Lucky lottery: 8, 10, 1, 44, 20, 26. Deadline pressure creates an aura of challenge and excitement. A relationship intensifies. You'll decide what should be done to promote harmony and happiness. Capricorn and Cancer play significant roles. Don't brush off a request as a mere formality.

Thursday, August 10 (Moon in Aquarius) The full moon position highlights philosophy, theology, and the ability to overcome distance and language barriers. Reach beyond the immediate, accenting correspondence. Learn what is happening in the world. After a burden is lifted, you'll be free to travel, publish, and love. Your lucky number is 9.

Friday, August 11 (Moon in Aquarius to Pisces 10:46 a.m.) You'll be saying, "What a way to begin the weekend!" You'll meet a dynamic Leo likely to have a name with these letters, initials: A, S, J. You'll learn more about showmanship, the use of color and sound, and the value of entertainment. A long-distance call provides excitement and spice.

Saturday, August 12 (Moon in Pisces) Lucky lottery: 12, 24, 7, 50, 9, 3. Attention revolves around the division of property, direction and motivation, family relationships, and marital status. Refuse to be limited by outmoded traditions. It's time to carve out your own fate and destiny. Capricorn and Cancer play dominant roles.

Sunday, August 13 (Moon in Pisces to Aries 2:41 p.m.) You'll be questioned about your theology as well as your taste in food and literature. Keep your sense of humor; highlight your diversity, curiosity, and appearance. A gift received in the late afternoon relates to your wardrobe or body image. Another Gemini who plays a significant role, and could have a name with these letters: C, L, U.

Monday, August 14 (Moon in Aries) A wish comes true in a dramatic way—you're able to revise, review, and to tear down in order to rebuild on a more suitable structure. An aggressive Aries is on your side and will serve as your private cheering section. In choosing colors, wear shades of red. Your lucky number is 4.

Tuesday, August 15 (Moon in Aries to Taurus 10:25 p.m.) Help your own cause by expressing feelings and ambitions via the written word. You possess hidden talent. You'll exude sex appeal; you'll attract allies by revealing that you most certainly are more than just a pretty face. The spotlight is on a change of scene, a variety of sensations.

Wednesday, August 16 (Moon in Taurus)   Those who took you for granted and thought they had you pigeonholed will be in for surprise. You'll win friends and influence people, you'll let others know that you are not without strength and allies. You'll hear these words: "We never saw you this way before!" Lucky lottery: 6, 12, 9, 7, 33, 35.

Thursday, August 17 (Moon in Taurus)   Define terms, outline boundaries, streamline procedures. It won't be easy for others to fool you, but you could fall victim to self-deception. Make an effort to see situations, places, and people as they actually are, not merely as you wish they were. Pisces and Virgo figure prominently.

Friday, August 18 (Moon in Taurus to Gemini 9:40 a.m.)   You might find yourself burdened with secrets. Keep in mind that discretion is the better part of valor. Focus on tradition, institutions, and dealings with older persons, some of whom say, "Do it the old way; it works out better!" A Cancer plays a memorable role.

Saturday, August 19 (Moon in Gemini)   Lucky lottery: 9, 5, 1, 10, 33, 22. Stress universal appeal, realizing you are free to experiment, to be vulnerable to love. Take special care around fires and electricity. A relationship that recently went off the track could be revived in a positive way. Stop carrying a burden that doesn't belong to you in the first place.

Sunday, August 20 (Moon in Gemini to Cancer 10:24 p.m.)   You'll look around and possibly say, "This is a fresh, new world!" The moon in your sign emphasizes your personality, originality, pioneering spirit, and sex appeal. Once again you'll be in sync. Wear shades of silver, green, and yellow. You'll come across fascinating reading material that could contain the solution to a perplexing problem.

Monday, August 21 (Moon in Cancer)   This is your kind of day. Ideas click, you reunite with a relative who left after an argument. Accent diplomacy, accept a dinner invitation. Check plumbing and repair mechanical parts, some of which connect with your car. You'll deal with a Capricorn who is likely to have a name containing these letters: B, K, T.

Tuesday, August 22 (Moon in Cancer)   You might be humming, "Pennies from heaven . . ." The focus is on your financial status, which is much improved. You'll locate what had been lost, missing, or stolen. A professional evaluation of your possessions shows they are worth more than you originally believed. A Cancer plays a key role.

Wednesday, August 23 (Moon in Cancer to Leo 10:13 a.m.) Lucky lottery: 4, 8, 44, 2, 20, 13. Catch up on tasks relating to tax and license requirements. Don't neglect a mechanical defect discovered yesterday. You're on solid ground—let others know how, why, and where you stand. Taurus, Leo, and Scorpio play significant roles.

Thursday, August 24 (Moon in Leo)   Accent showmanship, rich displays of color and product. Some will ask, "Aren't you going too far?" Your response, "Maybe too far for you, but not far enough for me!" You'll feel as if you've been released from prison—free, creative, maybe even in love. Virgo and another Gemini are in the picture.

Friday, August 25 (Moon in Leo to Virgo 7:50 p.m.)   Sharp dialogue takes place at home—be gentle but strong, calm but passionate, ready to have an open mind but refusing to be gullible. Attention revolves around the appearance of your home, a possible change of residence, the acquisition of property and a change of marital status. Your lucky number is 6.

Saturday, August 26 (Moon in Virgo)   The new moon in Virgo highlights the end of negotiations and the completion of a project. Property, home, and family relationships are also important today. You get a second chance and you'll be saying, "I will do it right this time!" The focus is on real estate, illusion and confusion, and an ability to see what is real and to do something constructive about it.

Sunday, August 27 (Moon in Virgo)   Be analytical; let a female member of your family know that you are not going to fall for a sob story. Offer tea and sympathy without becoming inextricably involved in a financial tangle. The emphasis is on responsibility, deadline pressure, and participation in a business enterprise. Your lucky number is 8.

Monday, August 28 (Moon in Virgo to Libra 3:15 a.m.) In a flash, you get what you want. A property settlement will favor you. A long-distance communication contains important references, so pay attention, taking nothing for granted. A Libra plays a role, and could have a name containing these letters: I and R. Your lucky number is 9.

Tuesday, August 29 (Moon in Libra) Focus on creativity, physical attraction, and your ability to win your way through charm and a degree of flirtation. The Libra moon equates to change, travel, variety, and your ability to climb the stairs of popularity. All stops are out, with no holding back now—you will gain a starring role. Leo is involved.

Wednesday, August 30 (Moon in Libra to Scorpio 8:12 p.m.) Lucky lottery: 2, 30, 6, 5, 42, 31. The emphasis is on personality, determination, and charm, and the opportunity to show off your creative style. You'll be saying, "This is my kind of day!" The scenario involves writing, travel, and restaurant trips. Be alive, alert, vulnerable to love. A Cancer is involved.

Thursday, August 31 (Moon in Scorpio) Focus on versatility and the ability to locate what had been lost, missing, or stolen. A love relationship requires review—there is danger that you might be taken for granted. Make it crystal clear that you will have none of that—put your foot down, saying "A new deal, and this time deal from the top of the deck!"

SEPTEMBER 1995

Friday, September 1 (Moon in Scorpio to Sagittarius 12:57 p.m.) On this Friday, the first day of the new month, it is appropriate that you make a fresh start, that you exercise independence of thought and action. Imprint your style, emphasizing creativity, inventiveness, and innovativeness. The Scorpio moon relates to your home environment, property, and the stability of a building.

Saturday, September 2 (Moon in Sagittarius) The emphasis is on cooperative efforts, your public image, your reputation and bank account, and getting your money's worth. The Sagittarius moon emphasizes legal maneuvers, license requirements, and rights and permissions. A lively Cancer puts forth a partnership proposal, and could have a name with these letters: B, K, T.

Sunday, September 3 (Moon in Sagittarius to Capricorn 3:45 p.m.) This is your kind of day! Permission is granted for a unique demonstration. The spotlight is on your marital status, partnership, and the conclusion of legal negotiations. A Sagittarian could prove instrumental in helping you strike it rich. Diversify, laugh at your own foibles, dress stylishly. Your lucky number is 3.

Monday, September 4 (Moon in Capricorn) A change of scene imminent—the Capricorn moon emphasizes the revelation of information about a partnership or a possible inheritance. Tear down in order to rebuild—sharpen your tools, test recipes. Taurus and Scorpio play dynamic roles and could have these letters in their names: D, M, V.

Tuesday, September 5 (Moon in Capricorn to Aquarius 5:47 p.m.) Play a conservative role to the hilt. The Capricorn moon highlights hidden material, a secret meeting, arrangements that are kept from you. You'll be dealing with artistic people, many of whom write—including Virgo, Sagittarius, and another Gemini. You'll have special good fortune by sticking with the number 5.

Wednesday, September 6 (Moon in Aquarius) Lucky lottery: 6, 2, 11, 22, 18, 7. People will comment, "You seem to have an uncanny gift for picking underdogs!" The key is to follow a hunch, refusing to be dismayed by someone who insists, "It's not in the stars; it's all pure luck!" You'll beautify your surroundings. Today's scenario features flowers, gifts, and music.

Thursday, September 7 (Moon in Aquarius to Pisces 8:08 p.m.) Protect your precious privacy. The number 7 astrological and numerical cycle, Neptune, blends with your Mercury ruler and this, combined with the Aquarian moon, promotes success in overcoming odds, restoring a love relationship, and winning a contest. Pisces and Virgo play outstanding roles.

Friday, September 8 (Moon in Pisces)   This can be your power-play day as the weekend begins. You learn more about money: where it comes from, how it's spent, and how to earn more of it. Someone in the know reveals a secret and you'll benefit as a result. You'll be dealing with Cancer and Capricorn likely to have these letters in their names: H, Q, Z.

Saturday, September 9 (Moon in Pisces)   The full moon position highlights career, business, and a completion of negotiations. Don't act completely on impulse—give logic equal time. Your professional superior is very emotional, and could say things that he or she later regrets. Know it, and keep your own perspective. Lucky lottery: 9, 12, 7, 20, 2, 32.

Sunday, September 10 (Moon in Pisces to Aries 12:14 a.m.)   The emphasis is on diversity, surprise visits, an original approach, and a meaningful compliment from an attractive person. Leo and Aquarius figure prominently, and could have a name that contains these letters: A, S, J. Take a risk to put your creative agenda across.

Monday, September 11 (Moon in Aries)   Forces that were scattered come back together—focus on responsibility, organization, property value, and serious consideration of your partnership or marital status. You'll enjoy gourmet dining tonight despite an annoying, minor digestive problem. Capricorn is in the picture.

Tuesday, September 12 (Moon in Aries to Taurus 7:21 a.m.)   This is your kind of day—you win friends and influence people, and your love life heats up. The Aries moon highlights your ability to make wishes come true, to state your views in a dynamic, original way. You'll gain at least one valuable friend as a result. Money comes your way via a third party.

Wednesday, September 13 (Moon in Taurus)   Lucky lottery: 4, 2, 20, 6, 17, 18. Fix things, correct mechanical-electrical defects. A secret arrangement involves a Taurus, who is likely to have these letters in his or her name: D, M,

V. Someone who claims to know it all actually has little knowledge. Respond accordingly.

Thursday, September 14 (Moon in Taurus to Gemini 5:48 p.m.) You'll participate in a unique learning process. You'll gain via the written word. Today's scenario features change, travel, variety, and flirtation. Virgo, Sagittarius, and another Gemini play significant roles. Make requests in writing—verbal overtures lack substance. Your lucky number is 5.

Friday, September 15 (Moon in Gemini) As the weekend begins, a complete housecleaning might be in order. The spotlight falls on a domestic adjustment that could involve a change of residence or marital status. Diplomacy wins. There's music in your life tonight. You'll also be dining on sumptuous hors d'oeuvres. Libra figures prominently.

Saturday, September 16 (Moon in Gemini) Lucky lottery: 7, 5, 3, 30, 14, 15. Define terms, make meanings crystal clear. There is an aura of subterfuge—be aware, alert, look behind the scenes. Your cycle is high. Your judgment and intuition are on target—you'll be at the right place at a crucial moment. Let others know you can be serious when events call for somber tone.

Sunday, September 17 (Moon in Gemini to Cancer 6:16 a.m.) Your cycle continues high, but wavers from personality to cash on the barrelhead. You'll be dealing with the barter system, payments and collections, and food preparation. You may have an opportunity to invest in a restaurant. Hold back on venture capital; play the waiting game. Capricorn and Cancer are involved in this exciting drama.

Monday, September 18 (Moon in Cancer) Reach beyond the immediate. Know that seeds planted approximately one month ago are now ready to bear fruit. Focus on universal appeal, the ability to gain a wider audience, and a sense of achievement. What you seek may be found overseas.—That's not as far away as you might imagine. Your lucky number is 9.

Tuesday, September 19 (Moon in Cancer to Leo 6:19 p.m.) A new approach brings positive financial results. Appraisal of property and possessions will be to your advantage—you might discover that you own a gem. A different kind of involvement is featured—it could include a hot romance with Leo or Aquarius.

Wednesday, September 20 (Moon in Leo)   Lucky lottery: 2, 10, 15, 38, 13, 50. At the track: post position special—number 6 P.P. in the fifth race. Pick six: 1, 5, 8, 5, 6, 4. In selecting names of potential winning horses and jockeys, be aware of these letters: B, K, T. Cancer and Capricorn figure in today's scenario.

Thursday, September 21 (Moon in Leo)   Dine out; diversify; show off your style, humor, wit, and wisdom. You'll star tonight, whether within the family circle or by participating in a political or charitable event. Your influence extends far and wide. You'll receive excellent news in connection with a publication. Your lucky number is 3.

Friday, September 22 (Moon in Leo to Virgo 4:01 a.m.)   You're on solid ground, so focus on property, large household products, and durable goods. A special hint: Check fixtures, mechanical objects, and your car. Oil and water figure prominently; symbolically, this also means that you should not attempt to bring together people who dislike each other.

Saturday, September 23 (Moon in Virgo)   Lucky lottery: 5, 41, 6, 13, 12, 30. The emphasis is on your marital status. You have a winning way with words. A dynamic Virgo plays a significant role, and is likely to have these letters in his or her name: E, N, W. Another Gemini helps resolve an embarrassing situation. Analyze character!

Sunday, September 24 (Moon in Virgo to Libra 10:50 a.m.)   It's an excellent day for a family gathering—the new moon in Libra emphasizes cooperation, balance, pressure, romance, and your marital status. There will be music in your life; you'll be musing, "Now I know indeed that life can be beautiful!" Taurus, Libra, and Scorpio are represented.

Monday, September 25 (Moon in Libra)   Look beyond the immediate; say to yourself, "All right, I will be vulnerable to romance and love!" You'll be quoting the bard, "Tis better to have loved and lost than never to have loved at all." The Libra moon stimulates the creative processes—Neptunian-7 influence brings dreams closer to realities.

Tuesday, September 26 (Moon in Libra to Scorpio 3:20 p.m.)   What appeared to be long ago and far away will materialize. You'll be made aware of a deadline. Justice will prevail in any legal situation. A relationship that means much to you does have thorns among the roses. You'll be dealing with a Cancer with these letters in his or her name: H, Q, Z.

Wednesday, September 27 (Moon in Scorpio)   Look beyond the immediate; understand that previous rules and regulations no longer apply. Love plays a major role. Your soul mate might be nearby. The Scorpio moon emphasizes basic issues, fitness, employment, pet ownership, and dependents. Aries and Libra play dynamic roles.

Thursday, September 28 (Moon in Scorpio to Sagittarius 6:30 p.m.)   It's an excellent day to make a fresh start, to meet people, to wear bright colors, to dress up your product. Accent originality; welcome a different kind of love. Vigor returns; people are drawn to you. Some comment, "Being near you revitalizes!" Leo and Aquarius are featured.

Friday, September 29 (Moon in Sagittarius)   You'll seriously consider a division of property, a major purchase, a partnership, your credit rating, or your marital status. Your sense of direction is regained. You'll learn more about the motivation of a family member. Special: Take extra precautions to avoid injury to your left eye. Your lucky number is 2.

Saturday, September 30 (Moon in Sagittarius to Capricorn 9:10 p.m.)   Lucky lottery: 3, 9, 33, 4, 12, 1. You'll receive a gift that adds to your wardrobe—you have quite a Saturday night in store. You'll be complimented; your innate wit and wisdom will surge forward. You'll make valuable contacts for both business and pleasure. Sagittarius and another Gemini are in the picture.

OCTOBER 1995

Sunday, October 1 (Moon in Capricorn)   Much of your attention revolves around the durability of goods and relationships. The emphasis is on family, cooperative effort, and expression of feelings. Focus on direction, motivation, and your marital status. A Cancer who plays a key role has a name with these letters: B, K, T.

Monday, October 2 (Moon in Capricorn to Aquarius 11:59 p.m.) You'll be saying, "The agreement made yesterday was a good thing and that is being proved today." Although it is Monday, you might feel as if it were Saturday night. You learn the truth about a hidden resource and the financial status of someone you trust.

Tuesday, October 3 (Moon in Aquarius) Throughout this month and especially on this day, you'll acknowledge your own value to yourself. This adds up to self-esteem, and to the ability to understand the dictum, "Physician, heal thyself." Taurus, Leo, and Scorpio play meaningful roles. Your lucky number is 4.

Wednesday, October 4 (Moon in Aquarius) Lucky lottery: 5, 45, 11, 22, 33, 7. You gain today through the use of words, spoken or written. Your natural talent as a reporter and analyzer of information and character will be used today and much of what you learn about others will add to your own self-knowledge. Virgo is involved.

Thursday, October 5 (Moon in Aquarius to Pisces 3:35 a.m.) Attention revolves around your family's financial structure. If you are single, you'll be concerned with a possible change of residence or marital status. Married or single, you might be concerned with the possibility of a long-term visitor or an addition to your family. Taurus is represented.

Friday, October 6 (Moon in Pisces) The answer to your question: Play the waiting game. What you want will be handed to you on a silver platter—if you don't force issues. The Pisces moon coincides with leadership, promotion, production, and getting the credit you earned and deserve. Pisces and Virgo persons play interesting roles.

Saturday, October 7 (Moon in Pisces to Aries 8:41 a.m.) What you lost yesterday will be returned today. Focus on money, payments, and collections. You might win a contest. Lucky lottery: 8, 13, 5, 4, 20, 1. You'll be dealing with

Capricorn and Cancer, who are likely to have these letters in their names: H, Q, Z.

Sunday, October 8 (Moon in Aries)   The full moon, lunar eclipse in Aries, translates to your eleventh house, which means that through unusual procedures, you get what you want even if at first you might feel that you lost. You'll upset the applecart. You'll pick long shots. A relationship will survive emotional fireworks.

Monday, October 9 (Moon in Aries to Taurus 4:05 p.m.)   The Aries moon continues to stimulate your creative process, helping you win friends and influence people and bringing you luck in matters of finance and romance. Begin a project, take the initiative in getting to the heart of matters, and participate in an innovative project. Leo plays a role. Your lucky number is 1.

Tuesday, October 10 (Moon in Taurus)   A family member announces, "Free at last!" Focus on hospitals, museums, institutions, and home care. The emphasis is on food, money management, and a secret arrangement. You might be saying, "More than I care to know!" A Cancer plays a role. The spotlight also falls on durable goods and large household products.

Wednesday, October 11 (Moon in Taurus)   Lucky lottery: 3, 20, 6, 16, 33, 22. A burden is lifted. This evening could feature fun and frolic. The key is diversification, versatility, and the willingness to experiment with different modes of transportation. You'll be dealing with an active Sagittarian likely to have these letters or initials in his or her name: C, L, U.

Thursday, October 12 (Moon in Taurus to Gemini 2:10 a.m.)   Be willing to tear down, revise, review, to rebuild, to be finished with outmoded methods, defective material. Because your cycle is high, you can trust your own judgment, heed your inner voice. Use elements of timing and surprise—advocate the unusual. Taurus, Leo, and Scorpio add spice to your life.

Friday, October 13 (Moon in Gemini)   This could be your lucky day! Your cycle is high; circumstances turn in your favor; you'll hear this comment at least once: "You have all the luck!" Wear shades of silver, green, and yellow. Make personal appearances, get your own views across in an entertaining, dramatic way. Your lucky number is 5.

Saturday, October 14 (Moon in Gemini to Cancer 2:20 p.m.) Attention revolves around music, harmony, and a reunion with a loved one. Although you won't exactly possess a money tree, a financial burden will be lifted. You'll have reason to celebrate because of that check arriving at a propitious moment. Lucky lottery: 11, 6, 4, 40, 13, 33.

Sunday, October 15 (Moon in Cancer) This is a day to be reflective, to meditate, to blend spirituality with the reality of your aspirations. Share unique collections with your family—display your product, let others know you are no stranger to poetry. Put on an aura of mystery, glamour, and intrigue—your hunch is on target.

Monday, October 16 (Moon in Cancer) What had been vague becomes clear—you'll be made aware of a deadline. A relationship becomes exciting, controversial, and durable. The spotlight falls on income potential, personal possessions, and professional appraisal of products. You'll be very much involved with business, career, money, and love.

Tuesday, October 17 (Moon in Cancer to Leo 2:46 a.m.) Finish what you start, reaching beyond previous expectations. Check a travel agency for a possible overseas journey. Focus also on your soul mate. Finish with a losing situation or relationship. A long-distance call informs that your views have been verified—you're the undisputed champion!

Wednesday, October 18 (Moon in Leo) The Leo moon highlights experimentation, showmanship, color coordination, and your ability to dress up your product. Make a fresh start, emphasizing originality, independence, and the willingness to take risks. A love relationship goes from medium to warm to hot. You'll be dealing with an excitable Leo who is likely to have these letters in his or her name: A, S, J.

Thursday, October 19 (Moon in Leo to Virgo 11:11 a.m.) You'll be designated as one who can bring order out of chaos. You'll hear these words, "We're counting on you to keep this family afloat!" You'll rediscover your sense of direction and motivation. You'll be dealing with an ambitious Capricorn, whose name has these letters: B, K, T.

Friday, October 20 (Moon in Virgo)   At the track: post position special—number 5 P.P. in the seventh race. Pick six: 3, 5, 7, 8, 5, 1. In selecting names of potential winning horses or jockeys, look for these letters—C, L, U. Diversify, experiment, get your ideas on paper. Another Gemini is helpful.

Saturday, October 21 (Moon in Virgo to Libra 8:15 p.m.)   Lucky lottery: 21, 4, 7, 5, 13, 50. Check for the hidden clause, keep your options open, tear down in order to rebuild on a more suitable structure. Some people will claim you are a loose cannon, mainly because you are different, creative, dynamic, and somewhat dangerous.

Sunday, October 22 (Moon in Libra)   Be ready for a surprising statement from a relative recently returned from a trip. Be diplomatic while standing tall for your principles. Today's scenario features creativity, style, a variety of experiences, and physical attraction. Virgo, Sagittarius, and another Gemini play outstanding roles. Your lucky number is 5.

Monday, October 23 (Moon in Libra)   A domestic adjustment is featured. A love relationship is accented. As creative juices stir, you express your ideas. Someone you are attracted to returns the compliment. You'll be dealing with a gentle Libran whose name has these letters: F, O, X. There's music in your life tonight by 11 p.m. You'll receive a token of affection and esteem.

Tuesday, October 24 (Moon in Libra to Scorpio 12:07 a.m.)   The new moon, solar eclipse in Scorpio, represents work issues to be contended with. It also emphasizes your physical fitness, pet ownership, and dependents. See people, places, and situations as they are, not merely as you wish they could be. Perfect techniques; get organized. Your lucky number is 7.

Wednesday, October 25 (Moon in Scorpio)   Lucky lottery: 20, 28, 2, 22, 33, 5. A deadline relates filling out forms with claims regarding lost luggage. A refund is due. A defective product caused concern and you deserve to be compensated for the time and disappointment involved. Capricorn figures prominently.

Thursday, October 26 (Moon in Scorpio to Sagittarius 1:56 a.m.) You get the green light for import-export activity. Refuse to be limited by outmoded methods, people who have no idea of what is original, or is stale. On a personal level, a love relationship is reactivated—a journey could be involved. Aries figures prominently.

Friday, October 27 (Moon in Sagittarius) A new deal is indicated in connection with your reputation and your credibility, legal rights, and permissions. This day marks a pivotal point in connection with love and marriage. A special note: Avoid heavy lifting. Express yourself. Be willing to take risks by participating in an unusual project. Your lucky number is 1.

Saturday, October 28 (Moon in Sagittarius to Capricorn 3:15 a.m.) You'll have luck today in connection with Cancer and Capricorn, who could have these letters in their names: B, K, T. You might also find these to be lucky lottery numbers: 2, 20, 8, 10, 5, 30. Your sense of directions is restored. A family member says, "Let us try to understand."

Sunday, October 29 (Moon in Capricorn; Daylight Saving Time Ends) Your position is fortified by one in charge of accounts. Someone in authority likes you, apologizes for the recent omission of your name in connection with credit. This message becomes crystal clear by 7 p.m. Diversify, accent humor, give full play to your intellectual curiosity.

Monday, October 30 (Moon in Capricorn to Aquarius 4:23 a.m.) Break free from those who are prisoners of preconceived notions. These are the people who frequently assert, "My mind is made up—don't disturb me with the facts!" Taurus, Leo, and Scorpio are involved, and could have these letters in their names: D, M, V.

Tuesday, October 31 (Moon in Aquarius) The emphasis is on a unique investigation. You can get points across via the written word. On this Halloween, you'll be reminded of past events and made aware of your future potential. An ambitious young person says, "I would like very much to be just like you!" Your lucky number is 5.

NOVEMBER 1995

Wednesday, November 1 (Moon in Aquarius to Pisces 8:17 a.m.) On this first day of November, optimism prevails. You'll be jovial. Travel plans could be on the horizon. Accent self-expression, reading and writing, publishing and advertising. A Sagittarian is involved, and could have a name with these letters: C, L, U. Test these lucky lottery numbers: 5, 50, 51, 8, 30, 32.

Thursday, November 2 (Moon in Pisces) On this second day of the month, you're on solid ground. The Pisces moon highlights creativity, style, leadership, promotion, and production. Be willing to revise, review, and remodel—test recipes, sharpen tools. You'll be dealing with Taurus and Scorpio, some of whom might have these letters in their names: D, M, V.

Friday, November 3 (Moon in Pisces to Aries 2:21 p.m.) It's an excellent day for reading and writing, for learning through the process of sharing and teaching others. Listen carefully: On this Friday night, a chance meeting, blind date, or flirtation might lead you along a path you never intended to trod. Don't be led astray by whispers of sweet nothings—they are worth exactly nothing.

Saturday, November 4 (Moon in Aries) Lucky lottery: 6, 16, 9, 19, 22, 33. At the track: post position special—number 2 P.P. in the fourth race. Pick six: 1, 5, 8, 2, 8, 8. The focus for you today will be on your property, marital status, direction, motivation, and plans for a possible sea cruise. A Cancer is involved.

Sunday, November 5 (Moon in Aries to Taurus 10:35 p.m.) Define terms, make notes—your desires are going to be fulfilled, but first you must get them on paper. Tonight you'll be asked, "Could you help us to help you by letting us know what you really want?" Focus on your ability to win friends and influence people. Your lucky number is 7.

Monday, November 6 (Moon in Taurus)   You'll surprise yourself by your ability to organize, to meet a deadline, to bring order out of chaos. An Aries who never lost faith in you takes the lead in promoting your cause. Use lessons learned during a recent experience involving a dishonest person who tried to steal your ideas.

Tuesday, November 7 (Moon in Taurus)   The full Taurus moon highlights secrets and special arrangements relating to income, investments, and the location of needed personnel and material. Finish what you start; go further than you originally anticipated. Focus on distance, language, and import-export activities. Aries is involved.

Wednesday, November 8 (Moon in Taurus to Gemini 8:55 a.m.)   Lucky lottery: 1, 12, 20, 18, 45, 7. You'll be doing business with Leo and Aquarius, whose names are likely to have these letters: A, S, J. Do your own thing. Don't follow others; let others follow you. A new love could be on the horizon. Wear shades of gold.

Thursday, November 9 (Moon in Gemini)   Focus on a partnership or reunion. You could find a real bargain at an auction. You'll be intrigued by watches and antique clocks. Property value is discussed; stand your ground. Do not give up something of value for nothing. Capricorn and Cancer play significant roles.

Friday, November 10 (Moon in Gemini to Cancer 8:57 p.m.)   You'll be saying, "This is my idea of how to begin the weekend—everything seems to be going my way!" Trust your judgment; follow through on a hunch. Circumstances will take a dramatic turn in your favor. There's a fine dining experience in store tonight. A Cancer is involved.

Saturday, November 11 (Moon in Cancer)   Lucky lottery: 4, 40, 3, 30, 2, 20. The cycle moves up where money is concerned. A lost article is located. A decision is made in connection with the sale or purchase of property or your participation in a commercial enterprise. Your marital status figures prominently. Play the waiting game.

Sunday, November 12 (Moon in Cancer)   Be analytical; seek reasons and motivations. The moon position highlights money, payments, collections, and credit received that previously was denied. Someone of the opposite sex sends your morale soaring with these words: "At times, I feel I can hardly keep my hands off you!" Virgo is involved.

Monday, November 13 (Moon in Cancer to Leo 9:37 a.m.)   The emphasis is on a domestic adjustment, flowers, music, and a decision relating to your property, home, and marriage. Special key: If you are diplomatic, you gain everything. Conversely, if you attempt to force issues, you could lose plenty. Taurus and Libra are involved. Your lucky number is 6.

Tuesday, November 14 (Moon in Leo)   Define terms, outline boundaries. A discussion with a relative is lively but need not deteriorate into an argument. Accent versatility, humor, and the ability to laugh at your own foibles. Keep an aura of mystery—don't tell all, but be discreet for best results. Pisces is involved.

Wednesday, November 15 (Moon in Leo to Virgo 9:02 p.m.)   Lucky lottery: 50, 8, 18, 17, 33, 26. At the track: post position special—number 8 P.P. in the eighth race. Pick six: 8, 5, 4, 4, 7, 2. In selecting names of potential winning horses and jockeys check for these letters: H, Q, Z. An older person will give you good advice.

Thursday, November 16 (Moon in Virgo)   The emphasis is on universal appeal, and the ability to answer the question, "Why am I here?" The spotlight is on the mantic arts and sciences, metaphysics, and recognition of spiritual values. Most important: Clear debris that represents a fire hazard at home. Someone close to you tends to be careless while lighting matches.

Friday, November 17 (Moon in Virgo)   Dark corners receive more light—your residence will be airy. You'll welcome people who smile, and who have a sense of humor and an abundance of talent and showmanship. Leo plays a major role and is likely to have a name with these letters: A, S, J. Your lucky number is 1.

Saturday, November 18 (Moon in Virgo to Libra 5:18 a.m.) Lucky lottery: 6, 12, 2, 20, 4, 40. Attention revolves around your home, property, and family, and your potential participation in a business requiring sales ability. Your sense of direction is restored. A reunion with a loved one tops the agenda. Down-to-earth matter: Plumbing requires special attention.

Sunday, November 19 (Moon in Libra) On this Sunday, some will say, "You certainly seem to be feeling your oats!" In reality, you are spiritual and happy, knowing once and for all that you are not alone in the universe. Focus on diversity, fitness, and the ability to communicate an important message in an entertaining, dynamic way.

Monday, November 20 (Moon in Libra to Scorpio 9:40 a.m.) Check details and references; study the fine print. Be willing to replace outworn machinery with an up-to-date product. Taurus and Scorpio talk about finances and business. A unique relationship could take you along the road of adventure. Your lucky number is 4.

Tuesday, November 21 (Moon in Scorpio) Be ready for change, travel, variety, a surprise gift. There's a declaration of love from someone who previously was reticent, even shy. You'll gain via words, both spoken and written. The moon position highlights work methods, basic issues, pet ownership, communication with someone who relies upon your special consideration, and generosity.

Wednesday, November 22 (Moon in Scorpio to Sagittarius 10:56 a.m.) The new moon in Scorpio coincides with a chance to do things in a new way. Focus on fitness, self-esteem, and attention to diet and nutrition. You might feel you are madly in love, but at the same time, realize you are asking for trouble by pursuing this urge.

Thursday, November 23 (Moon in Sagittarius) During this holiday, spiritual values will not be lost. The number 7 astrological and numerical cycle, plus the moon in Sagittarius, makes it crystal clear that you will genuinely give thanks on this Thanksgiving Day. Pisces and Virgo play prominent roles. An exciting reunion is in store for you!

Friday, November 24 (Moon in Sagittarius to Capricorn 10:48 a.m.) The holiday spirit prevails—the Sagittarian moon highlights your public image, reputation, credibility, partnership, cooperative efforts, and marital status. A signed agreement might relate to a journey, publishing, or participation in a spiritual mission. Capricorn and Cancer are represented.

Saturday, November 25 (Moon in Capricorn) Lucky lottery: 9, 10, 8, 44, 50, 1. Stress universal appeal; understand that previous rules, inhibitions, and regulations no longer apply to you. A burden is lifted. You're free to fly, to travel, and, most important, to love. Someone who took you for granted will pay a dear price.

Sunday, November 26 (Moon in Capricorn to Aquarius 11:15 a.m.) Focus on discovery, mystery, intrigue, ability to learn more about hidden values and about tax and license requirements. Although in whispered tones, a discussion relates to a possible inheritance. Don't permit yourself to be left out—speak your mind or forever hold your peace.

Monday, November 27 (Moon in Aquarius) The Aquarian moon accents an unorthodox approach. Surprise news arrives from someone previously close to you, possibly an old flame. The spotlight falls on property, public appearances, special payments and collections. But your marital status practically dominates today's scenario. Cancer is involved.

Tuesday, November 28 (Moon in Aquarius to Pisces 1:59 p.m.) This could be termed "my kind of day!" Focus on repartee, wit and wisdom, humor, a sense of the ridiculous. You'll meet lively people, especially Sagittarius and Gemini, who look upon you with wonderment. They are likely to have these letters in their names: C, L, U.

Wednesday, November 29 (Moon in Pisces) Lucky lottery: 4, 12, 7, 23, 5, 33. The Pisces moon highlights extra responsibility, leadership, promotion, production, and the ability to communicate with someone in power. The answer to your question: Yes, you are on firm emotional-financial ground. Scorpio plays a paramount role.

Thursday, November 30 (Moon in Pisces to Aries 7:51 p.m.) On this last day of November, you'll have more freedom of thought and action—you'll read and write, you'll learn through the process of sharing and teaching others. What begins as a mild flirtation could get out of hand, if you so permit. Virgo and another Gemini are in this picture.

DECEMBER 1995

Friday, December 1 (Moon in Aries)　　On this first day of December, you get things done, people rely upon your leadership, you learn rules in order to break them. Taurus, Leo, and Scorpio play paramount roles—some are likely to have these letters in their names: D, M. V.

Saturday, December 2 (Moon in Aries)　　Get ready for change, travel, variety, and an exciting discovery. The Aries moon coincides with the fulfillment of wishes and the ability to win friends and influence people. Aries becomes your strong ally. You'll be saying, "I know now that I am over the top!" Lucky lottery: 4, 40, 5, 10, 9, 27.

Sunday, December 3 (Moon in Aries to Taurus 4:40 a.m.)　　It's an excellent day for a family gathering, for beautifying your surroundings, for making dramatic changes that use color coordination, gaudy wrappings, flowers, and music. Your place will be the place to go. Before 6 p.m. you'll receive excellent news about money, especially potential income.

Monday, December 4 (Moon in Taurus)　　Define terms, make meanings crystal clear. Find out what's expected of you and what you can expect in return for your contributions. The emphasis is on visiting hospitals and museums, and on making secret arrangements. Pisces and Virgo play meaningful roles. Your lucky number is 7.

Tuesday, December 5 (Moon in Taurus to Gemini 3:35 p.m.)　　Focus on organization, responsibility, a relationship that grows warm. Business is part of today's scenario—use lessons learned in the recent past. Those who thought you would be a stranger to business acumen are in for a surprise. A Cancer and a Capricorn play significant roles. You'll have luck by sticking with the number 8.

Wednesday, December 6 (Moon in Gemini)   Lucky lottery: 9, 5, 30, 3, 33, 4. Emphasize universal appeal. Long-ago rules should not affect you. The Gemini moon highlights personality, initiative, originality, and your ability to get to the heart of matters. Let others know, "This is the cutoff point!" You'll be dealing with a rambunctious Aries who reminds you of a past favor.

Thursday, December 7 (Moon in Gemini)   The full moon in your sign coincides with emotional responses, romance, popularity, and the tendency to act on impulse and think about it later. The astrological and numerical cycle, number 1, relates to the sun. This combines with the full moon in your sign—on this day you could be involved in an explosive relationship. Dare to dream!

Friday, December 8 (Moon in Gemini to Cancer 3:44 a.m.)   At the track: post position special—number 6 P.P. in the fifth race. Pick six: 4, 2, 1, 6, 6, 8. In selecting names of potential winning horses and jockeys, be aware of these letters: B, K, T. Cancer, and Capricorn will play significant roles in your scenario.

Saturday, December 9 (Moon in Cancer)   The key is diversification. Be willing to take risks in order to give ideas a fair trial. Focus on trips, visits, relatives, a surprise visit from someone capable of elevating your morale. Sagittarius and another Gemini play outstanding roles. Lucky lottery: 3, 20, 4, 24, 33, 5.

Sunday, December 10 (Moon in Cancer to Leo 4:24 p.m.)   Be willing to revise, review, and remodel, to tear down in order to rebuild on a more suitable structure. The emphasis is on income, locating a lost article, meeting a Cancer who has your best interests at heart and will prove it—likely to have a name with these letters: D, M, V.

Monday, December 11 (Moon in Leo)   The Leo moon highlights fun, frolic, diversity, versatility, and humor. Someone you find extremely attractive will return the compliment. Be open to adventure, romance, and a meaningful relationship. It's an excellent day for reading and writing, teaching and learning—a chance meeting or blind date could lead to something significant.

Tuesday, December 12 (Moon in Leo)   Attention revolves around your home, music, security, family, and showmanship. Beautify your surroundings, say "Adios" to someone who is the prototype of a "Gloomy Gus." You'll win respect and admiration from those who appreciate your humor, courage, and integrity. Taurus, Libra, and Scorpio play significant roles.

Wednesday, December 13 (Moon in Leo to Virgo 4:26 a.m.) Lucky lottery: 17, 50, 5, 1, 7, 6. It's important to define terms and make meanings clear, to separate fact from fiction. Psychic impressions prove valid. You'll be given a chance to renovate, remodel, and rebuild, to create a profitable enterprise from a project on its last legs.

Thursday, December 14 (Moon in Virgo)   You already are planning ahead for a sensational holiday—Capricorn, Cancer, and Virgo are in your corner and will help you to succeed in whatever project you choose. You'll know that you are appreciated and loved, and that you do not stand alone.

Friday, December 15 (Moon in Virgo to Libra 2:09 p.m.)   Look beyond the immediate; plan ahead for travel; realize a property dispute will be settled in your favor—your physical presence will not be required. You have made an excellent point, but don't stay too long at the fair. A love relationship is at the smoldering state. Your lucky number is 9.

Saturday, December 16 (Moon in Libra)   Lucky lottery: 1, 7, 17, 20, 6, 15. Make a fresh start, stressing originality, inventiveness, and innovation. Someone who takes you for granted should be taught a lesson. A new kind of love is on the horizon. The Libra moon highlights creativity, variety, personal magnetism, and sex appeal.

Sunday, December 17 (Moon in Libra to Scorpio 8:07 p.m.)
The emphasis is on cooperative efforts, property values, partnership, publicity, and marital status. You'll exude a subtle kind of appeal—people will be drawn to you with their most intimate questions and problems. As if by magic, as you help others, your own emotional wounds will heal.

Monday, December 18 (Moon in Scorpio) The key is to diversify, experiment, and arrange a social affair that possibly relates to a charity or politics. You might be asked to direct a community project—check your wardrobe; keep resolutions about diet and nutrition. Whatever you do, don't neglect your health. Your lucky number is 3.

Tuesday, December 19 (Moon in Scorpio to Sagittarius 10:13 p.m.) Keep your options open—the emphasis is on employment, basic issues, pet ownership, communication from one who relies on your efforts, and generosity. Plans are subject to revision—someone once in charge could be told, "Get lost!" Remain in charge of your own fate and destiny. Your lucky number is 4.

Wednesday, December 20 (Moon in Sagittarius) You have word power, both spoken and written. The Scorpio moon emphasizes deep thoughts in connection with meaningful issues, work method, and employment. Someone is not telling the whole story—you could be the victim of false notions. Protect yourself in clinches; don't lead with your chin.

Thursday, December 21 (Moon in Sagittarius to Capricorn 9:46 p.m.) Accent your personal environment, the way your home looks, art objects, luxury items, and your marital status. Your credibility will be tested. You'll receive an offer that deserves serious consideration. Get promises in writing. Get together with someone who means much to you tonight. Your lucky number is 6.

Friday, December 22 (Moon in Capricorn) The numerical and astrological cycles, including the new moon, accent holiday preparations. Someone who had been far away makes it known: "I would like to be with you during the holidays." Make terms clear; don't hesitate to state your intentions. Focus also on legal affairs and marriage.

Saturday, December 23 (Moon in Capricorn to Aquarius 8:52 p.m.) Lucky lottery: 8, 10, 12, 32, 40, 1. The emphasis is on recognition of a time limitation. A relationship intensifies. Dig deep for information, check references, be aware of budgetary requirements. What had been hidden will be revealed to your advantage. A Capricorn figures prominently.

Sunday, December 24 (Moon in Aquarius) On this Christmas Eve, recognition of spiritual values plays an important role. You'll perceive potential; a quiet kind of optimism replaces recent ennui. You'll receive numerous gifts, more so than in previous years. You'll be most thankful for a gift of love from an Aries.

Monday, December 25 (Moon in Aquarius to Pisces 9:45 p.m.) On this Christmas Day, you feel spiritually refreshed and aware. You'll be listing resolutions, in advance of New Year's Eve. Among those resolves will be to make a fresh start in a new direction. Today's scenario features travel, romance, originality, unique decorations, and gifts. Your lucky number is 1.

Tuesday, December 26 (Moon in Pisces) Focus on family relationships and your ability to overcome distance and language barriers. A young person could steal the show. The rustle of gift wrappings will be heard loud and clear. The emphasis is also on dining with someone, possibly a family member, who returned from a journey to be with you during the holiday.

Wednesday, December 27 (Moon in Pisces) The key is diversification, the ability to control actions, to be sentimental without being maudlin. The Pisces moon coincides with a promotion, production, or participation in a spiritual ceremony. Check your guest list and New Year's Eve invitations. The element of luck rides with you. Lucky lottery: 3, 30, 10, 51, 48, 8.

Thursday, December 28 (Moon in Pisces to Aries 2:06 a.m.) Check details, be aware of costs; review plans for the upcoming holiday. What you thought was definite might turn out to be very flexible. A Pisces, who supposedly was in charge, is vacillating. Stay calm under pressure! Taurus and Scorpio can be helpful.

Friday, December 29 (Moon in Aries)   The moon moves to Aries, which equates with joy, fulfillment, friendship, and personal appeal. Today's scenario features discovery, excitement, personal magnetism, and a flirtation that adds spice. Get your thoughts and ideas on paper—by mid-afternoon, you'll feel like a new person.

Saturday, December 30 (Moon in Aries to Taurus 10:21 a.m.) Family members communicate; most are sincere, but others might feel that being obsequious is enough to ask. Be diplomatic without being weak—focus on decoration, remodeling, and beautifying your surroundings. There will be music as part of your scenario tonight. Your lucky number is 6.

Sunday, December 31 (Moon in Taurus)   On this New Year's Eve, the cycle shows deep reflection on your part, as well as sensitivity to the feelings of others. Realize that discretion is indeed the better part of valor. A quiet celebration is far more preferable than the other kind. Accent moderation, and keep private thoughts private. Pisces plays a major role. Happy New Year!

JANUARY 1996

Monday, January 1st (Moon in Taurus to Gemini 9:29 p.m.)   On this first day of 1996, you could be smiling due to financial good fortune. You solve a mystery, untie a Gordian knot, are in the mood to celebrate, and you'll be saying, "This certainly is not going to be a blue Monday!" Sagittarius and another Gemini figure in this scenario. Your lucky number is 3.

Tuesday, January 2 (Moon in Gemini)   At the track: Post position special—Number 4 P.P. in fourth race. Pick six: 3, 8, 1, 4, 5, 8. In choosing the names of horses or jockeys likely to be in the money, check for these letters or initials in names: D, M, V. Selections apply to all tracks. Scorpio is involved.

Wednesday, January 3 (Moon in Gemini)   Check dates and signatures—imprint your style, take the initiative in getting to the heart of matters. Because your cycle is high, and the moon is in your sign, you'll be at the right place at a crucial moment. Make personal appearances, wear Gemini colors—silver, green, and yellow. Lucky lottery numbers: 1, 5, 7, 8, 30, 50.

Thursday, January 4 (Moon in Gemini to Cancer 9:56 a.m.) On this Thursday, you'll beautify your surroundings, decorate and remodel, be close to a family member who for a time was distant, emotionally and literally. A domestic adjustment dominates, involves your lifestyle, residence, or marital status. The financial picture brightens. You'll have a reason to be pleased with yourself and a Taurus family member.

Friday, January 5 (Moon in Cancer) The moon in Cancer represents an area of your chart relating to finances and income, the ability to locate missing objects. Focus on food, security, family, value of property. Look for a Pisces with these letters or initials in his or her name: G, P, Y. Define terms, see people and places in a more realistic light.

Saturday, January 6 (Moon in Cancer to Leo 10:30 p.m.) Attention revolves around your career, a business arrangement, an intense relationship. You could be under pressure to meet a deadline. A Capricorn can be helpful. Look for these letters or initials in his or her name: H, Q, Z. What you seek could be in your own home. Lucky lottery numbers: 2, 4, 8, 17, 20, 22.

Sunday, January 7 (Moon in Leo) A long-standing disagreement or feud involving relatives will be settled. Focus on harmony, distance, language, a special invitation that could involve a journey. An apparent financial loss boomerangs in your favor within 24 hours. Aries is involved.

Monday, January 8 (Moon in Leo) What an unusual Monday! Focus on creativity, style, vigor, romantic inclinations. Make a fresh start. Erase previous losing patterns. Leo and Aquarius figure prominently. These letters or initials appear in their names: A, S, J. Your lucky number is 1.

Tuesday, January 9 (Moon in Leo to Virgo 10:29 a.m.) At the track: Post position special—Number 6 P.P. in fifth race. Pick six: 3, 6, 9, 1, 6, 8. Watch for these letters or initials in the names of potential winning horses

234

or jockeys: B, K, T. Selections apply to all tracks. Cancer and Capricorn figure in today's scenario.

Wednesday, January 10 (Moon in Virgo)   Focus on basic issues, employment, pet ownership, making a "different" arrangement with dependents. Sagittarius and another Gemini are involved, and have these letters or initials in their names: C, L, U. A gift received adds to your wardrobe and elevates your morale. Lucky lottery numbers: 3, 5, 6, 10, 36, 50.

Thursday, January 11 (Moon in Virgo)   At the track: Post position special—Number 4 PP. in fourth race. Pick six: 8, 4, 1, 4, 3, 8. In selecting potential winning horses or jockeys, keep these letters or initials in mind: D, M, V. Check signatures, and be aware of new information.

Friday, January 12 (Moon in Virgo to Libra 8:55 p.m.)   Within 24 hours favorable news is received concerning legal matters. Your romantic interests are heightened, which adds spice to your life. Focus on disseminating information, getting your thoughts on paper. Virgo, Sagittarius, and another Gemini play featured roles. Your lucky number is 5.

Saturday, January 13 (Moon in Libra)   Be diplomatic in connection with family affairs, domestic adjustment. The Libra moon highlights creativity, style, variety, and sensuality. There's music in your life tonight. Love takes on a more vibrant meaning. Libra plays a role. Lucky lottery numbers: 2, 6, 7, 12, 30, 51.

Sunday, January 14 (Moon in Libra to Scorpio 4:30 a.m.)   On this Sunday, it could be considered appropriate that spiritual values are emphasized. Creative juices stir, you gain rare insights. Pisces plays a role, and has these letters or initials in his or her name: G, P, Y. You'll have a backstage view. Your lucky number is 7.

Monday, January 15 (Moon in Scorpio)   Just 24 hours ago, you were concerned that "nothing is happening!" On this Monday, plenty occurs—including a business venture, an intense relationship. You'll also feel some deadline pressure. You'll be dealing with a Capricorn and Cancer with these letters or initials in their names: H, Q, Z.

Tuesday, January 16 (Moon in Scorpio to Sagittarius 8:25 a.m.) At the track: Post position special—Number 8 P.P. in first race. Pick six: 8, 2, 1, 3, 5, 9. In choosing names of potential winning horses or jockeys, watch for these letters or initials: I and R. Selections apply to all tracks. Aries figures prominently.

Wednesday, January 17 (Moon in Sagittarius) Love continues to dominate. You're due to make a decision about marriage. Take the independent course. Have the courage of your convictions. Try something new. Opportunities abound—enthusiam replaces indifference. An Aquarian is represented. Lucky lottery numbers: 1, 3, 7, 9, 30, 45.

Thursday, January 18 (Moon in Sagittarius to Capricorn 9:07 a.m.) The spotlight remains on the area of your chart associated with partnership, personal appearances, legal rights, and permissions. The emphasis is also on the sale or purchase of property or a home. Your marital status figures in today's dynamic action. Cancer and Capricorn play outstanding roles.

Friday, January 19 (Moon in Capricorn) You learn more about funds, tax and license requirements, the financial status of one close to you, including your business partner or mate. Diversify, ask questions, give full play to your intellectual curiosity. Advertise and publicize, bring your product or talent to the attention of more people.

Saturday, January 20 (Moon in Capricorn to Aquarius 8:15 a.m.) The new moon in Capricorn relates to your 8th House. Translated, this means you uncover hidden resources, could be an active participant in settling a dispute involving an inheritance. Today's scenario highlights mystery, intrigue, glamour, your sparkling personality. Lucky lottery numbers: 4, 8, 12, 33, 50, 51.

Sunday, January 21 (Moon in Aquarius) Sharpen tools, engage in a dialogue with a member of the opposite sex involving literature, theater, or restaurants. A clash of ideas proves stimulating and could lead to a romantic involvement. The Aquarian moon relates to publishing, advertising, communication, a possible journey.

Monday, January 22 (Moon in Aquarius to Pisces 8:02 a.m.) On this Monday, you are drawn in two directions—one would see you remaining close to home, the other involves advertising, publishing, travel. Focus on a domestic adjustment, income potential, flowers, music, the need to be on familiar ground. Libra is involved.

Tuesday, January 23 (Moon in Pisces) At the track: Post position special—Number 1 P.P. in sixth race. Pick six: 7, 3, 1, 4, 1, 1. In choosing potential winning horses or jockeys, look for these letters or initials in names: G, P, Y. Selections apply to all tracks. Pisces plays a role.

Wednesday, January 24 (Moon in Pisces to Aries 10:37 a.m.) The emphasis is on production, promotion, accepting the challenge of more responsibility, or a time limitation. The Pisces moon relates to your standing in the community, sudden changes affecting your ambition, career. Capricorn plays a distinguished role. Lucky lottery numbers: 4, 7, 8, 12, 22, 27.

Thursday, January 25 (Moon in Aries) A long-distance communication relates to friends, hopes, desires, the ability to have good fortune in finance and romance. You'll be idealistic in love, despite a bitter individual who says, "Love—there ain't no such animal!" Plant seeds that could blossom, resulting in an overseas journey.

Friday, January 26 (Moon in Aries to Taurus 5:16 p.m.) Make a fresh start, toss aside the status quo, reach beyond previous limitations. Today's Aries moon coincides with almost magical responses to your requests. You'll win friends and influence people. You'll inspire a loved one to action. Your lucky number is 1.

Saturday, January 27 (Moon in Taurus) A division of property could figure prominently. Focus on money, payments, and collections. A public appearance is aimed at improving your image. The moon accents the value of possessions, specialty items, the ability to transform a creative project into a profitable enterprise. Lucky lottery numbers: 1, 2, 12, 19, 20, 33.

Sunday, January 28 (Moon in Taurus)   On this Sunday, spiritual values surface. You'll know where you stand and what to do about it. Your cycle remains high, especially in matters of finance. An apparent loss boomerangs in your favor. Diversify, highlight humor, transportation, and art objects. Your lucky number is 3.

Monday, January 29 (Moon in Taurus to Gemini 3:43 a.m.)   You'll do the right thing at a crucial moment, the action will be where you are, you'll be independent, attractive, and sexy. Sharpen tools, do some mending, test recipes, be willing to revise, review, and remodel. Taurus and Scorpio figure in today's exciting scenario.

Tuesday, January 30 (Moon in Gemini)   The moon in your sign coincides with circumstances, events that favor your aspirations. Take the initiative, get to the heart of matters. Don't follow others—let them follow you! Be analytical: read, write, teach, disseminate information. Virgo plays an outstanding role.

Wednesday, January 31 (Moon in Gemini to Cancer 4:11 p.m.)   On this last day of January, beautify your surroundings, make your home more attractive and inviting. You'll receive a gift representing a token of affection or esteem. Within 24 hours, money comes your way in a surprising way. An object that had been lost will be discovered. Lucky lottery numbers: 6, 12, 17, 18, 20, 30.

FEBRUARY 1996

Thursday, February 1 (Moon in Cancer)   On this Thursday, the first day of February, you locate a "key" that was missing. A puzzle is solved, and the cash flows in. Be willing to revise, review, remodel, rebuild on a more suitable structure. You'll be dealing with Taurus and Scorpio, who are likely to have these letters or initials in their names: D, M, V.

Friday, February 2 (Moon in Cancer)   Focus on your ability to analyze, to determine character, to select quality over quantity. Your income potential is improved as a result of writing, reading, making your views and opinions known. You might be playing the role of investigative reporter. Your lucky number is 5.

Saturday, February 3 (Moon in Cancer to Leo 4:46 a.m.)
Focus on your home, lifestyle, residence, a major decision involving marriage. A trip involves a relative. Give full play to your intellectual curiosity. You'll be active, alert, and inquisitive—and that is as it should be. Libra is involved. Lucky lottery numbers: 4, 5, 6, 18, 33, 51.

Sunday, February 4 (Moon in Leo)   The Leo full moon relates to financial transactions, trading activities. A superficial relationship could culminate in a serious involvement. Define terms, realize that the element of deception could be part of today's scenario. Pisces is represented.

Monday, February 5 (Moon in Leo to Virgo 4:22 p.m.)   Accent showmanship, blend responsibility with color, entertainment, a promotional project. The astrological-numerical cycle relates to Saturn, discipline, the ultimate big payoff. Capricorn and Cancer are in the picture, and could have these letters or initials in their names: H, Q, Z.

Tuesday, February 6 (Moon in Virgo)   Accent universal appeal; refuse to be limited. Promote your product and talent. An overseas venture proves stimulating and exciting, guarantees a wider audience, bigger sales. Your relationship is ready to begin or end—there's little or no in-between. Aries plays a role.

Wednesday, February 7 (Moon in Virgo)   Make a fresh start, take the initiative, get to the heart of matters, let others know, "There are two ways to do things—the right way and my way!" Your cycle is favorable for pioneering a project, for getting your points across in a unique, original way. Lucky lottery numbers: 1, 5, 6, 16, 18, 37.

Thursday, February 8 (Moon in Virgo to Libra 2:30 a.m.)
Within 24 hours, as the moon enters Libra, your popularity increases, personal magnetism soars, sex appeal is much in evidence. Check details, read the fine print. Don't be intimidated by someone who claims to know it all but actually is small-minded, and knows little or nothing.

Friday, February 9 (Moon in Libra) Diversify, ask questions, entertain someone of the opposite sex who recently complained, "You don't pay enough attention to me!" There's music in your life today. You'll be feted, and many who were indifferent will now ask to be part of your inner circle!

Saturday, February 10 (Moon in Libra to Scorpio 10:35 a.m.) Be willing to rip apart outworn machinery, to add to your wardrobe, to read between the lines, to check references and signatures. The Libra moon continues to stimulate your creative juices. Someone of the opposite sex, possibly a musician, makes his or her feelings crystal clear. Lucky lottery numbers: 4, 6, 7, 12, 14, 20.

Sunday, February 11 (Moon in Scorpio) Focus on practicality, the ability to solve a dilemma by reading, writing, teaching, and absorbing information that previously escaped notice. A project involving a change of scene is featured—a young, dynamic individual plays a significant role. This person is likely to be another Gemini with these letters or initials in his or her name: E, N, W.

Monday, February 12 (Moon in Scorpio to Sagittarius 3:58 p.m.) A domestic adjustment is part of a scenario that involves a possible change of residence or marital status. Focus on harmony, music, a willingness to make intelligent concessions. A mechanical object that has been out of order will be repaired during the early evening hours.

Tuesday, February 13 (Moon in Sagittarius) A dilemma is resolved in connection with a legal agreement, partnership, public appearances, or marital status. Hold tight to your individuality. Avoid a tendency to compromise to such an extent that your principles are blurred. Pisces and Virgo figure in today's dynamic scenario. Your lucky number is 7.

Wednesday, February 14 (Moon in Sagittarius to Capricorn 6:30 p.m.) On this Valentine's Day, appropriately, the question of romance, love, and marriage commands attention. The number 8 astrological-numerical cycle blends Saturn with your Mercury rulership; translated, serious thought must be given to a deadline, legalities, the responsibility of commitment. Lucky lottery numbers: 7, 8, 9, 12, 19, 25.

Thursday, February 15 (Moon in Capricorn) Accent universal appeal. Reject a concept that promotes a limitation censorship, or inhibitions. Overcome distance and language barriers—be aware of import-export activities. A love relationship is strong, idealistic, and provides energy and inspiration. Your lucky number is 9.

Friday, February 16 (Moon in Capricorn to Aquarius 7 p.m.) Make a fresh start, let go of outworn concepts and methods. Be independent. Don't follow others, let them follow you. Leo figures prominently, with these letters or initials in his or her name: A, S, J. You'll receive news associated with the financial status of one close to you. The possibility of an inheritance should not be ruled out.

Saturday, February 17 (Moon in Aquarius) Dig deep for information. Be aware of the latest source material. Check records, signatures, tax and license requirements. The emphasis is also on idealism, philosophy, theology, and publishing. A Cancer is involved, with these letters or initials in his or her name: B, K, T. Lucky lottery numbers: 2, 5, 11, 20, 22, 33.

Sunday, February 18 (Moon in Aquarius to Pisces 7:09 p.m.) The Aquarius new moon coincides with a fresh approach to outdated concepts, queries, and dilemmas. Highlight the unorthodox, emphasize the elements of timing and surprise. Spiritual qualities surface. You'll look better and feel better and be in touch with your inner voice.

Monday, February 19 (Moon in Pisces) Stand your ground! Within 24 hours, you'll get approval for a project that seemed lost. Focus on leadership, confidence, the ability to rise above a petty dispute that threatened to sink you in the mud of mediocrity. Taurus, Leo, and Scorpio figure in today's dynamic scenario.

Tuesday, February 20 (Moon in Pisces to Aries 8:58 p.m.) At the track: Post position special—Number 3 P.P. in second race. Pick six: 4, 3, 7, 8, 5, 5. In selecting names of potential winning horses or jockeys, watch for these letters or initials: E, N, W. Selections apply to all tracks. Virgo plays a role.

Wednesday, February 21 (Moon in Aries)   The emphasis is on familiar ground. The spotlight is also on making a domestic adjustment that could change your lifestyle, residence, or marital status. Make intelligent concessions, without being servile. There's music in your life. A gift received represents a token of affection or esteem. Lucky lottery numbers: 6, 7, 12, 33, 40, 50.

Thursday, February 22 (Moon in Aries)   Almost as if by magic, circumstances take a dramatic turn in your favor. Focus on illusion, imagination, imagery, and meditation. Make your meanings crystal clear. Find out what is expected from you and what you can expect in return for your efforts and contributions.

Friday, February 23 (Moon in Aries to Taurus 2:08 a.m.)   Be aware of a time limitation. A relationship that runs hot-and-cold requires review. The Aries moon relates to your ability to win friends and influence people, powers of persuasion, and good fortune in matters of finance or romance. A Capricorn is involved, with these letters or initials in his or her name: H, Q, Z.

Saturday, February 24 (Moon in Taurus)   You'll have good reason to celebrate. It becomes evident that you possess a unique secret—the secret of popularity. Through contacts, personal and professional, you'll obtain a wider market, a bigger audience for your product or talent. Lucky lottery numbers: 8, 11, 12, 22, 33, 50.

Sunday, February 25 (Moon in Taurus to Gemini 11:14 a.m.)   On this Sunday, with the Taurus moon, give serious thought to deep spiritual convictions. What at first seems a lost cause will boomerang in your favor. Get to the heart of matters, stress independence of thought and action. Your lucky number is 1.

Monday, February 26 (Moon in Gemini)   Your cycle is high, so trust your own judgment and intuitive intellect. Make personal appearances, wear Gemini colors—silver, green, and yellow. The emphasis is on food, shelter, security, partnership, and marriage. You'll exude subtle vibrations of sex appeal. Check your plumbing!

Tuesday, February 27 (Moon in Gemini to Cancer 11:10 p.m.)   Focus on fun and frolic, intellectual curiosity, the ability to laugh at your own foibles. Stress versatility, diversity, different modes of transportation. The spotlight also falls on advertising, publicity, publishing, and articulating your beliefs. Sagittarius and another Gemini figure prominently.

Wednesday, February 28 (Moon in Cancer)   Within 24 hours, good news is received concerning financial support. Obstacles are removed, a lost article is located, a special communication verifies your views and flashes the "green light." Taurus, Leo, and Scorpio figure in today's scenario. Lucky lottery numbers: 4, 5, 6, 20, 31, 35.

Thursday, February 29 (Moon in Cancer)   The moon position, on this Leap Year day, highlights your potential for earning more money, for locating lost articles, for love and being loved. The emphasis is on food, shelter, security, the ability to transform your home into a place of harmony, beauty, and romance. Your lucky number is 5.

MARCH 1996

Friday, March 1 (Moon in Cancer to Leo 11:47 a.m.)   On this Friday, the first day of March, you could discover ways to earn more money. The emphasis is on teaching, disseminating information, talking and writing about people and places. You'll be dealing with a Virgo who is likely to have these letters or initials in his or her name: E, N, W. Your lucky number is 5.

Saturday, March 2 (Moon in Leo)   Attention revolves around relatives and basic issues concerning security, home, and marriage. Libra plays a prominent role, and is likely to have these letters or initials in his or her name: F, O, X. There's music in your life tonight. A gift is received from one who would like to become better acquainted. Lucky lottery numbers: 2, 4, 6, 13, 14, 17.

Sunday, March 3 (Moon in Leo to Virgo 11:13 p.m.) On this Sunday, spiritual values surface, you seek answers relating to who you are and why you are here. The lunar position emphasizes intellectual curiosity, experimentation, and various modes of transportation. Pisces and Virgo play memorable roles. Your lucky number is 7.

Monday, March 4 (Moon in Virgo) You become more aware of time, deadlines, the necessity for taking responsibility for your own destiny. As a relationship intensifies, focus on a commercial enterprise, your marital status. An older person lends the benefit of his or her experience, expresses confidence in your capability.

Tuesday, March 5 (Moon in Virgo) The full moon occurs in an area of your chart associated with building material, long-standing negotiations, the sale or purchase of property. Your marital status also figures prominently, along with a possible journey and a chance to gain a wider audience for your product or talent.

Wednesday, March 6 (Moon in Virgo to Libra 8:40 a.m.) Just 24 hours ago, you decided, "I am going to take steps into the future!" Today, Wednesday, you can make a fresh start, can chart a course that will do much to decide your future. Leo plays a featured role, and has these letters or initials in his or her name: A, S, J. Lucky lottery numbers: 1, 12, 13, 18, 22, 33.

Thursday, March 7 (Moon in Libra) Mysterious happenings dominate—among other things you'll be asking, "Is this déjà vu?" The emphasis is on extrasensory perception, the ability to know in advance what is going to occur. Pay serious attention to hunches and intuitive knowledge. A Cancer figures prominently.

Friday, March 8 (Moon in Libra to Scorpio 4:05 p.m.) After a burden is lifted, you'll have reason to celebrate. You'll be vital, vigorous, and optimistic. Your popularity zooms upward, and another Gemini is in picture. You'll receive an addition to your wardrobe. The spotlight is on creative endeavors, exciting discoveries. A special person may declare feelings of love.

Saturday, March 9 (Moon in Scorpio)   Get things done in a practical way—sharpen tools, test recipes, and mend clothes. Check signatures, and read instruction manuals. A Scorpio figures prominently, and could have these letters or initials in his or her name: D, M, V. Get going on a rebuilding program of either your character or your fitness level. Lucky lottery numbers: 1, 4, 7, 12, 15, 20.

Sunday, March 10 (Moon in Scorpio to Sagittarius 9:32 p.m.)   You'll be able to talk your way into and out of anything! The emphasis is on practical issues, work methods, employment prospects, pets, dependents, and fitness. A flirtation or a chance meeting lends spice, and is likely to involve a Virgo with these letters or initials in his or her name: E, N, W.

Monday, March 11 (Moon in Sagittarius)   Legal "pressure" is removed within 24 hours. The focus continues on contracts, agreements, partnership proposals, marital status. A domestic adjustment involves beautifying your surroundings, "making up" for speaking hurtful words. Your lucky number is 6.

Tuesday, March 12 (Moon in Sagittarius)   At the track: Post position special—Number 1 P.P. in sixth race. Pick six: 4, 2, 8, 5, 3, 1. In selecting names of potential winning horses or jockeys, keep these letters or initials in mind: G, P, Y. Selections apply to all tracks. Pisces plays a featured role.

Wednesday, March 13 (Moon in Sagittarius to Capricorn 1:08 a.m.)   Deal gingerly with those in power. What appears to be a broken promise merely represents a temporary delay. A Capricorn is involved, who has a name with these letters or initials: H, Q, Z. A deadline exists. Bring order out of chaos. Lucky lottery numbers: 3, 4, 8, 13, 19, 30.

Thursday, March 14 (Moon in Capricorn)   Look beyond the immediate. Toss aside preconceived notions. Accent universal appeal. Be idealistic in love. You can overcome distance or language barriers—the key is to be susceptible to romance. Read, write, and distribute information.

Friday, March 15 (Moon in Capricorn to Aquarius 3:15 a.m.) You begin this weekend in a dynamic way, exuding confidence and sex appeal. Wear yellow and gold, make personal appearances, get to the heart of matters. A special note: Avoid heavy lifting. Insist on a fair division of property or money. Your lucky number is 1.

Saturday, March 16 (Moon in Aquarius) Focus on direction, motivation, security, taking vitamin supplements. You'll be testing recipes, sharpening tools, mending, and repairing bridges recently "burned" in moments of anger. Capricorn and Cancer are part of today's action. Lucky lottery numbers: 2, 5, 7, 11, 22, 33.

Sunday, March 17 (Moon in Aquarius to Pisces 4:50 a.m.) On this St. Patrick's Day, you'll communicate with those in foreign lands. You'll also make plans (if only subconsciously) to participate in a journey that would take you to the "Old Sod." You'll be dealing with Gemini and Sagittarius, with these letters or initials in their names: C, L, U.

Monday, March 18 (Moon in Pisces) The moon in Pisces relates to your 10th House—translated, this spotlights career, business, dealings with community or church leaders. Be aware of the necessary documents or forms to be filled out, and the possibility of hidden clauses. Taurus, Leo, and Scorpio figure prominently.

Tuesday, March 19 (Moon in Pisces to Aries 7:15 a.m.) The new moon relates to your ability to attract the attention of those considered "high-and-mighty." You do this mostly through reading, writing, communicating, and expressing ideas or concepts in a unique, creative, original way. Your lucky number is 5.

Wednesday, March 20 (Moon in Aries) A domestic adjustment is necessary—a wish comes true, you'll get what you want. The key is to realize what it is you actually need. The Aries moon relates to an area of your chart associated with your ability to win friends and influence people. Lucky lottery numbers: 6, 9, 10, 18, 37, 40.

Thursday, March 21 (Moon in Aries to Taurus 11:59 a.m.) Define terms, outline boundaries, perfect techniques, and streamline procedures. You'll have good fortune in matters of romance and finance. Your popularity rating is very high, accelerating social activities. You'll be hobnobbing with the "bigwigs." Pisces is involved.

Friday, March 22 (Moon in Taurus)   Less than 24 hours ago, you uncovered a false rumor in connection with your motivation, direction, and ultimate goal. You now are in position to do something about it. Someone in authority backs your claims, assures that you will get credit due. Your lucky number is 8.

Saturday, March 23 (Moon in Taurus to Gemini 8 p.m.)   Today brings short trips, visits, relatives, ideas which can be developed into viable concepts. Focus on appealing to your crowd. Make time for romance, dining in an out-of-way place. Aries is involved.

Sunday, March 24 (Moon in Gemini)   Within 24 hours, your cycle moves up, you'll be at the right place at a crucial moment. You'll gain friends and followers from a wide spectrum, including the low and the lowly and the high and the mighty. Leo and Aquarius are in the picture, and have these letters or initials in their names: A, S, J.

Monday, March 25 (Moon in Gemini)   The emphasis is on food, music, family relationships, the ability to earn more money. Your cycle high, your judgment and intuition prove accurate. A Cancer figures prominently, with these letters or initials in his or her name: B, K, T. The spotlight is on direction, motivation, clearing of your name from possible scandal.

Tuesday, March 26 (Moon in Gemini to Cancer 7:06 a.m.)   You have reason to celebrate—legal rights prevail, you'll receive an offer to travel and could get a plum assignment. A love relationship sparkles. You'll desire further commitment, will eventually get it, but perhaps not on this Tuesday. Sagittarius is involved.

Wednesday, March 27 (Moon in Cancer)   The moon is in your "money House," personal possessions are evaluated, and are worth more than you originally anticipated. A wonderful day for going to an auction; you

247

could obtain a genuine bargain. Check the details, read between the lines, you'll get a boxlike object that could contain valuable material. Lucky lottery numbers: 7, 8, 13, 35, 40, 49.

Thursday, March 28 (Moon in Cancer to Leo 7:37 p.m.)   At the track: Post position special—Number 3 P.P. in second race. Pick six: 1, 3, 4, 4, 5, 8. In choosing names of potential winning horses or jockeys, keep these letters or initials in mind: E, N, W. Selections apply to all tracks. Virgo is represented.

Friday, March 29 (Moon in Leo)   A visit from a relative, intending to be a surprise, could be anticipated—within 24 hours. A domestic adjustment is due. There's music in your life tonight. A gift received represents a token of affection and esteem. Libra is involved, has these letters or initials in his or her name: F, O, X.

Saturday, March 30 (Moon in Leo to Virgo 7:15 a.m.)   Accent showmanship, color coordination, mystery, intrigue, and hidden values. A love relationship is once again on track. Define terms, make your intentions crystal clear. Wear shades of green. Let others know that you see clearly and will not be the target for false rumors. Lucky lottery numbers: 1, 5, 7, 10, 25, 33.

Sunday, March 31 (Moon in Virgo)   On this Sunday, the last day of March, the Leo moon coincides with trips, visits, ideas, relatives. Focus on responsibility and spiritual values. However, there is also some confusion and chaos in need of organization. Show how well you can handle the situation. You'll deserve a promotion and will get it soon. Your lucky number is 8.

APRIL 1996

Monday, April 1 (Moon in Virgo)   You will make clear that you're nobody's fool! The emphasis is on familiar ground, property value, a decision affecting long-range prospects. Deal with a family situation involving money, decorating, remodeling, or marital status. Libra plays a key role.

Tuesday, April 2 (Moon in Virgo to Libra 4:26 p.m.) Although no one can actually fool you, it is possible you could fall victim to self-deception. Define terms, see people, places, and situations as they are, not merely as you wish they might be. A backstage maneuver must not be translated into "back stabbing."

Wednesday, April 3 (Moon in Libra) Focus on organization, a strong love relationship, the necessity for getting your priorities in order. An older person, possibly a Capricorn, lends the benefit of his or her experience. Your morale is boosted by a vote of confidence. A Cancer is also in the picture. Lucky lottery numbers: 7, 8, 9, 12, 17, 22.

Thursday, April 4 (Moon in Libra to Scorpio 10:57 p.m.) The full moon, lunar eclipse in Libra, relates to an area of your solar horoscope associated with the adventure of discovery, physical attraction, a variety of sensations, sex appeal. A relationship—exciting but controversial—will be thoroughly tested. This involves children, challenge, and significant changes.

Friday, April 5 (Moon in Scorpio) What appeared to be lost will be recovered—including an apparent lost love. Take the initiative, get to the heart of matters, be direct, stress individuality and personal values. Leo and Aquarius are involved, having these letters or initials in their names: A, S, J.

Saturday, April 6 (Moon in Scorpio) Attention revolves around the need to "fix things up" at home. The emphasis is also on music, style, flowers, and gifts. A domestic adjustment relates to your home and marital status. Make intelligent concessions. A Capricorn is involved.

Sunday, April 7 (Moon in Scorpio to Sagittarius; Daylight Saving Time Begins) On this Sunday, spiritual values blend with intellectual curiosity. Focus on humor, versatility, diversity, different modes of transportation. You'll look better, feel better, receive news from a relative in transit. You're likely to dine on foreign cuisine.

Monday, April 8 (Moon in Sagittarius) The keynote is challenge. A deadline exists; there is utter confusion in some areas. You'll be relied upon to bring order out of chaos. Capricorn and Cancer figure prominently, having these letters or initials in their names: H, Q, Z. Check your bank account figures.

Tuesday, April 9 (Moon in Sagittarius to Capricorn 7:31 a.m.) Be an "investigative reporter." This means find out why things occur. Reject superficial explanations. A clash of ideas could lead to a meaningful, lasting relationship. Virgo, Sagittarius, and another Gemini play significant roles. Your lucky number is 5.

Wednesday, April 10 (Moon in Capricorn) You learn more about the funding process, a charitable organization, your ability to get the truth from one who professes to be on your side. Fight for the right to a fair division of money and property. Hidden resources come to light. Demand to know why you were kept in the dark. Lucky lottery numbers: 4, 6, 8, 10, 12, 50.

Thursday, April 11 (Moon in Capricorn to Aquarius 8:10 a.m.) Define terms, check real estate notices, be aware of money being held in trust or escrow. Take nothing for granted, get to the heart of matters, be direct, find out exactly what is expected from you and what you can anticipate in return. Your lucky number is 7.

Friday, April 12 (Moon in Aquarius) At the track: Post position special—Number 9 P.P. in eighth race. Pick six: 3, 4, 7, 5, 5, 8. In selecting names of potential winning horses, or jockeys, keep these letters or initials in mind: H, Q, Z. Selections apply to all tracks. A Cancer is involved.

Saturday, April 13 (Moon in Aquarius to Pisces 12 noon) Stress universal appeal. Previous rules and regulations no longer apply. Focus on distance, language, a love relationship that gets warm and cold. The search for your soul mate is ever-lasting. Aries figures prominently. Lucky lottery numbers: 7, 9, 11, 17, 18, 22.

Sunday, April 14 (Moon in Pisces) Get to the heart of matters, be direct, take the initiative, and avoid heavy lifting. A new love provides inspiration, substitutes enthusiasm for lethargy. By "new," this also means you could rediscover a current love. You'll exude creative force, sensuality, sex appeal. Your lucky number is 1.

Monday, April 15 (Moon in Pisces to Aries 4:43 p.m.) Today's emphasis is on partnership, marital status, a business enterprise, newfound allies. The Pisces moon relates to promotion, production, career, your standing in the community. Those who denigrated you will now plead, "Take us in!" Capricorn plays a major role.

Tuesday, April 16 (Moon in Aries) Suddenly, friends and allies appear and state in effect, "We are your obedient servants!" It is as if a genie rose from a bottle to become your personal representative. Plainly, this might appear to be a day of magic. Your lucky number is 3.

Wednesday, April 17 (Moon in Aries to Taurus 10:05 p.m.) The new moon, solar eclipse in Aries, represents your 11th House; translated, this means you are going to get your wishes, but it is necessary to prepare, so that you are not overrun or overwhelmed. Lucky lottery numbers: 1, 2, 10, 12, 20, 33.

Thursday, April 18 (Moon in Taurus) At the track: Post position special—Number 3 P.P. in second race. Pick six: 1, 3, 4, 4, 5, 8. Hot combinations, daily doubles: 2 and 3, 4 and 8, 5 and 9. Selections apply to all tracks. Virgo, Sagittarius, and another Gemini figure in today's dynamic scenario.

Friday, April 19 (Moon in Taurus) Backstage maneuvers involve family, property, security, valuables covering both art objects and luxury items. Focus on music, income, domestic adjustment involving where you live, your lifestyle, and marital status. Libra is in the picture, with these letters or initials in his or her name: F, O, X.

Saturday, April 20 (Moon in Taurus to Gemini 4:55 a.m.) Terms will be clearly defined. You'll locate a missing object, you'll determine what you can expect as result of your efforts and contributions. A clandestine arrangement involves Pisces and Virgo likely to have these letters or initials in their names: G, P, Y. Lucky lottery numbers: 1, 8, 10, 12, 14, 44.

Sunday, April 21 (Moon in Gemini)   Your cycle takes an upward turn. People who were distant suddenly become affectionate. The spotlight falls on organization, responsibility, a deadline, a strong love relationship. Make personal appearances and wear shades of silver, green, and yellow. Your lucky number is 8.

Monday, April 22 (Moon in Gemini to Cancer 4:25 p.m.)   Go directly to the heart of matters—take the initiative. Emphasize originality and inventiveness. Be willing to engage in a clash of ideas. Trust your own judgment, heed your inner voice. Your intuitive intellect now provides accurate information. Aries is involved.

Tuesday, April 23 (Moon in Cancer)   At the track: Post position special—Number 6 P.P. in fifth race. Pick six: 4, 2, 1, 3, 6, 5. In choosing potential winning horses or jockeys, look for these letters or initials in names: A, S, J. Leo and Aquarius play important roles and will help get a new project underway.

Wednesday, April 24 (Moon in Cancer)   The emphasis is on building materials, direction, motivation, the sale or purchase of property. A business venture is likely to succeed, following an initial delay. You'll receive proposals—business and marriage. A Cancer is involved. Lucky lottery numbers: 1, 2, 4, 17, 20, 40.

Thursday, April 25 (Moon in Cancer to Leo 4:44 a.m.)   A celebration tonight relates to money from a surprise source. Possessions are evaluated; they are worth more than you originally anticipated. Additions to your wardrobe improve your image, and transform your mental attitude from gloom to frivolity. Sagittarius and another Gemini play paramount roles.

Friday, April 26 (Moon in Leo)   A roadblock is removed. You'll have more space, your popularity surges upward. The Leo moon relates to trips, visits, relatives, the necessity for taking special care in traffic. Taurus, Leo and Scorpio figure in this scenario and have these letters or initials in their names: D, M, V. Your lucky number is 4.

Saturday, April 27 (Moon in Leo to Virgo 4:49

p.m.)   The accent is on words, compositions, character analysis, a clash of ideas that could lead to a meaningful relationship. You'll exude personal magnetism and sex appeal. A Virgo says, "You seem like a different person!" Lucky lottery numbers: 1, 5, 7, 10, 17, 51.

Sunday, April 28 (Moon in Virgo)   A family gathering relates to the numerical cycle, which is 6—which translates to Venus, Taurus, and Libra. Gifts are received; the spotlight is on flowers, music, the recognition of spiritual values. The Virgo moon verifies the numerical aspect, emphasizes domestic relationships, rebuilding of structure.

Monday, April 29 (Moon in Virgo to Libra 2:27 a.m.) Focus on your home, real estate, a partnership that requires more work or investment. The emphasis is also on your lifestyle, where you live, an agreement that results in decorating and remodeling, getting rid of outworn machinery. Do repair work, test tools and recipes.

Tuesday, April 30 (Moon in Libra)   On this last day of April, what was lost will be recovered. Focus on promotion, production, the awareness of a deadline. Capricorn and Cancer play outstanding roles, have these letters or initials in their names: H, Q, Z. Remember: If you don't blow your own horn, there will be no music!

MAY 1996

Wednesday, May 1 (Moon in Libra)   Throughout May, an aura of mystery and glamour dominates. On this first day, much of these indications are magnified. Maintain secrecy, be discreet, don't tell all. The Libra moon highlights sensuality, personality, physical attraction, and sex appeal. Lucky lottery numbers: 5, 7, 12, 14, 19, 50.

Thursday, May 2 (Moon in Libra to Scorpio 8:43 a.m.)   A lost article is replaced. You get credit previously withheld. A relationship is restored. You'll have more responsibility and greater financial reward. Someone of the opposite sex confides, "I'm finding it difficult to keep my hands off you!" A Cancer is involved.

Friday, May 3 (Moon in Scorpio)   The emphasis is on

universal appeal, the ability to overcome distance and language barriers. The full Scorpio moon coincides with completion of work, the ability to attract valuable allies. Focus on passion, creativity, competitiveness, style, and panache. Aries and Libra are in the picture.

Saturday, May 4 (Moon in Scorpio to Sagittarius 12:05 p.m.) The darker areas of your life receive more light. Focus on hidden resources, revelations concerning money and how it got that way. Partners are involved, including business or marriage. On this Saturday night, involvement with a "new love" is featured. Lucky lottery numbers: 8, 9, 12, 18, 22, 33.

Sunday, May 5 (Moon in Sagittarius) The emphasis is on family relationships, decisions affecting where you live, your lifestyle, structure, design, marriage. A legal agreement requires scrutiny. Play the waiting game; refuse to be cajoled into making a snap decision. A Capricorn figures prominently.

Monday, May 6 (Moon in Sagittarius to Capricorn 1:54 p.m.) Diversify, accent humor. Blend wisdom with your ability to laugh at your own foibles. The lunar emphasis is on how you look to the world and how the world appears to you. Obviously, gaining the proper perspective is of the utmost importance. Another Gemini plays a paramount role. Your lucky number is 3.

Tuesday, May 7 (Moon in Capricorn) What was in disarray will fall into place, as iron filings respond to a giant magnet. Stand your ground, read between the lines. Check facts and figures, as well as source material. Insist on a division of property. Get legal counsel. An inheritance could figure in today's scenario.

Wednesday, May 8 (Moon in Capricorn to Aquarius 3:39 p.m.) You get more space, your words command attention and admiration. What was hidden will be revealed—to your advantage. Be ready for change, challenge, children, variety, processing written material. Virgo, Sagittarius, and another Gemini play significant roles. Lucky lottery numbers: 5, 10, 12, 13, 33, 50.

Thursday, May 9 (Moon in Aquarius)   The focus is on a domestic adjustment. A long-distance communication relates to a unique invitation that involves a journey. The lunar emphasis is on philosophy, theology, higher education. Refuse to be satisfied with the status quo—imprint your own style. There's music in your life tonight. Taurus and Libra are involved.

Friday, May 10 (Moon in Aquarius to Pisces 6:29 p.m.)   On this Friday, you might be musing, "Long ago and far away . . ." The key is to realize that what seemed "far away" could be practically at your doorstep. Spiritual values surface, psychic capabilities multiply. You'll suddenly know where to go and what to do. Pisces is involved.

Saturday, May 11 (Moon in Pisces)   Attention revolves around production, promotion, time limitation, involvement in a situation that demands timing and discipline. Your key word is "leadership." People close to you will rely upon your judgment, integrity, and intuitive intellect. Lucky lottery numbers: 8, 12, 13, 18, 20, 33.

Sunday, May 12 (Moon in Pisces to Aries 11 p.m.)   This Sunday might seem as if it was "Friday" repeating itself—mysterious, shades of déjà vu. Focus on distance, language, foreign cuisine, the ability to shake off a losing proposition. The search for a soul mate might be nearing an end. Aries and Libra are involved.

Monday, May 13 (Moon in Aries)   Within 24 hours, many of your hopes and wishes could become realities. You'll influence people, win allies, blend humor with wisdom. On this day, Monday, you'll be inspired to make a fresh start in a different direction. Focus on initiative, independence, creativity, and sex appeal.

Tuesday, May 14 (Moon in Aries)   Confidential information obtained relates to your home, property, a business venture. The spotlight is on partnership, cooperative efforts, public relations, your marital status. Cancer and Capricorn figure prominently, and could have these letters or initials in their names: B, K, T. Your lucky number is 2.

Wednesday, May 15 (Moon in Aries to Taurus 5:25 p.m.) On this Wednesday, you might be regarded as a "social lion." People vie to wine and dine you. The spotlight is on celebration, versatility, humor, published material. Sagittarius and another Gemini play leading roles, with these letters or initials in their names: C, L, U. Lucky lottery numbers: 3, 4, 6, 9, 16, 30.

Thursday, May 16 (Moon in Taurus) Stand your ground! The Taurus moon relates to institutions, hospitals, theaters, galleries, communication with someone temporarily in cramped quarters. Study reference material, build on a solid base, get the networking process underway with the cooperation of a Scorpio.

Friday, May 17 (Moon in Taurus to Gemini 1:48 p.m.) The new moon position highlights drama, a secret meeting, the need to be discreet. The focus is also on a clash of ideas, special investigation, the necessity for taking notes. Keeping a diary will prove valuable in any future business or law dispute. A Virgo figures prominently.

Saturday, May 18 (Moon in Gemini) Attention revolves around initiative, independence, the ability to get to the heart of matters relating to domestic affairs. Today's scenario features music, harmony, luxury items, and large household products. The moon in your sign coincides with good fortune in finance or romance. Lucky lottery numbers: 5, 8, 13, 22, 40, 50.

Sunday, May 19 (Moon in Gemini) On this Sunday, it is appropriate that your spiritual values surface—you'll see people in a new light, and many will perceive you as a new person. The moon in your sign, plus the number 7 astrological-numerical cycle, makes this one of your most memorable times. Pisces is involved.

Monday, May 20 (Moon in Gemini to Cancer 12:16 a.m.) Within 24 hours, you could hit the financial jackpot! The cycle is high, your intuitive intellect is on target. You'll meet a deadline. A love relationship is intense, controversial, and durable. Capricorn is involved, with these letters or initials in his or her name: H, Q, Z. Your lucky number is 8.

Tuesday, May 21 (Moon in Cancer)   At the track: Post position special—Number 8 P.P. in first race. Pick six: 8, 4, 1, 3, 6, 9. In choosing potential winning horses or jockeys, watch for these letters or initials in names: I and R. Selections apply to all tracks. Aries and Libra figure in today's exciting scenario.

Wednesday, May 22 (Moon in Cancer to Leo 12:28 p.m.)   An excellent day for a fresh start, maintaining individuality, imprinting style, welcoming new experience and love. You'll be dealing with a Leo, who is likely to have these letters or initials in his or her name: A, S, J. An Aquarian also plays a role. Lucky lottery numbers: 1, 2, 4, 20, 38, 40.

Thursday, May 23 (Moon in Leo)   Be analytical, welcome the opportunity to revive a relationship with a family member recently returned from a trip. Focus also on direction, motivation, making an unusual public appearance, during which you act as spokesperson for someone. A Cancer is involved.

Friday, May 24 (Moon in Leo)   Protect yourself in close quarters—an obsequious individual would like you to fail. Forces are scattered; strive to bring order out of a chaotic situation. Your popularity increases. New apparel lifts your spirits. Sagittarius and another Gemini figure in today's scenario. Your lucky number is 3.

Saturday, May 25 (Moon in Leo to Virgo 12:58 a.m.) Within 24 hours, you'll be on more solid ground, property will be evaluated, your marital status clarified. A relative says, "I feel you now are getting your life in order!" You'll be dealing with Taurus and Scorpio, with these letters or initials in their names: D, M, V. Lucky lottery numbers: 1, 4, 5, 10, 13, 40.

Sunday, May 26 (Moon in Virgo)   Read, write, teach, and disseminate information. Focus on home, family, the ability to transform obstacles into stepping-stones. A Taurus exerts considerable influence, has these letters or initials in his or her name: E, N, W. A backstage maneuver takes place. Surprisingly, you benefit as a result.

Monday, May 27 (Moon in Virgo to Libra 11:34 a.m.)   Attention revolves around music, harmony, excellent cuisine, a domestic adjustment involving your lifestyle or marital status. The Virgo moon coincides with fixing things at home, getting rid of superfluous material, reviewing the fine print in a legal agreement. Your lucky number is 6.

Tuesday, May 28 (Moon in Libra)   Terms will be defined. You'll know what is expected of you and what you can anticipate in return. The Libra moon coincides with vitality, personal magnetism, physical attraction, and sex appeal. Caution: Don't start anything you don't expect to finish! Pisces is involved.

Wednesday, May 29 (Moon in Libra to Scorpio 6:30 p.m.)   Be aware of a deadline. Get payments in the mail relating to your mortgage or automobile insurance. You'll be dealing with a Capricorn who is likely to have these letters or initials in his or her name: H, Q, Z. A reward is at the end of the rainbow! Lucky lottery numbers: 6, 7, 11, 29, 40, 51.

Thursday, May 30 (Moon in Scorpio)   At the track: Post position special—Number 8 P.P. in first race. Pick six: 8, 8, 1, 1, 7, 8. Older horses tend to win; veteran jockeys will have a field day. Keep these letters or initials in mind when choosing potential winners: H, Q, Z. Selections apply to all tracks.

Friday, May 31 (Moon in Scorpio to Sagittarius 9:43 p.m.)   On this last day of May, you'll feel revitalized. A recent break from tradition proved worthwhile and profitable. Work methods improve. You'll inspire others to live up to their potential. Leo and Aquarius help you fulfill your destiny. Your lucky number is 1.

JUNE 1996

Saturday, June 1 (Moon in Sagittarius)   On this Saturday, the full moon in Sagittarius relates to public appearances, legal agreement, partnership, and marital status. As June gets underway, vitality returns, enthusiasm replaces boredom. Capricorn and Cancer play important roles, have these letters or initials in their names: H, Q, Z. Lucky lottery numbers: 6, 8, 12, 14, 35, 40.

Sunday, June 2 (Moon in Sagittarius to Capricorn 10:29 p.m.)   Spiritual values surge forward—extend your influence far and wide. Previous rules and regulations no longer apply. You're free to travel, to love, to make inquiries about a possible change of address. The search for your soul mate becomes more than symbolic.

Monday, June 3 (Moon in Capricorn)   Within 24 hours, financial arrangements will be made, you'll feel more secure as a result. Defy the odds, imprint your own style, stress independence of thought and action. Leo plays a dramatic role, and is likely to have these letters or initials in his or her name: A, S, J. Your lucky number is 1.

Tuesday, June 4 (Moon in Capricorn to Aquarius 10:45 p.m.)   Insist on additional information relating to tax or license requirements. Focus on investment, the money position of one close to you, including your partner or mate. Read between the lines, check references and signatures. Taurus and Scorpio figure in today's scenario.

Wednesday, June 5 (Moon in Aquarius)   Diversify, keep your options open, check the invitation list of a social affair. A gift received during the late afternoon adds to your wardrobe, improves your image. A Sagittarian provides information previously kept secret. Another Gemini also plays an active role. Lucky lottery numbers: 3, 5, 12, 36, 40, 45.

Thursday, June 6 (Moon in Aquarius)   At the track: Post position special—Number 4 P.P. in fourth race. Pick six: 1, 2, 4, 5, 6, 8. In selecting potential winning horses or jockeys, watch for names with these letters or initials: D, M, V. Selections apply to all tracks. Scorpio plays a role.

Friday, June 7 (Moon in Aquarius to Pisces 12:19 a.m.)   Attention revolves around change, travel, a variety of sensations and experiences. Gain is achieved as result of the written word—get this message across. Protect formats, concepts, and ideas. A chance meeting or blind date could lead to a lasting relationship. Your lucky number is 5.

Saturday, June 8 (Moon in Pisces)   The emphasis is on painting, music, remodeling. An important domestic adjustment could involve your lifestyle, where you live, your marital status. You'll be dealing with a Pisces likely to have these letters or initials in his or her name: F, O, X. Lucky lottery numbers: 6, 12, 18, 22, 33.

Sunday, June 9 (Moon in Pisces to Aries 4:23 a.m.)   The emphasis is on spirituality, psychic impressions, contacts with people you respect and who respect you so much so that you could be told, "Without you there is not much of anything!" Keep your proper perspective. Blend humor with profundity. Virgo is involved.

Monday, June 10 (Moon in Aries)   You could be humming, "Everything is going my way!" Today's Aries moon relates to your powers of persuasion, winning friends and influencing people. Good fortune exists in matters of romance and finance. You'll help a teacher, or someone in authority, to earn additional credits or funds.

Tuesday, June 11 (Moon in Aries to Taurus 11:11 a.m.) Reach beyond previous restrictions. Be vulnerable to love. Know with certainty that what you imagine can become real. Investigate the possibility of participation in import-export activities. A significant communication will be received from someone in a foreign land.

Wednesday, June 12 (Moon in Taurus)   Make a fresh start, take the initiative in getting to the heart of matters. Maintain your self-esteem. Make this declaration: "When you see me, you are looking at the very best!" Leo and Aquarius figure in today's dynamic scenario.

Thursday, June 13 (Moon in Taurus to Gemini 8:16 p.m.)   At the track: Post position special—Number 6 P.P. in fifth race. Pick six: 1, 5, 3, 2, 6, 7. In selecting potential winning horses or jockeys, watch for these letters or initials in names: B, K, T. Capricorn and Cancer figure in this exciting scenario.

Friday, June 14 (Moon in Gemini)   Within 24 hours, your cycle moves up. You'll be at the right place. You'll gain added recognition. You'll rewrite the script and be in charge of your own fate and destiny. The emphasis today is on your popularity, wardrobe, and body image, your ability to make people laugh, even through their tears.

Saturday, June 15 (Moon in Gemini)   The moon in your sign coincides with initiative, the ability to be at the right place at the right time. Imprint your own style, make personal appearances, and wear shades of silver, green, and yellow. Circumstances take a turn in your favor. Your goal is closer than you expected. Lucky lottery numbers: 3, 7, 11, 13, 22, 50.

Sunday, June 16 (Moon in Gemini to Cancer 7:08 a.m.)   The new moon in Gemini coincides with your personality and showmanship. You can attract a wider audience for your product or talent. The numerical cycle relates to your ruling planet Mercury; this means reading, writing, teaching, learning, and disseminating information. Sagittarius is involved.

Monday, June 17 (Moon in Cancer)   There is music in your life tonight. You'll locate an object that was lost, missing, or stolen. The moon in your 2nd House means a chance for more money, for getting a favorable estimate on your home or property. A business partnership or marriage or both figure in today's scenario.

Tuesday, June 18 (Moon in Cancer to Leo 7:22 p.m.)   On this Tuesday you'll hear sound of your inner voice. You might receive an answer to the eternal question "Why am I here?" The Cancer moon is associated with food, security, income, locating your lost articles, marital status. Pisces and Virgo play outstanding roles. Your lucky number is 7.

Wednesday, June 19 (Moon in Leo)   Be aware of a time limitation, discuss plans with a relative, and keep your options open. It might be necessary to make a short trip in order to locate a needed document. Capricorn and Cancer figure in this scenario. Lucky lottery numbers: 1, 5, 8, 10, 16, 50.

Thursday, June 20 (Moon in Leo)   Those who thought they could fool you will be in for a rude awakening. A communication received from far away verifies your views, lets you know what is going on and why. You'll be rid of a foolish obligation and be free to love, travel, and create.

Friday, June 21 (Moon in Leo to Virgo 8:07 a.m.) Within 24 hours, attention will revolve around your home, property, long-standing negotiations, and marital status. On this Friday, imprint your style, make a fresh start, be vulnerable to love. A special note: avoid heavy lifting! Leo and Aquarius play significant roles.

Saturday, June 22 (Moon in Virgo)   The spotlight is on where you live, your lifestyle, a business or marriage partner. Insist on fair play in connection with the division of property. A Cancer helps obtain funding, opening new doors of opportunity. Overcome the temptation to look back—move forward. Lucky lottery numbers: 2, 7, 11, 13, 29, 40.

Sunday, June 23 (Moon in Virgo to Libra 7:37 p.m.)   Attempting to reignite an old flame could cause embarrassment or loss. The focus is on spirituality, foreign lands, The adventure of discovery. Avoid getting mired down in the past. Keep these words in mind: "That was then, this is now!" Another Gemini is in the picture.

Monday, June 24 (Moon in Libra)   Tear down, in order to rebuild. The Libra moon emphasizes creativity, style, change, travel, a variety of sensations and experiences. Read and write, disseminate information, stick to your own style. Taurus and Scorpio figure in today's scenario. Your lucky number is 4.

Tuesday, June 25 (Moon in Libra)   You'll be musing, "This is one of my most active, unusual Tuesdays!" Focus in style, panache, change, travel, variety, sensuality, and sex appeal. Virgo, Sagittarius, and another Gemini are in the picture, and have these letters or initials in their names: E, N, W. Your lucky number is 5.

Wednesday, June 26 (Moon in Libra to Scorpio 3:54 a.m.)   On this Wednesday, attention revolves around your home, decoration, remodeling, household products, music, and marital status. The 5th House moon in Libra coincides with your ability to draw to you fascinating, creative people. You might be saying, "I have the best of everything!" Lucky lottery numbers: 5, 6, 7, 12, 30, 50.

Thursday, June 27 (Moon in Scorpio)   The key word—"reflections." The emphasis is on inner feelings. The Scorpio moon tells of basic issues, a question regarding ordinarily routine work, and people. The number 7 astrological-numerical cycle (Neptune) coincides with your Mercury significator, and this means blending of reasoning powers with imagery and extrasensory perception.

Friday, June 28 (Moon in Scorpio to Sagittarius 8:01 a.m.)   At the track: Post position special—Number 8 P.P. in ninth race. Pick six: 8, 5, 1, 3, 2, 7. In choosing names of potential winning horses or jockeys, watch for these letters or initials: H, Q, Z. Selections apply to all tracks. Capricorn is represented.

Saturday, June 29 (Moon in Sagittarius)   Lucky lottery numbers: 3, 4, 9, 19, 22, 30. Stress universal appeal, refuse to be limited by previous rules or regulations. Today, you write your own script, take charge of your own fate or destiny. Aries is in the picture, with these letters or initials in his or her name: I and R.

Sunday, June 30 (Moon in Sagittarius to Capricorn 8:47 a.m.)   The emphasis is on independence, style, creativity, the recognition of spiritual values. The Sagittarius moon highlights your reputation, public image, legal rights, partnership, and marriage. Leo and Aquarius figure in today's scenario, and have these letters or initials in their names: A, S, J. Your lucky number is 1.

JULY 1996

Monday, July 1 (Moon in Capricorn)   You begin one of your most memorable months of 1996. The full Capricorn moon relates to inheritance, information regarding hidden resources, a lost love. Focus on universal appeal, travel, revival of interest in a project long dormant. Your lucky number is 9.

Tuesday, July 2 (Moon in Capricorn to Aquarius 8:05 a.m.)   You'll be saying, "This is more like it!" You discover resources previously hidden. A new love could be on the horizon. You'll imprint your own style and take charge of your destiny. Leo and Aquarius play roles, and are likely to have these letters or initials in their names: A, S, J.

Wednesday, July 3 (Moon in Aquarius)   The family structure is featured. Long-distance news assures you that a loved one is safe, possibly in a foreign land. Others will be made to realize you are willing to fight when the cause is right. A Cancer is involved. Lucky lottery numbers: 2, 4, 11, 20, 22, 33.

Thursday, July 4 (Moon in Aquarius to Pisces 8:07 a.m.)   On this holiday, you'll be flattered by many who are surprised by your knowledge of history. Focus on power, authority, the enjoyment of the Fourth of July celebration. Another Gemini is in the picture and could have these letters or initials in his or her name: C, L, U. Your lucky number is 3.

Friday, July 5 (Moon in Pisces)   Someone who once betrayed you will again seek your favor. Today's lunar position highlights leadership, vindication, your standing in the community. Taurus, Leo, and Scorpio are involved, with these letters or initials in their names: D, M, V. You'll have luck with number 4.

Saturday, July 6 (Moon in Pisces to Aries 10:42 a.m.)   As a Gemini, you'll feel in tune with this Saturday—for you, it's number 5, a number associated with Mercury. That is "your planet." You'll disseminate information and be complimented on your humor and charm. Lucky lottery numbers: 3, 15, 22, 35, 41, 45.

Sunday, July 7 (Moon in Aries)   A gift received during the early evening represents a token of affection or esteem. Psychic impressions prove valid. A Pisces plays an outstanding role in your plans. Look for these letters or initials in his or her name: G, P, Y. Make a domestic adjustment, including decorating, remodeling, and color coordination.

Monday, July 8 (Moon in Aries to Taurus 4:43 p.m.) Those who claimed you were "one step behind" will be in for a rude awakening. You not only catch up, you move far ahead. An apparent loss boomerangs in your favor. Define terms, perfect techniques, and streamline procedures. Don't wait for others to make up their minds—be a self-starter.

Tuesday, July 9 (Moon in Taurus) A Capricorn in a position of authority lets you in on a secret. Maintain your equilibrium, utilize data so generously provided. Realize you are going to the top despite detractors. Focus on production, promotion, the ability to perceive future trends. Your lucky number is 8.

Wednesday, July 10 (Moon in Taurus) Accent universal appeal, don't be limited by previous rules or regulations. Break free from a situation or relationship that is purely negative. Aries and Libra are on your side, and have these letters or initials in their names: I and R. A lost love is found. Lucky lottery numbers: 2, 6, 9, 12, 18, 40.

Thursday, July 11 (Moon in Taurus to Gemini 1:52 a.m.) Make a fresh start. Your cycle moves up, and you'll be at the right place at a crucial moment. Take the initiative, get to the heart of matters. Spotlight originality, pioneering spirit, the courage of your convictions. A Leo figures prominently, with these letters or initials in his or her name: A, S, J.

Friday, July 12 (Moon in Gemini) At the track: Post position special—Number 6 P.P. in fifth race. Pick six: 4, 2, 1, 1, 6, 5. In choosing names of potential winning horses or jockeys, be alert for these letters or initials: F, O, X. Selections apply to all tracks. A Cancer is involved.

Saturday, July 13 (Moon in Gemini to Cancer 1:08 p.m.) Make personal appearances. Start a dialogue with a Sagittarian who does not always agree, but who has your best interests at heart. Stress personality, ask questions, be analytical, and allow yourself to be vulnerable to love. Accent diversity. Lucky lottery numbers: 3, 5, 12, 18, 30, 50.

Sunday, July 14 (Moon in Cancer) Today's lunar position highlights personal possessions, basic values, the ability to locate items that are lost, missing, or stolen. Circumstances turn in your favor. Money comes from unusual source. You'll be more confident and secure. You'll look and feel fit. Scorpio is involved.

Monday, July 15 (Moon in Cancer)   The new moon in your "money House" could mean you hit the financial jackpot. A Cancer figures prominently. Look for these letters or initials in his or her name: E, N, W. Be selective, choose quality over quantity. You'll profit from the written word. Your lucky number is 5.

Tuesday, July 16 (Moon in Cancer to Leo 1:31 a.m.) Within 24 hours, you'll have a dialogue with a Leo whose ideas prove startling but productive. A short trip could be on your agenda. You'll be stimulated, your creative juices stir. Tonight, you get rid of a roadblock and be free from the prison of preconceived notions. Your lucky number is 6.

Wednesday, July 17 (Moon in Leo)   You might be inspired to quote another Gemini, Sir Arthur Conan Doyle, who declared, "The day a man's mind closes is the day of his mental death!" Define terms, give full play to your intellectual curiosity and extrasensory preception. Lucky lottery numbers: 3, 7, 16, 18, 45, 51.

Thursday, July 18 (Moon in Leo to Virgo 2:17 p.m.)   You have things your own way—the key is to seek the answer to "What is my way?" The emphasis is on added responsibility, the pressure of a deadline, the need to bring order out of chaos. Capricorn and Cancer figure in today's exciting action. Your lucky number is 8.

Friday, July 19 (Moon in Virgo)   The completion of "building project" is clearly indicated. What had been moribund will be revitalized. Highlight universal appeal, broaden areas of interest, be willing to love and be loved. Aries plays a dominant role, and can be identified by these letters or initials in his or her name: I and R.

Saturday, July 20 (Moon in Virgo)   Take the initiative in getting to the heart of matters. Imprint your style; don't follow others, let them follow you. The Virgo moon highlights homes, security, rebuilding process, and marital status. Leo and Aquarius play outstanding roles. Lucky lottery numbers: 1, 5, 6, 7, 17, 50.

Sunday, July 21 (Moon in Virgo to Libra 2:14 a.m.) A family gathering brings desired results. There's a restoration of harmony and frank discussions relation to financial security. Within 24 hours, the moon position will encourage change, children, challenge, variety, and physical attraction. On this Sunday evening gourmet dining will be featured.

Monday, July 22 (Moon in Libra) You might be asking, "Why couldn't every day be this way?" Number 3 of one astrological-numerical cycle blends with the Libra moon, which coincides with a physical attraction, vitality, an exciting love relationship. Social activities are due to accelerate. Your popularity rating soars upward.

Tuesday, July 23 (Moon in Libra to Scorpio 11:43 a.m.) On this Tuesday you get things done. Taurus and Scorpio individuals prove helpful and could have these letters or initials in their names: D, M, V. The moon position stresses creativity, style, panache, and sex appeal. Musical notes are part of today's unusual scenario.

Wednesday, July 24 (Moon in Scorpio) Read and write, disseminate information, welcome a clash of ideas with another Gemini who can be identified by these letters or initials in his or her name: E, N, W. It is important to analyze character and to study handwriting and signatures. Lucky lottery numbers: 4, 5, 8, 12, 13, 22.

Thursday, July 25 (Moon in Scorpio to Sagittarius 5:24 p.m.) Family finances could occupy more than usual attention. Stress diplomacy. Realize you cannot get your way by attempting to force issues. Conversely, you win a major point via a diplomatic approach. Taurus, Libra, and Scorpio play "interesting" roles.

Friday, July 26 (Moon in Sagittarius) Decisions reached 24 hours ago relating to property, home, and finances could be crystallized by tonight. Define terms, look beyond the immediate, check plumbing and toilet facilities. Pisces and Virgo are in the picture, with these letters or initials in their names: G, P, Y.

Saturday, July 27 (*Moon in Sagittarius to Capricorn 7:17 p.m.*) You'll bring order out of chaos. A love relationship is controversial, but durable. Capricorn and Cancer play major roles, with these letters or initials in their names: H, Q, Z. Property values "slide" up and down in accordance with today's volatile market. Lucky lottery numbers: 8, 9, 12, 38, 40, 50.

Sunday, July 28 (*Moon in Capricorn*) Your psychic faculties surface—you'll "see" tomorrow. Long-range projects are reactivated, which relate to import-export activities. By letting go of a losing proposition, situation, or relationship, you open the door to new, more exciting experiences or relationships. Your lucky number is 9.

Monday, July 29 (*Moon in Capricorn to Aquarius 6:47 p.m.*) The answer to a question: It is time for a fresh start in a new direction, time to be more independent in thought and action. Dig deep for information, check recipes and signatures. There is a strong possibility that inheritance will play a major role. Leo is represented.

Tuesday, July 30 (*Moon in Aquarius*) The full moon (blue moon) in Aquarius represents a journey, education, idealism in connection with a romance; it also means the revival of a love affair. Stand tall, and don't permit others to take you for granted. Get your message across via advertising or publishing. A creative project could become a profitable enterprise.

Wednesday, July 31 (*Moon in Aquarius to Pisces 6 p.m.*) New clothes help improve your image—you look good, fit, and are able to blend humor with profundity. Accent versatility, exprimentation, communication, and different modes of transportation. Sagittarius and another Gemini figure prominently. Lucky lottery numbers: 3, 11, 18, 22, 36, 51.

AUGUST 1996

Thursday, August 1 (*Moon in Pisces*) On this first day of August, you dispose of challenges and roadblocks with panache, grace, and style. Accent independence, have the courage of your convictions. Today's Pisces moon highlights your career and business activities. You could have a successful promotion. Leo will play a paramount role.

Friday, August 2 (Moon in Pisces to Aries 7:05 p.m.) Puzzle pieces fall into place. You get an inside view of business prospects, property value, as one result of a relationship. Gourmet dining is on tap tonight, A Cancer figures prominently. You'll be told, "It is so much fun to be with you!" Your lucky number is 2.

Saturday, August 3 (Moon in Aries) Focus on diversity, versatility, humor, a reason for celebration. Today's Aries moon coincides with your ability to win friends, influence people, to make dreams come true in a dramatic way. Good fortune is indicated in finance and romance. Lucky lottery numbers: 1, 3, 10, 19, 40, 50.

Sunday, August 4 (Moon in Aries to Taurus 11:33 p.m.) Someone who seemed flighty expresses the desire to settle down. Revise, review, check your facts and figures. Get familiar with tax and license requirements. Romance could be "too hot not to cool down." You're on solid ground, so don't be dismayed by one who knows the price of everything, the value of nothing.

Monday, August 5 (Moon in Taurus) On this Monday, creative juices stir—self-expression is important. You'll read and write and communicate and perhaps prepare an itinerary relating to advertising and publishing. Virgo, Sagittarius, and another Gemini play dominant roles.

Tuesday, August 6 (Moon in Taurus) Focus on music, harmony, lifestyle, domestic adjustment, receipt of flowers or gifts representing tokens of affection. Your financial picture brightens. The sale or purchase of art objects and luxury items is featured. A secret meeting tonight involves your income potential. Taurus is represented.

Wednesday, August 7 (Moon in Taurus to Gemini 7:49 a.m.) Steer clear of a get-rich-quick scheme. Pisces and Virgo play interesting roles, and are likely to have these letters or initials in their names: G, P, Y. Your cycle is high, the moon in your sign coincides with initiative and sex appeal. Lucky lottery numbers: 6, 7, 9, 16, 18, 22.

Thursday, August 8 (Moon in Gemini)   A power play today! An apparent loss boomerangs in your favor. Some will comment, "You seem to have the Midas touch!" The Gemini moon highlights your personality, gregariousness, charm, and intellect. Deal with an older person who is willing to share the benefit of his or her experience. A Cancer is involved.

Friday, August 9 (Moon in Gemini to Cancer 6:57 p.m.)   Stress universal appeal, and investigate markets for products and talents. Within 24 hours, you'll be more independent, you'll make a fresh start, and you'll settle questions about personal relationships. Tonight open lines of communication, let others be aware of your true feelings.

Saturday, August 10 (Moon in Cancer)   Take a new approach to marketing, advertising, and promotion. You could have fantastic results. Emphasize originality and innovativeness. Be willing to go the extra mile. Leo plays a major role. Look for these letters or initials in his or her name: A, S, J. Lucky lottery numbers: 1, 5, 10, 12, 18, 50.

Sunday, August 11 (Moon in Cancer)   On this Sunday, the puzzle pieces fall into place. A family member relents, declares, "I am going to cooperate, I want to be an integral part of this plan!" A lost article will be located. The manner in which it is found will be a cause for a humorous reaction.

Monday, August 12 (Moon in Cancer to Leo 7:29 a.m.) Release yourself from an obligation that was foolish to assume in the first place. Let go of a losing proposition. Free yourself from a relationship that drains you emotionally and financially. If you do this, you'll have reason to celebrate. Sagittarius and another Gemini are represented.

Tuesday, August 13 (Moon in Leo)   Be willing to revise, review, and remodel, to present a product in a different light. Today's Leo moon highlights showmanship, music, and entertainment. Be willing to let others test claims. A short trip involves a relative. Accent diversity and versatility. Scorpio is involved.

Wednesday, August 14 (Moon in Leo to Virgo 8 p.m.)   A new deal involves trips, visits, and relatives who want to cooperate, but "just can't find the time." Accent self-reliance. Know once again that if you want something done, ask a busy person. A Sagittarian is involved. Lucky lottery numbers: 1, 2, 5, 13, 20, 37.

Thursday, August 15 (Moon in Virgo)   At the track: Post position special—Number 6 P.P. in fifth race. Pick six: 4, 2, 1, 5, 6, 7. In choosing potential winning horses or jockeys, check for these letters or initials in names: F, O, X. Selections apply to all tracks. Libra plays a role.

Friday, August 16 (Moon in Virgo)   The emphasis is on real estate, definition of terms, large household products. It's important to see people and places as they are, not merely as you wish they might be. A Pisces plays a significant role. Look for these letters or initials in his or her name: G, P, Y. Your lucky number is 7.

Saturday, August 17 (Moon in Virgo to Libra 7:55 a.m.)   Get rid of dead wood! The emphasis is on production, promotion, selectivity, and discrimination. Insist on the best, despite those who might whine about making an extra effort. You'll have more responsibility, a chance to hit the financial jackpot. Lucky lottery numbers: 2, 4, 5, 8, 34, 48.

Sunday, August 18 (Moon in Libra)   On this Sunday, spiritual values surge forward. Today's Libra moon highlights creativity, style, integrity, physical attraction, the ability to provide inspiration. Music and harmony are featured. A domestic adjustment involves children, change, challenge, and variety. Aries is represented.

Monday, August 19 (Moon in Libra to Scorpio 5:50 p.m.)   Make a fresh start, imprint your own style, permit yourself to be vulnerable to love. You'll attract dynamic, fascinating persons, very likely Leo, Aquarius, and Libra, who have these letters or initials in their names: A, S, J. Your lucky number is 1.

Tuesday, August 20 (Moon in Scorpio)   At the track: Post position special—Number 6 P.P. in fifth race. Pick six: 8, 5, 3, 1, 6, 4. Watch for these letters or initials in names of horses or jockeys: F, O, X. Selections apply to all tracks. Your marital status and a possible change of residence dominates today's scenario.

Wednesday, August 21 (Moon in Scorpio)   You'll have more working room. The elements of timing and surprise prove beneficial. Your popularity is on the rise. You could win on the athletic field or in the political arena. Sagittarius, another Gemini figure in today's scenario. Lucky lottery numbers: 3, 4, 8, 12, 18, 40.

Thursday, August 22 (Moon in Scorpio to Sagittarius 12:48 a.m.)   Within 24 hours, you'll receive more information about legal rights or permissions. Today, check facts, figures, and accounting procedures. You'll be dealing with Taurus and Scorpio, who could have these letters or initials in their names: D, M, V. Your lucky number is 4.

Friday, August 23 (Moon in Sagittarius)   Focus on reading, publishing, writing, and distribution. Someone of the opposite sex asserts, "You seem different today, very attractive, I can hardly keep my hands off you!" Be analytical, keep compliments in proper perspective. Protect yourself where signatures are concerned.

Saturday, August 24 (Moon in Sagittarius to Capricorn 4:22 a.m.)   A domestic adjustment could include where you live, your lifestyle, decorating, remodeling, income, and marital status. There's music in your life tonight—you'll feel very good because someone you admire seeks to wine and dine you. Lucky lottery numbers: 1, 3, 6, 9, 30, 50.

Sunday, August 25 (Moon in Capricorn)   You'll be told, "Just being with you is an adventure!" Focus on mystery, intrigue, glamour, spirituality. Keep in mind that discretion is the better part of valor. This means don't tell all, despite urgings from those only in a position to "hold your coat" if a battle royal results.

Monday, August 26 (Moon in Capricorn to Aquarius 5:10 a.m.)   The emphasis on medical prescriptions, organization, responsibility, the necessity for meeting a deadline. Attention also revolves around the financial status of someone who would be your partner or mate. Watch for information concerning a possible inheritance. A Capricorn is involved.

Tuesday, August 27 (Moon in Aquarius)   All points indicate education, spirituality, travel, expansion of horizons. You'll be engaged in philosophy, theology, New Age subjects. Overcome distance and language barriers. Be with people who speak more than one language, who are open-minded. Libra is represented.

Wednesday, August 28 (Moon in Aquarius to Pisces 4:49 a.m.)   The full moon in Aquarius relates to your ability to reach beyond previous limitations. Focus on the unusual, the metaphysical, mantic arts and sciences that include astrology and numerology. Today's full moon also highlights romance, creativity, the courage of your convictions. Lucky lottery numbers: 1, 4, 11, 13, 20, 22.

Thursday, August 29 (Moon in Pisces)   A family member surprises you, responds in a way to make you ponder, "Am I doing the right thing? Maybe I should wait." Study facts and figures, and refuse to be deterred by someone with a faint heart who is a natural naysayer. Cancer and Capricorn figure in this scenario.

Friday, August 30 (Moon in Pisces to Aries 5:16 a.m.) Within 24 hours, you'll gain a definite advantage over your competitors. You are on brink of winning friends among the high and mighty, of closing a deal successfully. For now, highlight diversity and versatility. Use different modes of transportation. Your lucky number is 3.

Saturday, August 31 (Moon in Aries)   On this last day of August, the Aries moon relates to speculation, adventure, romance, winning ways, and personality. There's a chance to hit the jackpot in money and love. You might be musing, "I wish every day could be this way!" Taurus, Leo, and Scorpio play outstanding roles. Lucky lottery numbers: 7, 9, 10, 11, 17, 48.

Sunday, September 1 (Moon in Aries to Taurus 8:19 a.m.) A realization hits home concerning family values, property, security, your marital status. Today's Aries moon relates to your ability to win friends and influence people, to have good fortune in matters of finance and romance. There's gourmet dining tonight!

Monday, September 2 (Moon in Taurus) Diversify, know that you do have allies behind the scene. Someone who is financially secure sincerely wants to help you attain a goal. A Taurus figures prominently, helps make contacts that ordinarily would be out of reach. Luck rides with you tonight!

Tuesday, September 3 (Moon in Taurus to Gemini 3:08 p.m.) At the track: Post position special—Number 4 P.P. in fourth race. Pick six: 8, 5, 1, 4, 3, 7. In selecting the names of potential winning horses or jockeys, watch for these letters or initials: D, M, V. Selections apply to all tracks. Scorpio plays a major role.

Wednesday, September 4 (Moon in Gemini) Your cycle is high, so take the initiative in getting to the heart of matters. Emphasize reading and writing, disseminating information. Be open to adventures resulting from a clash of ideas. Virgo, Sagittarius, and another Gemini are represented. Lucky lottery numbers: 1, 5, 7, 13, 14, 40.

Thursday, September 5 (Moon in Gemini) Attention revolves around your ability to fix things in the house, to set a value on art objects, luxury items, and on your own time. Circumstances make a turn in your favor. Financial gain is the direct result. Libra, Aries, and another Gemini play roles. Your lucky number is 6.

Friday, September 6 (Moon in Gemini to Cancer 1:29 a.m.) Within 24 hours, an opportunity presents itself in connection with payments, collections, refunds, investments. Today you locate a missing link, missing ingredients; your confidence is restored as a result. Let go of preconceived notions—old rules no longer apply. Pisces figures prominently.

Saturday, September 7 (Moon in Cancer)   What appeared to be a loss will boomerang in your favor. Be aware of time. A deadline does exist. The moon in Cancer relates to food, shelter, participation in a profitable enterprise. A Capricorn is involved, with these letters or initials in his or her name: H, Q, Z. Lucky lottery numbers: 8, 9, 10, 12, 18, 44.

Sunday, September 8 (Moon in Cancer to Leo 1:54 p.m.)   Accent universal appeal, refuse to be limited by those who lack talent or faith. Open lines of communication—an opportunity might exist in connection with overseas travel or assignment. Spiritual values will be much in evidence. Aries is involved.

Monday, September 9 (Moon in Leo)   Today you'll be musing, "Everything seems new, I'm going to be more independent, original, and I will be vulnerable to love!" Imprint your own style, lead rather than follow, have the courage of your convictions. Today's Leo moon emphasizes relatives, trips, visits, the necessity for locating special documents.

Tuesday, September 10 (Moon in Leo)   A mystery is solved in connection with direction, motivation. Attention revolves around property, home, basic issues, your marital status. Accent versatility and personality, make special appearances. Wear yellow and gold. Cancer and Capricorn play instrumental roles.

Wednesday, September 11 (Moon in Leo to Virgo 2:28 a.m.)   You might be asked to take charge of an entertainment program relating to a political or charitable project. A gift received in the late afternoon adds to your wardrobe and helps remove doubts about your body image. A Sagittarian involved. Lucky lottery numbers: 3, 4, 6, 7, 22, 35.

Thursday, September 12 (Moon in Virgo)   The new moon in Virgo relates to home, boundary lines, the necessity for being selective, discriminating, insisting on quality goods. Taurus and Scorpio play major roles, are likely to have these letters or initials in their names: D, M, V. Check reference material and signatures.

Friday, September 13 (Moon in Virgo to Libra 1:51 p.m.) This will be your lucky day! You'll be released from an obligation you should not have assumed in the first place. Stay on familiar ground, let others know, "If and when I decide to move, it will be my decision!" Virgo and another Gemini figure in the scenario.

Saturday, September 14 (Moon in Libra) There's music in your life tonight—you'll be able to say with confidence, "I march to the beat of my own drum!" Taurus, Libra, and Scorpio are involved, have these letters or initials in their names: F, O, X. Funds will be obtained. Lucky lottery numbers: 1, 6, 9, 12, 18, 45.

Sunday, September 15 (Moon in Libra to Scorpio 11:20 p.m.) Play the waiting game, don't equate delay with defeat. The Libra moon highlights creativity, style, and physical attraction. Spiritual values surface. You'll feel at one with the universe. Pisces and Virgo show appreciation, give love, and are likely to have these letters or initials in their names: G, P, Y.

Monday, September 16 (Moon in Scorpio) What was out of reach could become suddenly available. Conditions change sharply within 24 hours. The financial status of a young person, perhaps your child becomes startlingly clear. Hold back on a speculative venture. A Cancer will soon share pertinent information, which results in more financial security.

Tuesday, September 17 (Moon in Scorpio) You'll be rid of a burden. You'll be free to express your feelings in a dynamic, dramatic way. Pay attention to import-export activities. Seek a larger market, audience for your product or talent. You'll "glow" in the realization that love is not a stranger. Your lucky number is 9.

Wednesday, September 18 (Moon in Scorpio to Sagittarius 6:31 a.m.) Many will seek enlightenment through your words and actions. What usually seems ordinary could become extraordinary with you at the helm. Stress innovativeness, independence, originality, your pioneering spirit.

276

Key words should be, "All stops out!" Lucky lottery numbers: 1, 4, 8, 12, 18, 22.

Thursday, September 19 (Moon in Sagittarius)   At the track: Post position special—Number 6 P.P. in fifth race. Pick six: 1, 7, 3, 8, 6, 5. Winning horses or jockeys are likely to have these letters or initials in their names: F, O, X. Veteran jockeys should be riding winners. Selections apply to all tracks. Capricorn is involved.

Friday, September 20 (Moon in Sagittarius to Capricorn 11:12 a.m.)   Diversify, welcome any opportunity to prove your ability to reach beyond previous limitations. The lunar, numerical cycles highlight public appearances, written agreements, where previously there were only verbal statements. The emphasis is on partnership, cooperative efforts, and marital status.

Saturday, September 21 (Moon in Capricorn)   The emphasis is on practicality, proofreading, details that usually escape your attention. You'll be dealing with hidden resources, financial potential, interpreting words associated with a possible inheritance. Be willing to revise, review, or remodel, to rebuild on a more suitable structure. Lucky lottery numbers: 1, 4, 7, 19, 22, 40.

Sunday, September 22 (Moon in Capricorn to Aquarius 1:39 p.m.)   An opportunity exists to show off material, product, or talent. You'll benefit from using words, verbal and written. A flirtation or chance meeting could result in a clash of ideas that, in return, leads to physical attraction and a relationship. Ultimately this could become a lasting friendship or marriage.

Monday, September 23 (Moon in Aquarius)   Focus on idealism, romance, music, an evaluation of your property, lifestyle, residence, marital status. The key is diplomacy. Money due will be paid, if you don't equate delay with defeat. Libra figures prominently. Look for these letters or initials in his or her name: F, O, X.

Tuesday, September 24 (Moon in Aquarius to Pisces 2:43 p.m.)   Today's scenario features mystery, intrigue, and glamour. Keep in mind on this day that discretion is the better part of valor. You'll see things you were not supposed to observe. If you're careless, you could pay dearly and so it behooves you to play dumb. Virgo is involved.

Wednesday, September 25 (Moon in Pisces) The spotlight is on your ability to meet a deadline, to bring order out of chaos. The Pisces moon activates your 10th House, that section of your horoscope associated with your career, your standing in the community, promotion, and prestige. Capricorn is represented. Lucky lottery numbers: 4, 7, 8, 12, 17, 30.

Thursday, September 26 (Moon in Pisces to Aries 3:46 p.m.) You'll be saying, "I fooled myself, I didn't know I could go this far. Truly the sky is the limit and now I know it for sure!" Someone previously indifferent will now express enthusiasm and might ask, "Where have you been all my life?" Your lucky number is 9.

Friday, September 27 (Moon in Aries) The full moon, lunar eclipse in Aries relates to your House of hopes, wishes, desires, powers of persuasion. What you wished for 24 hours ago could be completely different. Many past inhibitions and limitations will be eradicated. Leo is involved.

Saturday, September 28 (Moon in Aries to Taurus 6:24 p.m.) Focus on the division of property, domestic conditions, motivation, public appearances, dealings with women. The spotlight also falls on partnership, public relations, and marriage. Cancer and Capricorn figure prominently. Look for these letters or initials in their names: B, K, T. Lucky lottery numbers: 1, 10, 12, 20, 33, 40.

Sunday, September 29 (Moon in Taurus) There should be joy in your heart! Someone who disappeared now returns and makes a family gathering complete. Food, frolic, an awareness of spirituality are featured. You'll rebuild bridges burned in moments of impulse or carelessness—this means friendships, family relationships are restored.

Monday, September 30 (Moon in Taurus) On this last day of September, you're on solid ground, your views are verified, your prestige is restored. The Taurus moon highlights secret meetings, galleries, motion pictures, antiques, clandestine arrangements involving money. Taurus, Leo, and Scorpio figure prominently.

OCTOBER 1996

Tuesday, October 1 (Moon in Taurus to Gemini 12:01 a.m.) Where previously you felt restricted, you'll experience greater freedom of thought and action. Another Gemini figures prominently. Look for these letters or initials in his or her name: C, L, U. An excellent day for planning a social affair or entertainment.

Wednesday, October 2 (Moon in Gemini) Check signatures, read between the lines. Examine the latest source material. Circumstances turn in your favor. Events transpire to bring you closer to your ultimate goal. Taurus and Scorpio figure prominently. Lucky lottery numbers: 1, 3, 8, 20, 30, 40.

Thursday, October 3 (Moon in Gemini to Cancer 9:14 a.m.) Money comes your way as result of refunds, royalties, back pay, a legal decision. An addition to your wardrobe improves your appearance. You are capable of bringing joy to others, even though you're undergoing emotional turmoil. A Sagittarian plays a paramount role.

Friday, October 4 (Moon in Cancer) Attention revolves around home, family, security, large household products. Check accounting procedures, be alert to tax or license requirements. Your income potential shows a marked improvement. There's music tonight, and restoration of harmony on the domestic front. Your lucky number is 6.

Saturday, October 5 (Moon in Cancer to Leo 9:12 a.m.) Define terms, see people and places as they are, not merely as you wish they might be. Someone you trust could be involved in an element of deception. Protect yourself in emotional clinches. Pisces and Virgo are represented. Lucky lottery numbers: 2, 13, 18, 20, 22, 47.

Sunday, October 6 (Moon in Leo) Within 24 hours, news is received from a relative in transit. This results in a sudden change of itinerary. Focus on versatility, diversity, different modes of transportation. The spotlight is on organization, responsibility, setting up priorities. Your lucky number is 8.

Monday, October 7 (Moon in Leo) You'll be complimented on your appearance, color coordination, sense of showmanship. Accent universal appeal, refuse to be limited by someone who complains, "It was never done that way before!" Your response: "It is going to be done this way now and it is my way!"

Tuesday, October 8 (Moon in Leo to Virgo 9:49 a.m.) New experiences are featured; a love relationship provides inspiration amid controversy. Accent independence, originality, a willingness to take risks in order to stick to your principles. Leo and Aquarius play significant roles. Look for these letters or initials in their names: A, S, J.

Wednesday, October 9 (Moon in Virgo) Today's Virgo moon highlights property values. Long-standing negotiations will be completed to your advantage. Check the sturdiness of a product—choose quality over quantity. Capricorn and Cancer are in the picture. Look for these letters or initials in their names: B, K, T. Lucky lottery numbers: 5, 6, 15, 29, 30, 51.

Thursday, October 10 (Moon in Virgo to Libra 9 p.m.) You'll have more space. Optimism replaces boredom. Criticism received at home should be regarded as helpful, not destructive. The emphasis is on your ability to relieve pressure by getting rid of an unnecessary burden. Sagittarius and another Gemini are in the picture. Look for these letters or initials in their names: C, L, U.

Friday, October 11 (Moon in Libra) At the track: Post position special—Number 4 P.P. in fourth race. Pick six: 8, 5, 7, 4, 3, 9. Watch for these letters or initials in names of potential winning horses or jockeys: D, M, V. Selections apply to all tracks. Check signatures and be alert for deception, deliberate or otherwise.

Saturday, October 12 (Moon in Libra)   The new moon, solar eclipse in Libra, aspects a section of your chart relating to creativity, style, variety, and physical attraction. A love relationship becomes more exciting, upsetting, or controversial. Virgo, Sagittarius, and another Gemini figure prominently. Lucky lottery numbers: 1, 5, 7, 10, 18, 50.

Sunday, October 13 (Moon in Libra to Scorpio 5:46 a.m.)   A family relationship is strained. The healing process gets underway early this evening. Domestic harmony is restored after a brief intermission. Taurus and Libra become your staunch allies—don't resist a necessary transformation.

Monday, October 14 (Moon in Scorpio)   Hidden values and resources dominate. A clandestine arrangement comes to light; you'll be indignant, but don't show it. Play the waiting game. Time is on your side. Get rid of clutter. Streamline procedures. Pisces and Virgo play strong roles.

Tuesday, October 15 (Moon in Scorpio to Sagittarius 12:07 p.m.)   The emphasis is on production, promotion, dealings with Cancer and Capricorn. Look for these letters or initials in their names: H, Q, Z. Be organized in all that you do. A controversial love relationship is out in the open. Before this day is over, you will bring order out of chaos.

Wednesday, October 16 (Moon in Sagittarius)   News from a distance helps overcome language and other barriers. Focus on idealism, a love relationship, a search for your soul mate. The spotlight is on partnership, public relations, the ability to successfully use your powers of persuasion. Lucky lottery numbers: 3, 5, 9, 19, 30, 41.

Thursday, October 17 (Moon in Sagittarius to Capricorn 4:37 p.m.)   A clash of ideas with a Leo becomes an interesting, fascinating relationship; these letters or initials are involved: A, S, J. Get to the heart of matters, stress independence, originality, your pioneering spirit. Your public image is important. Proposals will be offered, both business and marriage.

Friday, October 18 (Moon in Capricorn)   You'll be asking, "Is this déjà vu?" Today's scenario features familiar faces and places. The spotlight is on property value, direction, motivation, family relationships, and marital status. You'll uncover hidden values and you could receive news about an inheritance. A money mystery is solved!

Saturday, October 19 (Moon in Capricorn to Aquarius 7:51 p.m.)   Diversify, accept a social obligation that could involve entertainment for a political or charitable organization. Improve your body image by adding to your wardrobe. Synchronize humor with profundity. Another Gemini figures in today's scenario. Look for these letters or initials in his or her name: C, L, U. Lucky lottery numbers: 3, 5, 6, 18, 30, 51.

Sunday, October 20 (Moon in Aquarius)   News received during the early evening hours concerns distribution, production, display, a possible journey. Be willing to revise, review, remodel, to tear down in order to rebuild. Make corrections, do some mending, test tools and recipes. Scorpio figures prominently.

Monday, October 21 (Moon in Aquarius to Pisces 10:22 p.m.)   Distribute books and pamphlets—you'll gain through words, both verbal and written. A flirtation or chance meeting could lead to a meaningful relationship. Virgo, Sagittarius, and another Gemini figure prominently. Look for these letters or initials in their names: E, N, W. Your lucky number is 5.

Tuesday, October 22 (Moon in Pisces)   Attention revolves around your ability to beautify your surroundings, home, family, marriage. What begins as a creative hobby could be transformed into a profitable enterprise. Accent music, rhythm, style, design, and architecture. Within 24 hours, your emotional wounds will heal.

Wednesday, October 23 (Moon in Pisces)   Terms will be clearly defined; within two months, you'll be saying, "I'm happy I agreed, despite initial reservations." Psychic faculties surge forward. You could be acquiring the nickname, "Nostradamus." Lucky lottery numbers: 7, 12, 14, 18, 23, 40.

Thursday, October 24 (Moon in Pisces to Aries 12:50 a.m.)   Use lessons learned from recent experience. The Pisces moon relates to career, business enterprise, elevation of your standing in the community. Make this your power play day—all stops are out, bet on your own capabilities. Capricorn and Cancer figure prominently.

Friday, October 25 (Moon in Aries)   On this Friday, you complete a project, inspire others, exalt in knowledge that your wishes are coming true and that you are winning friends and influencing people. You'll strike pay dirt in an amazing, unorthodox way. Aries and Libra figure in today's dramatic scenario.

Saturday, October 26   Make a fresh start, get to the heart of matters, let go of the status quo. A new love could be on the horizon. Your creative juices stir, you'll assume a leadership role. You'll have good fortune in matters of romance and finance. Leo is represented. Lucky lottery numbers: 1, 4, 11, 19, 20, 33.

Sunday, October 27 (Moon in Taurus; End of Daylight Saving Time)   You'll locate a lost article. A family member returns from a journey and makes it clear, "I missed you so very much!" The spotlight falls on property, security, building material, partnership, and marriage. A secret meeting results in the settlement of a financial dispute. Your lucky number is 2.

Monday, October 28 (Moon in Taurus to Gemini 8:35 a.m. EST)   The full moon in Taurus coincides with information marked "Confidential." You might be involved in a stock market transaction relating to a home product or information especially valuable to women. Focus on backstage practice involving drama or voice. Another Gemini is involved.

Tuesday, October 29 (Moon in Gemini)   At the track: Post position special—Number 4 P.P. in fourth race. Pick six: 8, 5, 7, 4, 3, 3. Hot combinations, daily double: 4 and 6, 8, and 5, 4 and 4, 3 and 7. Watch for names with these letters or initials in choosing winning horses or jockeys: D, M, V. Selections apply to all tracks.

Wednesday, October 30 (Moon in Gemini to Cancer 4:56 p.m.)   You get your way—more important, you learn "what is my way." Your cycle is high, your judgment and intuition are on target. Express your personality, all stops are out. Accent versatility, humor, diversity, different modes of transportation. Virgo, Sagittarius, and another Gemini play dynamic roles. Lucky lottery numbers: 3, 5, 14, 22, 30, 33.

Thursday, October 31 (Moon in Cancer)   Stay close to home, if possible. Arrange entertainment which appeals to both children and adults on this Halloween. The Cancer moon relates to money, payments, collections, and luck in finance. Stress music, design, and costumes. You'll hear these whispered words, "You are a magnificent person!"

NOVEMBER 1996

Friday, November 1 (Moon in Cancer)   Gather facts and figures, synthesize results, and make a plan of action that will carry you through the entire month. You'll be on solid ground. Don't be intimidated by one who knows the price of everything, the value of nothing.

Saturday, November 2 (Moon in Cancer to Leo 4:16 a.m.) Disseminate information. Explore ideas with someone associated with publishing or journalism. Stretch your mental wings! Today's scenario features a change of venue, travel, investigation, the adventure of discovery. Lucky lottery numbers: 4, 5, 11, 21, 27, 40.

Sunday, November 3 (Moon in Leo)   Attention revolves around your home, harmony, music, children, and creative endeavors. Be close to your family, express your feelings, and don't permit a discussion about money to deteriorate into an argument. Taurus, Libra, and Scorpio are involved. Look for these letters or initials in their names: F, O, X.

Monday, November 4 (Moon in Leo To Virgo 4:57 p.m.) Liberate yourself from someone who takes you for granted, and gives nothing in return. Focus on trips, visits, intellectual curiosity, diversity, and versatility. Spotlight mystery, glamour, and intrigue. Keep hidden values hidden. Pisces is represented.

Tuesday, November 5 (Moon in Virgo) This could be a day of accomplishment. It's an excellent time for a business venture, buying and selling, attending an auction. Practical measures succeed; look for potential real estate investments, sales and purchases of homes or products for homes. A Cancer can be helpful.

Wednesday, November 6 (Moon in Virgo) A project will be completed in an unusual manner—distance and language challenges are involved. Emerge from any emotional cocoon, speak up, and wear shades of red. Use your critical faculties. Strive to enter the international market. Lucky lottery numbers: 6, 7, 8, 13, 25, 51.

Thursday, November 7 (Moon in Virgo to Libra 4:29 a.m.) Within 24 hours, your scenario could feature creativity, style, variety, a love relationship. Make your impact now— make a fresh start, in a new direction. Be independent, and willing to face reality. The secret of your success could be color coordination, entertainment, showmanship—make room for the new!

Friday, November 8 (Moon in Libra) On this Friday, welcome the challenge of meeting a deadline. Stress creativity, dealings with young persons, a physical attraction, sex appeal. Focus also on direction, motivation, a relationship with an older female family member. Gourmet dining is featured tonight.

Saturday, November 9 (Moon in Libra to Scorpio 1:02 p.m.) Entertainment is highlighted; fun and frolic. You'll be more pleased with your image after a recent purchase of apparel. Your creative juices stir, you might be saying, "I didn't plan it this way but maybe I am in love!" Sagittarius is involved. Lucky lottery numbers: 6, 7, 27, 35, 42, 45.

Sunday, November 10 (Moon in Scorpio)   Information long awaited will be received, involving a mechanical object, reference material, prices of foreign products. Test tools and recipes, do some mending, rebuild bridges burned during impulsive moments. Work methods are different from the usual, but they'll prove both productive and profitable.

Monday, November 11 (Moon in Scorpio to Sagittarius 6:27 p.m.)   The new moon in Scorpio relates to fitness, style, pets, dependents, the ability to appeal to a large segment of the public, from the low and the lonely to the high and the mighty. Be ready for a written notice: "You are appealing, attractive, and dynamic, but some changes are necessary instantly!"

Tuesday, November 12 (Moon in Sagittarius)   Attention revolves around partnership, public relations, changes in a domestic area that revolves around your home or marriage. You'll be invited to dine out; an admirer seeks to wine and dine you. Be diplomatic, but don't abandon your principles. Libra plays a role.

Wednesday, November 13 (Moon in Sagittarius to Capricorn 9:44 p.m.)   The spotlight is on how the world looks to you, how you appear to the world. Look behind the scenes, see people and places as they are, not merely as you wish they might be. Don't fall victim to self-deception. Be aware of the 7th House moon, which relates to partnership, cooperative efforts, public relations, and marriage. Lucky lottery numbers: 3, 7, 9, 26, 30, 51.

Thursday, November 14 (Moon in Capricorn)   You'll be asked to meet a deadline, accept a challenge, bring order out of a chaotic situation. Funding is obtained in less than 24 hours. A legal agreement is valid despite objections from those who claim, "You are getting all the best of it and you should agree to revisions!"

Friday, November 15 (Moon in Capricorn) This Friday, you gain the secret of universal appeal. Today's scenario includes a possible inheritance, funding, partnership, strong sexual desires. Be discriminating. Choose carefully. Protect yourself in emotional clinches. Aries and Libra play roles. Look for these letters or initials in their names: I and R.

Saturday, November 16 (Moon in Capricorn to Aquarius 12:14 a.m.) On this Saturday, you make a fresh start. You'll learn the secret of assessing the value of possessions. A love relationship sparkles. Express your personality and will. Don't permit others to take charge of your destiny. Insist on an accounting. Others might attempt to denegrate your contributions—don't let it happen!

Sunday, November 17 (Moon in Aquarius) The Aquarian moon relates to travel, unorthodox procedures, communication from one recently arrived at an overseas destination. The spotlight also falls on property value, home, family relationships, the ability to bring order out of a chaotic situation. A Cancer is involved.

Monday, November 18 (Moon in Aquarius to Pisces 3 a.m.) All indications point to celebration, publishing, "journeys of the mind." Even if you do not move an inch geographically, your intellectual curiosity will be stirred. You'll exude a subtle kind of sex appeal. Sagittarius and another Gemini figure in today's exciting scenario.

Tuesday, November 19 (Moon in Pisces) You'll be on top of your game. Taurus, Leo, and Scorpio play vital roles, and could have these letters or initials in their names: D, M, V. Check references, read the fine print, be willing to revise, review, remodel, and to replace outworn machinery.

Wednesday, November 20 (Moon in Pisces to Aries 6:34 a.m.) Today's Pisces moon highlights leadership, promotion, and production. A unique honor is presented by members of a club, organization, or community. The key is to disseminate information, to gain knowledge through reading and writing. Get your views on record! Lucky lottery numbers: 7, 12, 13, 20, 27, 31.

Thursday, November 21 (Moon in Aries)   The moon in Aries relates to your ability to take the initiative in winning friends and influencing people. Attention revolves around home and family members who provide inspiration and offer services or funds. Taurus, Libra, and Scorpio are involved. Look for these letters or initial in their names: F, O, X.

Friday, November 22 (Moon in Aries to Taurus 11:12 a.m.)   On this Friday, you decide, "I will not be a stranger in my own universe!" Allies are aggressive in your behalf. Pay back by improving techniques, streamlining procedures, getting rid of clutter, and cutting down expenses. Pisces and Virgo persons play outstanding roles.

Saturday, November 23 (Moon in Taurus)   Be aware of a time limitation or deadline. Let others know, "We are going to make it with plenty to spare!" Your ability to inspire others proves invaluable. Capricorn and Cancer play fascinating roles. Lucky lottery numbers: 2, 8, 11, 12, 15, 20.

Sunday, November 24 (Moon in Taurus to Gemini 5:20 p.m.)   What was held back will be revealed—to your advantage. A secret cache is likely to be involved. You'll learn more about money and how it got that way. Review tax and accounting methods. Long-distance news resolves a dilemma associated with travel, language, foreign customs, or career aspirations.

Monday, November 25 (Moon in Gemini)   The full moon in your sign is properly interpreted as your ability to finish what you start, to gain greater public recognition, to resolve an emotional dilemma. New Love is on the horizon. Be vulnerable to the creative urge. Cancer and Capricorn play prominent roles.

Tuesday, November 26 (Moon in Gemini)   Take advantage of your high cycle. Get to the heart of matters. The action will be where you are. A financial dispute is settled, and you'll be more secure as a result. Focus on direction, motivation, sumptuous dining tonight that features foreign cuisine. Your lucky number is 2.

Wednesday, November 27 (Moon in Gemini to Cancer 1:37 a.m.)   Within 24 hours, money "arrives." The lunar position highlights personal possessions, basic values, a relation to a historic event. Sagittarius and another Gemini are featured, with these letters or initials in their names: C, L, U. Lucky lottery numbers: 3, 6, 13, 30, 40, 50.

Thursday, November 28 (Moon in Cancer)   At the track: Post position special—Number 4 P.P. in fourth race. Pick six: 8, 5, 3, 4, 1, 7. In selecting names of potential winning horses or jockeys, look for these letters or initials: D, M, V. Hot combinations, daily doubles: 4 and 4, 7 and 1, 8 and 1. Selections apply to all tracks.

Friday, November 29 (Moon in Cancer to Leo 12:30 p.m.)   The spotlight is on reading and writing; a clash of ideas, public speaking. You'll earn more respect and money. A former teacher or employer gets in touch to say, "Very proud of you!" Virgo, Sagittarius, and another Gemini play meaningful roles. Look for these letters or initials in their names: E, N, W.

Saturday, November 30 (Moon in Leo)   The moon in Leo highlights showmanship, personality, color coordination, entertainment related to charity or political activities. Focus on home, domestic arrangements, flowers, music, gifts, marital status. A serious discussion ensues during the early evening hours, relating to a possible change of residence or lifestyle.

DECEMBER 1996

Sunday, December 1 (Moon in Leo)   On this Sunday, the first day of the last month of 1996, communication with a Leo relative is of utmost importance. You will regard this finally as "my kind of day!" The emphasis is on reading, a study group, an exciting clash of ideas. Another Gemini plays a significant role.

Monday, December 2 (Moon in Leo to Virgo 1:11 a.m.)   The emphasis is on flowers, music, decisions relating to a domestic adjustment or your marital status. Within 24 hours, you'll learn more about your property value, long-standing negotiations, residence, or legal arrangement. Taurus and Libra figure prominently.

Tuesday, December 3 (Moon in Virgo)   Push aside situations that are confusing, that draw from you financially and emotionally. Make your meanings crystal clear. Define terms and arrangements. Understand what others expect from you and what you can anticipate in return. Your lucky number is 7.

Wednesday, December 4 (Moon in Virgo to Libra 1:23 p.m.)   All indications point to practicality, resourcefulness, using lessons learned during past experiences. An older person steps forward and declares, "You are more valuable than you yourself might believe!" Lucky lottery numbers: 4, 7, 8, 12, 13, 22.

Thursday, December 5 (Moon in Libra)   The emphasis is on universal appeal, idealism in romance, personal magnetism, and sexual attraction. Look beyond the immediate. Previous limitations no longer apply. Be open to an invitation that could send you on a journey involving an overseas assignment. Aries is represented.

Friday, December 6 (Moon in Libra to Scorpio 10:39 p.m.)   Make a fresh start in a new direction. Permit the sun to shine in your living quarters. Music and entertainment are in your life tonight. Someone you admire could profess love and declare, "You thrill and excite me!" Leo and Aquarius are featured. Look for these letters or initials in their names: A, S, J.

Saturday, December 7 (Moon in Scorpio)   Focus on real estate, a sea cruise, improved health, attention revolving around pet ownership, dependents, and employment. A special note: Investigate plumbing facilities, at home and elsewhere. A Cancer says, "You are such fun to be with, please join me for dinner!" Lucky lottery numbers: 2, 4, 6, 20, 22, 25.

Sunday, December 8 (Moon in Scorpio)   Communication with a family member is essential. Don't permit your pride to deter progress or happiness. Take steps to bring about a reunion. Focus on organization, experience, wisdom, investment, time limitation, and marital status. Your lucky number is 3.

Monday, December 9 (Moon in Scorpio to Sagittarius 3:59 a.m.)   What occurred 24 hours ago proves relevant to conditions on this Monday. Check details, keep your options open; sudden changes occur relating to those previously in leadership roles. Bring source material up to date. Avoid squandering resources. Scorpio is involved.

Tuesday, December 10 (Moon in Sagittarius)   The new moon in Sagittarius relates to partnership, public relations, enlightenment, marriage. What appeared to be a defeat will rebound in your favor—don't give up the ship! Accent a variety of experiences and sensations. A flirtation or chance meeting could lead eventually to a meaningful relationship.

Wednesday, December 11 (Moon in Sagittarius to Capricorn 6:15 a.m.)   A legal agreement is spotlighted. Read between the lines. Refuse to be hemmed in. Attention revolves around basic issues, income, art objects, luxury items, large household products, as well as living quarters, and marital status. Lucky lottery numbers: 6, 7, 9, 12, 20, 33.

Thursday, December 12 (Moon in Capricorn)   The view "backstage" proves entertaining and informative. Remember this aphorism, "Discretion is the better part of valor!" You'll see things usually obscured from view. You could be subject to an embarrassing moment. Pisces and Virgo are involved. Look for these letters or initials in their names: G, P, Y.

Friday, December 13 (Moon in Capricorn to Aquarius 7:14 a.m.)   At the track: Post position special—Number 8 P.P. in ninth race. Pick six: 4, 4, 5, 1, 6, 8. Watch for these letters or initials in names of potential winning horses or jockeys: H, Q, Z. Selections apply to all tracks. Capricorn and Cancer play meaningful roles.

Saturday, December 14 (Moon in Aquarius)   The emphasis is on communication, the ability to overcome distance and language obstacles. Be in touch with someone who is familiar with foreign markets. Today's Aquarian moon relates to the unorthodox association with people who are creative, dynamic, and original. Lucky lottery numbers: 2, 5, 9, 11, 22, 47.

Sunday, December 15 (Moon in Aquarius to Pisces 8:44 a.m.)   Spiritual values surface. The 9th House moon coincides with "the Source." Focus on individuality, spirituality, a fresh start, the transformation of ideas concerning love. Imprint your own style, let others know, "I will not budge from my ideals and principles!" Leo is represented.

Monday, December 16 (Moon in Pisces)   What was lost yesterday will be found during the early evening hours. The Pisces moon relates to prestige, standing in community, restoration of self-confidence. The spotlight falls on discovery of your soul mate during a journey. There could be a clash of ideas with a sensitive Cancer. Your lucky number is 2.

Tuesday, December 17 (Moon in Pisces to Aries 11:55 a.m.)   Diversify, participate in an entertainment program associated with charity or politics. Add to your wardrobe, fulfill resolutions made involving diet and nutrition. People are drawn to you with their problems; as you help heal the emotional wounds of others, your own wounds heal, too.

Wednesday, December 18 (Moon in Aries)   Focus on rebuilding, remodeling, transforming the plain-and-dreary into a colorful, attractive base. Today's Aries moon relates to your powers of persuasion, the ability to obtain funding, to win friends and influence people. Lucky lottery numbers: 1, 4, 9, 10, 19, 40.

Thursday, December 19 (Moon in Aries to Taurus 5:10 p.m.)   As the holiday season approaches, high spirits prevail. The lunar position continues to accent popularity, good luck in finance and romance. There is plenty of excitement, including gift purchases, change, travel, a variety of experiences. Sagittarius is involved.

Friday, December 20 (Moon in Taurus)   Music is in your life. Romance and drama are featured. You get more than you anticipated and it will be necessary to be diplomatic. Candy is featured, as are luxury items, art objects, and declarations of love. This is one Friday you won't soon forget! Taurus and Libra are involved.

Saturday, December 21 (Moon in Taurus)   Psychic faculties surface. You see beyond the immediate. Today's scenario features intrigue and clandestine arrangements. The spotlight is on theater, drama, showmanship, galleries, communication with someone temporarily confined to home or hospital. Lucky lottery numbers: 1, 5, 7, 12, 14, 26.

Sunday, December 22 (Moon in Taurus to Gemini 12:17 a.m.)   On this Sunday, puzzle pieces fall into place—faith is restored. A relationship gets back on track. Capricorn and Cancer play major roles, and are likely to have these letters or initials in their names: H, Q, Z. Within 24 hours, your cycle moves up. You'll be at the right place. Your judgment and intuition will be on target.

Monday, December 23 (Moon in Gemini)   The moon in your sign coincides with correct judgment, intuitive intellect, the ability to be at the right place at a crucial moment. Focus on universal appeal, travel, vulnerability to love. Aries and Libra play outstanding roles, and are likely to have these letters or initials in their names: I and R.

Tuesday, December 24 (Moon in Gemini To Cancer 9:14 a.m.)   On this Christmas Eve, the full moon is in your sign, number 1 numerical cycle, which translates to an exciting discovery, exchange of gifts, romance, and fulfillment of desires. Accent showmanship and creativity. There's a special relationship with Leo and Aquarius.

Wednesday, December 25 (Moon in Cancer) Merry Christmas! Today's moon in Cancer represents gifts, relatives, "found money." The cycle is high for style, romance, a reunion with people who went out of your life not long ago. The emphasis is on home, property, security, your marital status. A Cancer is involved.

Thursday, December 26 (Moon in Cancer to Leo 8:09 p.m.) An aura of confusion exists; budget is involved, a possible journey looms large. Accent diversity, versatility, the ability to laugh at your own foibles. The Cancer moon coincides with funding, property value, romance and marriage, and possible anticipation of an addition to your family.

Friday, December 27 (Moon in Leo) Within 24 hours, you'll participate in a short trip involving a relative in search of a document. Your cycle continues high. You'll be on solid ground. Competition melts. You'll receive credit previously denied. Taurus, Leo, and Scorpio play major roles.

Saturday, December 28 (Moon in Leo) Focus on dissemination of information. A chance meeting or blind date could lead to a meaningful relationship. Another Gemini figures prominently, and is likely to have these letters or initials in their names: E, N, W. Lucky lottery numbers: 1, 5, 7, 10, 12, 15.

Sunday, December 29 (Moon in Leo to Virgo 8:45 a.m.) The emphasis is on the domestic areas of your life—family, music, marriage. An inquisitive relative apparently feels better equipped to run your life than you yourself. Be patient, diplomatic, but know when to draw the line. Your lucky number is 6.

Monday, December 30 (Moon in Virgo) New Year's Eve planning requires revision. A Pisces who supposedly was in charge of organizing pulls a "disappearing act." Have alternatives at hand; be sure to include a designated driver. Follow through on a hunch!

Tuesday, December 31 (Moon in Virgo)   New Year's Eve: The Virgo moon relates to home, security, familiar ground, dealings with people who feel they must "let themselves go!" A Capricorn and Cancer who are usually conservative, decide to let off steam on this night before the New Year. You'll hear these words—HAPPY NEW YEAR!

ABOUT THIS SERIES

This is one of a series
of twelve Day-to-Day Astrological Guides
for the signs of 1996
by Sydney Omarr

ABOUT THE AUTHOR

Born on August 5, 1926, in Philadelphia, Omarr was the only person ever given full-time duty in the U.S. Army as an astrologer. He also is regarded as the most erudite astrologer of our time and the best known, through his syndicated column (300 newspapers) and his radio and television programs (he is Merv Griffin's "resident astrologer"). Omarr has been called the most "knowledgeable astrologer since Evangeline Adams." His forecasts of Nixon's downfall, the end of World War II in mid-August of 1945, the assassination of John F. Kennedy, Roosevelt's election to the fourth term and his death in office ... these and many others are on record and quoted enough to be considered "legendary."